Annual Index 2022

Series Editor: Danielle Lobban

Complete A-Z index

independence
educational publishers

First published by Independence Educational Publishers

The Studio, High Green

Great Shelford

Cambridge CB22 5EG

England

Copyright

Photocopy licence

ISBN-13: 978 1 86168 875 0

Printed in Great Britain

Zenith Print Group

#iwill campaign **382**.14, 18
#MeToo movement **364**.9–10, **380**.19
#normalizenormalbodies **375**.37
#TimeTogether campaign **384**.33

'2.4 children' **363**.8
7/7 bombings **355**.41
9/11 bombings **355**.3, 41
10 Minute Shake Up Campaign **307**.39
10 R's of sustainable living **368**.10–11
100,000 Genomes Project **352**.11–13

A

A4 Challenge **307**.19
abiotic stress resistance **352**.3
abode, right of **382**.2, 4
abortion **367**.1, **392**.7, 23
   alternatives **302**.19
   availability **367**.3
   complications **367**.16–17
   confidentiality **302**.5
   conscientious objection **367**.3
   costs **302**.23
   decisions about **367**.1–2
   decriminalising **367**.11–12, 26
   deprivation **302**.2
   devolution of law **302**.33, 39
   early **302**.2, 17
   eligibility for **367**.1, 3
   emotional responses to **302**.3–5
   failures **302**.7
   further pregnancy **302**.7
   gender selection **302**.30–2, 37
   help and counselling **302**.4–5, 6, 17, 18, 19, 27
   human rights **302**.11, 34, 35, 36, **372**.35–8
   incomplete **367**.16
   increase in rate of **367**.28–31
   late **302**.3, 17, 26–9
   legislation **302**.1, 2, 11–13, 21, 25, 26, 29–31, **367**.3, 10–11
   medical **302**.2, 3, 6, 10, 23–4, **367**.2, 15
   men's responsibilities **302**.39
   men's rights **302**.37–9
   and mental health **302**.1, 4, 27
   moral status **302**.13
   NHS provision **302**.2–4, 11, 16, 21
   in Northern Ireland **367**.3, 10, 19–20
   objections to **367**.3, 9–10, 13–15
   in Poland **367**.21–2
   and politics **367**.13–15
   and poverty **367**.31–2
   prenatal screening **302**.36–7
   private provision **302**.2, 3, 4
   procedure **367**.2
   pro-choice movements **302**.16
   providers **367**.1
   refusals **302**.5, 20, 21, 24, 29
   and religion **367**.13, 31–2
   repeat **302**.2, 10
   restrictions **302**.11–15, 23–7, 31, 34, 35
   risks **302**.1, 3, 7, 14, 23, 24–7, 30–1, 34, 35, **367**.2
   secularism **302**.15
   selective **367**.24
   statistics **367**.4–6, 28–30
   stigma **302**.13
   and stress **302**.17–18
   surgical **302**.2–3, 6–7, **367**.2, 15–16
   time limits **302**.4, 15, 26, 29
   travel abroad for **302**.23, 34, 35
   two agreements for **302**.1, 5, 25, 33
   unmarried status **302**.1
   unsafe **302**.15, 22, 25, 26, **367**.15–17, 26–7
   unviable foetuses to term **302**.34, 35, 36
   views on **367**.7–8
   waiting times for **302**.5
   and women's rights **302**.15, 27, 39
Abortion Act 1967 **302**.1, 2, 29–31, **367**.3, 10–11
absolute poverty **305**.30, **306**.27–8, 35, **377**.1, 3, 41
abstinence **379**.3, 13
abuse
   in childhood **354**.18–19, **373**.2–3
   definitions **388**.1, 4–5
   digital **409**.41
   elder **311**.21, 22, **370**.19, 41, **378**.22, 41
   financial **354**.28, **370**.1, 41
   gang **379**.30
   in later life **388**.3–4, 27
   of men and boys **388**.3, 20–1

Vol. numbers appear first (in bold) followed by page numbers; a change in volume is preceded by a semi-colon.

Vol. 305	Globalisation – Good or Bad?
Vol. 314	HIV & AIDS
Vol. 316	Marriage
Vol. 347	The Censorship Debate
Vol. 348	World Health
Vol. 349	Gambling Culture
Vol. 350	Lifestyle Diets
Vol. 351	The Anxiety Epidemic
Vol. 352	Biotech & Bioethics
Vol. 353	Education
Vol. 354	Relationships
Vol. 355	Terrorism
Vol. 356	British Armed Forces
Vol. 357	The Climate Emergency
Vol. 358	Religion Today
Vol. 359	Migration & Immigration
Vol. 360	Government
Vol. 361	Cyberbullying
Vol. 362	Euthanasia
Vol. 363	Population Change
Vol. 364	The Gender Equality Debate
Vol. 365	Tourism Today
Vol. 366	Crime in the UK
Vol. 367	Discussing Abortion
Vol. 368	Sustainable Living
Vol. 369	LGBT+ Issues
Vol. 370	Domestic Violence and Abuse
Vol. 371	The Internet and Us
Vol. 372	Our Human Rights
Vol. 373	Drug Use and Abuse
Vol. 374	Animal Rights
Vol. 375	Body Image
Vol. 376	Racism
Vol. 377	Poverty
Vol. 378	Ageing
Vol. 379	Understanding Sexual Health
Vol. 380	About Bullying
Vol. 381	Business
Vol. 382	Active Citizenship
Vol. 383	The Privacy Debate
Vol. 384	Health & Fitness
Vol. 385	Waste & Recycling Issues
Vol. 386	Sexualising Society
Vol. 387	Fertility Issues
Vol. 388	Discussing Child Abuse
Vol. 389	Sleep
Vol. 390	Eating Disorders
Vol. 391	Money
Vol. 392	National Health
Vol. 393	Disability
Vol. 394	Pregnancy
Vol. 395	Teen Self-Care
Vol. 396	UK Housing
Vol. 397	Alcohol Issues
Vol. 398	Homelessness
Vol. 399	Discussing Cannabis
Vol. 400	Suicide & Self-Harm
Vol. 401	War & Conflict
Vol. 402	Endangered Species
Vol. 403	Student Options
Vol. 404	Depression
Vol. 405	Employability
Vol. 406	Smoking
Vol. 407	Bereavement
Vol. 408	Healthy Eating
Vol. 409	Online Safety
Vol. 410	Addiction
Vol. 411	Sport
Vol. 412	Rights of the Child
Vol. 413	Energy
Vol. 414	Consumerism
Vol. 415	Mental Health

and mental health **388**.27–9
non-recent **388**.32
non-verbal **361**.41
online **371**.14–15, 26–7, **388**.23–4, 36, 38, **409**.33–4
and poverty **377**.2
of power **405**.36
prevalence of **388**.3
in relationships **354**.28
sharing sexual images **361**.25–6
sources of support **388**.39
statistics **388**.2–4, 25
verbal **361**.27, 41, **393**.16–17
see also domestic abuse; emotional abuse; neglect;
   physical abuse; sexual abuse
abuser programmes **370**.38–9, 41
academic freedom **347**.5
academic performance, and cannabis use **399**.18–19
academies **353**.2–3, 5–6, 28, 41
Academies Act 2010 **353**.5
Acas *see* Advisory, Conciliation and Arbitration Service (Acas)
accents, and bullying **380**.26–7
accessibility **393**.6–8, 30–1, 41
acetycholine **406**.9
acid (LSD) *see* LSD
acne **394**.7, **395**.22–3
Acquired Immune Deficiency Syndrome *see* AIDS
acrylonitrile butadiene styrene (ABS) **385**.29
ActionAid **306**.32
Action for Children **306**.12
Action on Elder Abuse **311**.21–2
Action on Smoking and Health (ASH) **406**.2–5, 19, 27, 30–1,
   34, 38–9
active euthanasia **362**.1, 16, 41
activism **371**.10, **372**.35–8, **382**.16–17, 38, 41
Activities of Daily Living (ADL) **378**.4
activity levels **411**.11–13, 41
actors, pressures on **375**.26–7
Acts of Parliament **360**.3, 6–8, 41
acupressure **343**.7
acupuncture **343**.6, 16–17, 21, 41
addiction **406**.8–10, 21, 33, 41
cannabis **399**.3, 4, 13, 17, 21, 41
causes **410**.1
and children **410**.32–3
consequences of **373**.2, 32–3
and crime **373**.1
definition **373**.1, 41, **410**.2, 41
as a disease **410**.4
environmental factors **373**.2–3
gambling **349**.26–7
and gender **410**.3
genetic factors **373**.2
as health/medical issue **301**.29, 32
heroin **301**.34
illegal drugs **301**.33, 37
impact on family and friends **301**.38
internet pornography **318**.33
over-the-counter medicines **301**.10
physical **373**.1, **410**.1, 2
pornography **318**.32
psychological **373**.1, **410**.1, 2
quitting **410**.37–9
recognising **410**.1, 35–6
rehabilitation **373**.12, 33, 35–9
risk factors **301**.36–7, **373**.3, 31–2
services **301**.35
signs of **373**.2
stereotypes **410**.8
stereotyping **373**.32–3
symptoms **410**.1
understanding **410**.2, 5
withdrawal **373**.1, 3, 41
see also alcohol; substance misuse
addictive personality **410**.3
Additional Member System (AMS) **360**.25
additives **408**.14–15, 17, 20, 41
admissions to university *see* UCAS (Universities and Colleges
   Admissions Service)
adolescent marriage *see* child marriage
adoption **354**.13
adrenaline **389**.2, 3, **406**.9
adult gaming centres (AGCs) **349**.1
adulthood
legal age of **354**.1
milestones **354**.1
adventure tourism **365**.1
adverse childhood experiences **388**.31
advertising **381**.4, **397**.34, **414**.34, 41
and body image **375**.16, 19, 21–3, 25, 33
and gambling **349**.6, 12, 17, 25, 34–5
gender stereotypes in **364**.32–3
junk food **392**.24
online **371**.4
and sexualisation **386**.21–5, 27–8
smoking **406**.1
and tobacco **349**.17
tobacco **392**.23
see also marketing; media
Advertising Standards Authority (ASA) **364**.41, **375**.33, 41
on gender stereotypes **364**.32–3
Advisory, Conciliation and Arbitration Service (Acas)
on age discrimination **311**.6
on workplace bullying **380**.18–19
aerobic exercise **384**.22–3
aesthetic labour **375**.26–7
aesthetic surgery *see* cosmetic surgery
affluence *see* wealth
affordable housing **396**.2
Afghanistan
armed forces in **356**.15, 27
war and conflict **401**.4, 5, 16, 17, 19–20, 31–3
aflatoxin **348**.19
Africa
employment rights **405**.33
fertility rates **363**.26, 31
global poverty **306**.28
HIV **314**.2, 5, 18
life expectancy **378**.5, 6
medicine **343**.8–9
nutrition **348**.4
population growth **363**.20–1, 27–9
poverty **377**.21–2
retirement age **378**.12–14
war and conflict **401**.24
and women's unequal labour **364**.1
African National Congress (ANC) **355**.2
age
of adulthood **354**.1

and cohabitation **316**.18
compulsory school age **353**.1–2, 7–8
of consent **354**.33–4
of criminal responsibility **354**.1
discrimination **311**.6, 16–17, **378**.19, 41, **380**.4
and internet use **371**.1
milestones **354**.1
of raised participation **353**.4
restrictions **349**.1–2
stereotypes **378**.22–3
see also ageing; older people
ageing **311**.1, 3, 16, 25
brain **311**.38
community **311**.17
definition **378**.41
economic contribution **311**.17
employment **311**.23
families **311**.26, 36
fitness **311**.17, 23
health **311**.11, 17, 35–6
housing **311**.17, 24, 37
memory **311**.39
pensions **311**.7, 8
social isolation **311**.35
in urban areas **311**.25–7
volunteering **311**.17
see also life expectancy; older people
ageing population **363**.4–5, 6, 12, 41, **378**.1–3, 20, 41,
  392.29–35
and economics **378**.2
ageism **393**.13
agency workers **405**.33
age-related macular degeneration (AMD) **392**.30
Age UK
on elder abuse **370**.19
on old age care **378**.29, 31
on sexually transmitted infections (STIs) **379**.19
aggression **380**.17, 19, **397**.2, **415**.33
agnosticism **358**.14, 19, 41
agoraphobia **351**.4, 41
agricultural biotechnology **352**.2
see also crops
agricultural intensification **402**.8
agriculture **357**.24–7
net zero targets **357**.37
see also farming
aid **305**.22–3
and global poverty **305**.22
and healthcare **305**.22, 23
and sanctions **305**.14
AIDS (Acquired Immune Deficiency Syndrome) **314**.1, 11, 12,
  39, **348**.17, **379**.16–17, **392**.2
and animal experimentation **374**.15
death **314**.2, 3, 6, 14, 15
global investment in **314**.3
innate defence **314**.36
memorials **314**.27
misinformation **314**.24
and mortality **363**.20
stigma **314**.11
timeline **314**.6
see also HIV (human immunodeficiency virus)
airbrushing **307**.11, 16, 18, 25, **375**.30, 41
airlines

budget **365**.6, 12
frequent flyers **365**.24–5
air pollution **348**.3, 5, 6, 10, 11–12, 41, **365**.30, **412**.16,
  413.15, 37
incinerators **385**.16–17
see also emissions
airstrikes **401**.6–7
air travel **365**.24
alcohol **354**.1, **356**.9, 26, **373**.9, 14–15, **392**.22, **394**.15,
  410.41
addiction **373**.2, **397**.3–4, 10–20, 14, 38–9, 41, **410**.4, 7,
  34–9
advertising **397**.34
and assaults **309**.27
and cannabis **399**.9–10
consumption trends **301**.4, 6
definition **397**.41
and dental health **395**.25
as a drug **397**.10–11
effects of **397**.1–3
and fertility **387**.21–2, 29
labels **397**.2
and the law **301**.19
legislation **397**.4, 26–7
mixing with drugs **397**.3
and mood **397**.24
parental influence **301**.4
during pregnancy **394**.10
public health/economic costs of **301**.7
risks of **397**.1, 3, 8–9, 12–13
safety guidelines **397**.4, 12
and self-harm **400**.21
and sleep **389**.2, 5–6, 39
and social media use **397**.33
substitutes **301**.31
units **397**.2, 41
withdrawal **397**.11
see also drink driving
alcohol by volume (ABV) **397**.41
alcoholic liver disease **397**.6
alcohol-related deaths **397**.5–7
alcohol use disorder (AUD) **397**.16
alcopops **397**.2, 3
A-levels **353**.18–19, 41, **403**.1, 10–11, 41
choosing **403**.13
grade inflation **403**.16–17
requirements for **403**.2–4, 7, 10–11
vocational equivalents **403**.9
Alexa devices **383**.26–31
see also smart speakers
Alexander Technique **343**.11
Algeria, censorship in **347**.11
algorithms **381**.4
Alien Restriction (Amendment) Act 1919 **382**.2–3
allergies, food **350**.27–9, 41
Allergy UK **350**.27
All-Party Parliamentary Groups (APPGs) **360**.41
All Saints' Day **358**.23
All Souls' Day **358**.23
almshouses, history of **306**.5
al-Qaeda **355**.3, 4, 5, 41, **401**.24, 31
ALS (Amyotrophic Lateral Sclerosis) **392**.33
Al-Shabaab **355**.15–16
Alternative Dispute Resolution (ADR) scheme **414**.10

alternative therapies **343**.1–17
alternative tourism **365**.41
Alternative Vote (AV) **360**.24–5
altruism **382**.27
   see also volunteering
aluminium cans **385**.12, 25, 28
alumni networks **405**.6
Alzheimer's disease **389**.15, **392**.31, **408**.10
Amazon **381**.3, 36, **383**.26–31
Amazon rainforest **357**.6, 16
American Civil War (1861-1865) **401**.3
American Revolution (1775-1783) **401**.3
Amnesty International **300**.17–18, 20–1, **369**.24, **372**.35–6
   on abortion **302**.35–6, **367**.10
   on impacts of war **401**.25–6
   on prostitution **318**.3–5, 6, 7, 13
amphetamines **373**.5, 22, 28, 41, **399**.11, 22
amyl nitrates (poppers) **301**.19, 30
anabolic steroids **301**.14, 15–16, **373**.4, 22, **411**.34, 41
anaemia **390**.20, **394**.17, **408**.28
anaerobic digestion **413**.19
anaerobic exercise **384**.22–3
anal cancer **309**.25
anarchist terrorism **355**.6, 7
Andrea Adams Trust **405**.36
androgynous **386**.41
anencephaly **302**.35
anger **415**.4, 5
Anglo-Indian Wars (1766-1849) **401**.1
angst **415**.41
Animal Boarding Establishments Act 1963 **303**.2
Animal Defenders International (ADI) **303**.10, 26, **374**.20
   on badger culling **303**.27
   on hunting **303**.27
   on primates as pets **303**.28
Animal Health and Welfare (Scotland) Act 2006 **374**.5, 8
Animal Protection Index (API) **374**.6–7
animals
   gene editing **352**.38–9
   research and experiments **303**.13, 14, 33, 35, 36, **374**.14–25, 41
      banning cosmetics tests **303**.38–9
      cost–benefit analysis **303**.13
      and firebombing **303**.13

      and GM animals **303**.15–16, 35
      and legislation **303**.39
      to replace, refine, reduce **303**.33–4, 35
   rights **303**.6, 12, 13, 14, 24, 25, 37–8, **350**.8
      consent **374**.38–9
      defining **374**.1, 41
      dog racing **303**.16
      extremists **374**.41
      firebombing **303**.13
      fur farming **303**.30, 31–2
      hunting **303**.27
      legislation **303**.21, 27
      and moral judgments **374**.3–4
      personhood **303**.22–3, 24–5
      petting zoos **303**.22
      poaching **303**.27
   sentience **374**.9
   suffering **374**.1, 9, 19
   welfare **303**.1, 6, 7, 9, 12, 13, 14, 15, 17–18, 29, **350**.8, 12–13, 34
      Animal Protection Index (API) **374**.6–7
      badger culling **303**.27–8
      banning primates as pets **303**.11, 28
      bullfighting **303**.5
      circuses **374**.26
      dog festival **303**.17–18
      dog fighting **303**.8–9
      dog trafficking **303**.3, 4
      elephant riding trips **303**.29
      fur farming **303**.30–2
      legislation **303**.1–2, 10, 26, 27, **374**.5, 8
      live exports **303**.15–16
      overweight **303**.19–20
      and pets **374**.5, 8, 12–13
      puppy farms **303**.3, 4
      trophy hunting **374**.28–9
      wild animals in circuses **303**.10, 26–7, 29
      zoos **374**.33–5
Animal Welfare Act 2006 **303**.1, **374**.5, 8, 41
Annual Bullying Survey 2020 **380**.7–9
Annual Population Survey (2018), on non-religious population **358**.18
Annual Survey of Hours and Earnings (ASHE) **364**.15
anonymity, and cyberbullying **361**.18–19

Vol. numbers appear first (in bold) followed by page numbers; a change in volume is preceded by a semi-colon.

Vol. 305	Globalisation – Good or Bad?	Vol. 368	Sustainable Living	Vol. 392	National Health
Vol. 314	HIV & AIDS	Vol. 369	LGBT+ Issues	Vol. 393	Disability
Vol. 316	Marriage	Vol. 370	Domestic Violence and Abuse	Vol. 394	Pregnancy
Vol. 347	The Censorship Debate	Vol. 371	The Internet and Us	Vol. 395	Teen Self-Care
Vol. 348	World Health	Vol. 372	Our Human Rights	Vol. 396	UK Housing
Vol. 349	Gambling Culture	Vol. 373	Drug Use and Abuse	Vol. 397	Alcohol Issues
Vol. 350	Lifestyle Diets	Vol. 374	Animal Rights	Vol. 398	Homelessness
Vol. 351	The Anxiety Epidemic	Vol. 375	Body Image	Vol. 399	Discussing Cannabis
Vol. 352	Biotech & Bioethics	Vol. 376	Racism	Vol. 400	Suicide & Self-Harm
Vol. 353	Education	Vol. 377	Poverty	Vol. 401	War & Conflict
Vol. 354	Relationships	Vol. 378	Ageing	Vol. 402	Endangered Species
Vol. 355	Terrorism	Vol. 379	Understanding Sexual Health	Vol. 403	Student Options
Vol. 356	British Armed Forces	Vol. 380	About Bullying	Vol. 404	Depression
Vol. 357	The Climate Emergency	Vol. 381	Business	Vol. 405	Employability
Vol. 358	Religion Today	Vol. 382	Active Citizenship	Vol. 406	Smoking
Vol. 359	Migration & Immigration	Vol. 383	The Privacy Debate	Vol. 407	Bereavement
Vol. 360	Government	Vol. 384	Health & Fitness	Vol. 408	Healthy Eating
Vol. 361	Cyberbullying	Vol. 385	Waste & Recycling Issues	Vol. 409	Online Safety
Vol. 362	Euthanasia	Vol. 386	Sexualising Society	Vol. 410	Addiction
Vol. 363	Population Change	Vol. 387	Fertility Issues	Vol. 411	Sport
Vol. 364	The Gender Equality Debate	Vol. 388	Discussing Child Abuse	Vol. 412	Rights of the Child
Vol. 365	Tourism Today	Vol. 389	Sleep	Vol. 413	Energy
Vol. 366	Crime in the UK	Vol. 390	Eating Disorders	Vol. 414	Consumerism
Vol. 367	Discussing Abortion	Vol. 391	Money	Vol. 415	Mental Health

anorexia athletica **390**.41

anorexia nervosa **307**.16, **350**.18–20, **390**.3–4, 6, 9, 20, 22–5, 34–6, 41, **415**.3

antenatal checks **394**.17–18

antenatal depression **351**.22–3

antibiotic resistance **348**.16, 37–8

antibiotics **352**.2

   herbal **343**.31–2

   prescription **343**.32–3

Anti-Bullying Alliance **380**.14–15, 25

anti-bullying app **361**.27

Anti-Bullying Week **380**.14–15

anticipatory grief **407**.16

antidepressants **314**.37, **351**.24, **373**.13–14, **400**.41, **404**.3, 5, 13, 16, 27, 29, 41, **415**.24–5, 41

   see also medications

anti-doping policies **411**.34–6

anti-English sentiment **376**.24–5

anti-immigration policies **359**.27

antimicrobial resistance (AMR) **348**.41

anti-racist practices **376**.28, 39

antiretroviral therapy (ART) **314**.4–6, 8–9, 17–18, 29, **348**.1

   antibody trials **314**.35

   global statistics **314**.3

   and other conditions **314**.31

   and viral suppression **314**.8–11, 24, 26, 35

anti-Semitism **355**.17, **376**.12, 41

antisocial behaviours **399**.10

anti-terrorism see counter-terrorism

anti-vaccine stories **395**.11

anti-virus software **371**.26

anxiety **380**.20, **384**.32, **395**.36, 41, **400**.13–14, 34, 41, **404**.11, 41, **415**.3, 5, 16, 35–6, 41

   accessing treatment **351**.25

   and alcohol **397**.24

   avoiding **351**.2

   awareness of **351**.6–7

   causes of **351**.1–2, 6, 37

   disorders **351**.3–5, 35–6

   and eating disorders **390**.2

   epidemic **351**.6–7

   explaining **351**.1, 41

   inherited **351**.2

   in the modern world **351**.6

   and mortality **351**.7

   and physical health **351**.12

   and poverty **351**.17–18

   self-help for **351**.24

   and sleep **389**.9–11, 16, 20, 27

   and smoking **406**.8

   statistics **351**.10–11

   symptoms **351**.1–2, 20–1, 37

   in teenagers **351**.26–7

   treatments for **351**.7, 9, 24–5, 28–9, 32, 35, 37–9

   triggers **351**.18–20, 30, 37

'anxiety economy' **351**.7–9

appearance

   and gene editing **352**.9–10

   see also body image

appetite changes **394**.4

appetite loss **395**.19

appetite research **408**.38–9

Apple

   encryption **383**.28

   online security **383**.5

   privacy policy **383**.13

   privacy violation **383**.34

   technology **317**.21–2, 34

Application Specific Integrated Circuits (ASIC) **391**.35

Applied General Qualifications **403**.14–15

applied relaxation therapy **351**.24

apprenticeships **403**.1–2, 9, 18, 19, 22, 29–31, 41, **405**.1, 23, 41

   inequality **308**.38, 39

apps **307**.21, 22–3, **351**.9

   anonymous **361**.18–19

   anti-bullying **361**.27

   anti-racist tools **308**.37–8

   disclaimers **307**.21

   gaming **307**.21–2

   sleep-tracking **389**.10–11, 13

   see also social media

App Tracking Transparency (ATT) **383**.13

Arab-Israeli War (1967-1988) **401**.2

Arab Spring **401**.5, 13

Arafat, Yasser **355**.2

arcades **349**.1, 17

Arcadia **381**.19–21

architecture, new homes **396**.28–32

Argentina, employment rights **405**.33

arguments

   in families **354**.9–10

   with friends **354**.23

   in relationships **354**.15–16, **379**.27

Aristotle **360**.1

armed conflict see war and conflict

Armed Forces **372**.7

   attitudes to **356**.3–4, 20

   definition **356**.41

   as heros **356**.3–4

   recruitment approaches **356**.5–7, 9–11

   role in society **356**.20

   support for **356**.20

   transition from **356**.30–9

   see also military; war and conflict

Armed Forces Day **356**.3, 20

Army Foundation College **356**.11

aromatherapy **343**.6, 41, **351**.32, 37–9

arranged marriage **316**.21, **388**.16

arsenic **374**.15

arson **366**.2

art

   artistic freedom **347**.36–9

   therapy **343**.6

arthritis **392**.29

artificial intelligence (AI) **357**.23, **383**.25–6

   in care homes **378**.26

   in ecommerce **381**.4

   rights of **382**.12

artificial reproductive technology (ART) **387**.41

artisan roles **405**.2

arts, GCSE & A-levels **403**.4, 5

arts and crafts **395**.35

Ascension Day **358**.22

asexuality **369**.2, 13, 41

Ash Wednesday **358**.22

Asia

   Asian history in Britain **376**.35

employment rights **405**.33
global poverty **306**.28
HIV **314**.18
life expectancy **378**.5, 7, 10
population decline **363**.27–9
population growth **363**.20, 27–9
retirement age **378**.13–14
Asia-Pacific region, and religion **358**.2
AS-levels **403**.10–11
aspirin **311**.14–15
gastrointestinal bleeding **311**.15
heart disease **311**.14, 15
stroke **311**.14, 15
assertiveness **307**.31, 35
assimilation **359**.26, 41
assisted dying
definitions **362**.4, 8, 19, 41
see also assisted suicide; euthanasia
Assisted Dying bills **362**.3, 13
Assisted Dying for the Terminally Ill Bill **362**.2
assisted suicide
countries permitting **362**.4, 8–9
as criminal act **362**.8, 28
definitions **362**.1, 4, 8, 16, 19, 41
and dignity in death **362**.32
and disabled people **362**.18–20, 38
legislation **362**.1–5, 7, 10–14, 16, 21
public view of **362**.6–7, 21, 28, 30
statistics **362**.5–6
and terminal illness **362**.18, 20, 32–6
see also assisted dying; euthanasia; physician-assisted suicide (PAS)
Association of Zoos and Aquariums (AZA) **374**.34
Assumption of Mary **358**.23
asteroids **402**.2
asthma **392**.28, 29–30, **406**.14, 17
asylum
applications **359**.2, 30, 35–6, 41
asylum seeker status **359**.30–1, 35–6
refugee status **359**.30–1
Syrian refugees **359**.31
worldwide statistics **359**.31–4
asylums **392**.2
asylum seekers **359**.30–1, 35–6, 41, **380**.4, **415**.17
see also refugees
asymptomatic viral shedding **379**.3
atheism **316**.7, **355**.41, **358**.2, 13–14, 19, 41
attachment **354**.12–13, **409**.24–5
Attachment-based Compassion Therapy (ACT) **343**.22
Attenborough, David **357**.17, 31, **368**.19, 22
attendance, school **353**.22–3
attention deficit hyperactivity disorder (ADHD) **384**.32, **393**.3, 5
attention spans **371**.8
atypical anorexia **390**.5
AUKUS **401**.20
austerity **305**.33, **306**.21, **391**.15
policies **377**.14, 41
and poverty **306**.4, 9, 11, 23, **318**.2
and work **306**.21
Australia
abortion **302**.15
AIDS **314**.11–12
compulsory voting **360**.17

globalisation **305**.8–9
Great Barrier Reef **357**.17
healthcare **392**.16–17
high temperatures **357**.29
human rights issues **372**.30–1
immigration statistics **359**.3–4
international trade **305**.35
Islamophobia **308**.37
online privacy **383**.10
prostitution **318**.27–8
racism **308**.37
retirement age **378**.13–14
and voluntary euthanasia **362**.9
Austria
immigration statistics **359**.4
online privacy **317**.38
waste statistics **385**.3
autism spectrum disorders (ASD) **343**.35–6, **351**.28, **393**.3–4, 41, **415**.16
autistic burnout **404**.8
automatic facial recognition (AFR) **383**.14–15, 17–22
automation **383**.4
autonomous deliveries **381**.4
avatars **386**.6
aviation **357**.37
see also air travel
avoidance **351**.2, 21
Avon Longitudinal Study of Parents and Children (ALSPAC) **354**.14
AWOL (absent without leave) **356**.41
Ayurveda **358**.21

B

babies and birth
birth rates **358**.3
and HIV **314**.2, 24, 29–30
life expectancy **311**.4
mortality **306**.27
premature babies **302**.26
see also fertility; postnatal depression
baby boom **363**.3, 8
baby boomers **368**.5
drug abuse **373**.14–15
and meat-free diets **350**.4–5
backbenchers **360**.41
backpacking **365**.38–9
back pain **343**.2, 4, 11, **394**.5
bacteria **348**.16, 19
bacterial genes **352**.30
badgers, culling **303**.27–8
bad news, coping with **404**.34–5
bags for life **385**.27
Baha'i faith **303**.37, **358**.2, 8–9, 31
Bahrain
immigration statistics **359**.3
waste statistics **385**.4
baiting **380**.3, 41
balanced diet **350**.23
see also diet; healthy eating
bamboo **357**.18
BAME see Black, Asian and minority ethnic (BAME)
bananas **408**.13

banknotes **391**.1, 4
Bank of England **391**.3, 15, 30
banks **305**.38, **306**.12, 34, **391**.3, 15, 21–2
    basic accounts **306**.37
    central banks **391**.30–1
    charges **306**.37
    creating new money **391**.15, 21
    debt with **306**.9
    protectionism **305**.32
banter, and bullying **380**.2, 41
Barbie
    gender inclusive dolls **364**.37
    images **307**.13
    surveillance **317**.37
barbiuturates **373**.22
Barclays **356**.38–9
Barnardo's, on child poverty **306**.13
bartering **391**.2
basal temperature **394**.4
basic income **377**.35–6
Battersea Dogs and Cats Home, on puppy farms **303**.4
BBC, and gender discrimination **364**.17
B-Corps **381**.27–8, 41
beaches, littering of **385**.6, 10–11
beauty pageants **386**.41
'beauty sleep' **389**.3
beavers **402**.30
Beck Depression Inventory **404**.18
bedded down
    see also rough sleeping
beef, and climate change **357**.24–7
bees **352**.17
'before and after' photographs **375**.17
begging **300**.6–7
Begum, Shamima **355**.25–7
behavioural addiction **410**.9–10
Belgium
    and euthanasia **362**.9, 26–7
    immigration statistics **359**.4
beliefs
    versus faith **358**.16
    nature of **358**.16–17
    philosophical **358**.16–17
    see also humanism; religion; individual religions
Belly Button Challenge **307**.19
benefits system **377**.1, 3, 5, 7, 19, 41, **393**.25
    access to **382**.3
benzodiazepines **351**.24, **373**.5, 13, 22
Bercow, John **308**.32, **360**.10
bereavement **400**.6, 24, 37–8, 41, **407**.16, 24–5, 38, **415**.41
    see also grief
Bermuda, waste statistics **385**.4
beta-blockers **351**.24
Better2Know, on sexual health **379**.3
betting
    age restrictions **349**.2
    Fixed-Odds Betting Terminals (FOBTs) **349**.1, 17, 26–30
    pools **349**.2, 41
    and World Cup **349**.14
    see also gambling
Bevan, Aneurin **392**.1
Beveridge Report **392**.1
bias **364**.41
    unconscious **364**.3

Bible **358**.13, 31, 34
Biden, Joe **401**.15, 18, 20–1
Big Brother **383**.41
Big Brother Watch **383**.21–2
Big Butterfly Count **357**.34
big cats circuses **303**.10, 26
    endangered **303**.27
    hunting of **303**.27
big data **408**.38–9
Big Fat Gypsy Weddings (TV) **308**.7
Big Issue **398**.6
bikes see cycling
Bill of Rights **360**.14, **372**.5
Bills, process through Parliament **360**.6–8, 41
binge drinking **397**.13, 33, 41, **399**.9–10
binge eating disorder (BED) **390**.3, 5, 6, 41, **400**.16, 18, **415**.3
bingo **349**.2, 7, 41
biocapacity **368**.4
biodegradable waste **368**.4, 23, 41, **385**.41
biodiversity **357**.34, **402**.41
    and overpopulation **363**.22–3
    targets **357**.1
biodiversity loss **402**.2–6, 10–11, 39
bioethics **352**.3–4, 31–9
biofuel energy **352**.3
biofuels **413**.2, 5, 9, 41
biogas energy **413**.38
biohacking **352**.21–2, 32, 41
biological clock **389**.12
biological sex **369**.2, 3
biological warfare **355**.4, **401**.33, 41
biomass **413**.5, 38–9, 41
biometrics **383**.14, 41
biomonitoring **352**.7
biotechnology
    agricultural **352**.2
    applications **352**.2–3, 7
    definition **352**.1, 41
    in food **352**.19
    and forests **352**.26–8
    industrial **352**.3
    and inequalities **352**.33
    medical **352**.1–2
    in medicine **352**.11–13, 16, 23–4
    pharmaceutical drugs **352**.1, 3
bioterrorism **352**.34
bioweapons **357**.23
biphobia **369**.13
biphobic bullying **380**.5
bipolar disorder **388**.29, 33, **404**.3, 41, **415**.4, 5, 19, 41
BirdLife International, on slaughtered birds **303**.9
birds
    feeding **357**.33
    as pets **374**.13
    at risk of extinction **402**.13, 22–3, 34–5
    slaughter of **303**.9, 12
Birmingham, and tourism **365**.4
birth see babies and birth
birth control see contraception
birth rates **363**.2–3, 7–11, 29, 36–7, 41, **387**.11, 41, **394**.19, 41
'birth strikers' **363**.38–9
bisexuality **369**.2, 12, 13, 15, 20–3, 41
    see also LGBTQIA+ community
Bisphenol A **379**.7

Bitcoin **391**.30, 32–6
Black, Asian and minority ethnic (BAME) **308**.9–10, 18, 19, **381**.29–32, **382**.6, 14, 41, **398**.14
  education **308**.16, 28
  employment **308**.12, 27, 38–9
  films **308**.9, 32
  hate crime **308**.12
  inequality **308**.9, 12
  labelling as white **308**.31
  marriage **316**.26
  and mental health **415**.28
  racial stereotyping **308**.31–2
  violence **308**.37–8
Black disabled representation **393**.29–30
Black Friday **414**.24–6, 41
blackheads **395**.22–3
Black history, in Britain **376**.1, 35
Black Lives Matter **376**.4, 6, 9–10, 13–14, 26, **381**.29
'blacksplaining' **376**.33
bladder control **394**.31
blaming
  in relationships **354**.28
  see also control
blasphemy **347**.1, 4, 6, **358**.36–7, 41
bleeding **394**.7, 20, 23, 31
  unexplained **395**.19
blindness **392**.30
bloating **394**.5, **395**.19
blockchain **391**.32–6
blocking, on social media **409**.14–15, 30
blogging **350**.19–20
  freedom of speech **347**.1
  and online privacy **317**.39
blogs **409**.26, 41
blood
  donation **382**.30–1
  effects of cannabis **399**.15
  pressure, high **392**.32–3
  tests **394**.17
  transfusions, and HIV **314**.2
Blue Badge holders **393**.17, 41
blue light **389**.15, 41
'Blue Planet' effect **368**.19, 23
BMI (body mass index) **307**.3, 16, **390**.25, 36, 41, **408**.41

board games **378**.33
bodybuilding **375**.14–15
body clock **404**.17
body dysmorphic disorder **415**.3, 5
body dysmorphic disorder (BDD) **307**.8, 9–12, 13–14, **351**.3, **375**.3, 6, 11, 21, 41, **390**.2, 41
body fat content (BFC) **384**.4
body image **307**.1, 2, 3, 5, 13, 15, 28, **369**.36, **379**.1, **380**.4, **386**.3, **390**.2, 6, 15, 18, 25, 41, **395**.41, **408**.35
  and airbrushing **307**.16, 18, 25, **375**.30
  and anorexia **307**.16
  and Barbie images **307**.13
  and BMI **307**.3, 16
  body positive campaigns **307**.17–18
  comparing to others **375**.2, 24
  comparisons **307**.6–7
  cosmetic surgery **307**.20, 21–4
  definition **375**.1, 41
  and disability **375**.19
  dissatisfaction with **375**.4–5, 10, 16, 31
  emotions **307**.26, 27
  friendship **307**.7
  getting help **307**.2
  humour **307**.27–8
  impact of lockdown **375**.18
  infantilisation **307**.26–7
  influences on **375**.1
  marginalisation **307**.27, 28
  media alternatives **307**.15
  media pressure **307**.1, 4
  and mental health **375**.1–2
  narcissism **307**.6
  'normal' parameters **307**.26
  safety **307**.26
  social pressure **307**.19, 27
  status **307**.6
  teasing **307**.1–2
  see also sexualisation
body language, and consent **379**.31
body mass index (BMI) **384**.1–2, 4, 6–7, 41, **394**.17
  and fertility **387**.21–3, 29
body positivity **375**.3, 17, 29, 35–9, **386**.4
body weight
  and contraceptive pill **309**.3

Vol. numbers appear first (in bold) followed by page numbers; a change in volume is preceded by a semi-colon.

Vol. 305	Globalisation – Good or Bad?	Vol. 368	Sustainable Living	Vol. 392	National Health
Vol. 314	HIV & AIDS	Vol. 369	LGBT+ Issues	Vol. 393	Disability
Vol. 316	Marriage	Vol. 370	Domestic Violence and Abuse	Vol. 394	Pregnancy
Vol. 347	The Censorship Debate	Vol. 371	The Internet and Us	Vol. 395	Teen Self-Care
Vol. 348	World Health	Vol. 372	Our Human Rights	Vol. 396	UK Housing
Vol. 349	Gambling Culture	Vol. 373	Drug Use and Abuse	Vol. 397	Alcohol Issues
Vol. 350	Lifestyle Diets	Vol. 374	Animal Rights	Vol. 398	Homelessness
Vol. 351	The Anxiety Epidemic	Vol. 375	Body Image	Vol. 399	Discussing Cannabis
Vol. 352	Biotech & Bioethics	Vol. 376	Racism	Vol. 400	Suicide & Self-Harm
Vol. 353	Education	Vol. 377	Poverty	Vol. 401	War & Conflict
Vol. 354	Relationships	Vol. 378	Ageing	Vol. 402	Endangered Species
Vol. 355	Terrorism	Vol. 379	Understanding Sexual Health	Vol. 403	Student Options
Vol. 356	British Armed Forces	Vol. 380	About Bullying	Vol. 404	Depression
Vol. 357	The Climate Emergency	Vol. 381	Business	Vol. 405	Employability
Vol. 358	Religion Today	Vol. 382	Active Citizenship	Vol. 406	Smoking
Vol. 359	Migration & Immigration	Vol. 383	The Privacy Debate	Vol. 407	Bereavement
Vol. 360	Government	Vol. 384	Health & Fitness	Vol. 408	Healthy Eating
Vol. 361	Cyberbullying	Vol. 385	Waste & Recycling Issues	Vol. 409	Online Safety
Vol. 362	Euthanasia	Vol. 386	Sexualising Society	Vol. 410	Addiction
Vol. 363	Population Change	Vol. 387	Fertility Issues	Vol. 411	Sport
Vol. 364	The Gender Equality Debate	Vol. 388	Discussing Child Abuse	Vol. 412	Rights of the Child
Vol. 365	Tourism Today	Vol. 389	Sleep	Vol. 413	Energy
Vol. 366	Crime in the UK	Vol. 390	Eating Disorders	Vol. 414	Consumerism
Vol. 367	Discussing Abortion	Vol. 391	Money	Vol. 415	Mental Health

and exercise **307**.39
see also overweight and obesity
bogong moth **402**.21
Boiler Upgrade Scheme **413**.28
Boko Haram **355**.15–16, **401**.24
bongs **399**.1
bookmaker **349**.41
books, and censorship **347**.31–5
booze cruises **365**.11
borderline personality disorder **404**.36
borderline personality disorder (BPD) **415**.5
borders, and migration **318**.38–9
Born Free **374**.26, 28–9
borrowing *see* debt
Botswana
    government **360**.39
    and SDGs **314**.9
boundaries **395**.39, **404**.9
bovine TB, and badger culling **303**.27–8
bowel health **395**.20
boyfriends **354**.26–7
    see also romantic relationships
boys and young men
    and body image **307**.15
    education inequality **364**.19
    and gender equality **314**.32
    and HIV **314**.16–17
    and homelessness **398**.6, 22, 33
    and pornography **318**.34, 35
    and self-esteem **307**.38
    and selfies **318**.35
    and sex **309**.29
    and sexual dysfunction **309**.16
    smoking statistics **406**.1
    and social media **409**.5
    stages of puberty **395**.27, 29
    and STIs **309**.25
braces and orthodontics **395**.26
brain
    and animal research **303**.33–4
    and cannabis **301**.11
    death **407**.1, 4–5
    and depression **404**.14–16
    development, in teenagers **400**.8
    effects of cannabis **399**.2, 14–15, 16
    impacts of drugs on **373**.4
    and memory **311**.38
    reward systems **373**.1, 28
brain drain **305**.6
brain injury **411**.14–16
brain training, online **311**.20–1
brands **305**.7–8
    clothing label sizes **305**.8–9
Brazil
    and abortion **302**.24
    and animal research **303**.38
    and body image **307**.23–4
    CO_2 emissions **357**.3
    rainforest **357**.16
breaches of children's rights **412**.28–9
bread, wholegrain **408**.12–13
breakfast clubs **306**.17, 36
breaking up **354**.38–9, **379**.28
breast cancer **395**.17, 19

breast-feeding **408**.1
breastfeeding **394**.38–9
breasts, changes in pregnancy **394**.4–5
breathing techniques **351**.37–8
breathlessness **395**.19
Breeding and Sale of Dogs (Welfare) Act 1999 **303**.2
Breeding of Dogs Acts **303**.2
Brexit **360**.10, 11, 28, **382**.1–2, 8, 10, 18, 24, 41
    and anxiety **351**.13–14
    and European Union (EU) citizens **359**.13–14
    and globalisation **305**.20, 21, 36, 38–9
    and human rights **372**.6
    immigration **359**.22–5
    impact on business **381**.5–6, 9–11
    impact on tourism **365**.7
    and racism **376**.1–2
    risks to health **348**.38–39
Bristol Energy Cooperative (BEC) **413**.34–5
Bristol Stool Chart **395**.20
British Army **356**.41
    'Belonging' campaign **356**.6
    equality and diversity **356**.16
    partners **356**.29
    recruitment **356**.6
    Royal Engineers **356**.14
    women in **356**.13
British Association for Counselling and Psychotherapy (BACP) **404**.39
British Bill of Rights **300**.30, 33, 36–7
British Board of Film Classification (BBFC) **347**.24
British citizenship **382**.1–5
    see also citizenship
British Empire **382**.8–9
British Gas **413**.21
British Humanist Association (BHA)
    on animal welfare **303**.7
    on marriage **316**.6, 10
British identity **308**.4, 5, **382**.6–11
    and globalisation **305**.7–8
British Medical Association (BMA)
    on assisted dying **362**.29
    on HIV **314**.23
British Nationality Act 1948 **382**.9
British Nationality Act 1981 **382**.1, 3
British Pregnancy Advisory Service (BPAS) **367**.1
British Social Attitudes (BSA) survey
    on euthanasia **362**.6
    on non-religious population **358**.18
    on religion **358**.1
British Summertime **389**.12
British traits **382**.10–11
British Union for the Abolition of Vivisection (BUAV) **374**.21
Broken Plate Report **408**.30, 32
bronchitis **392**.30–1
Brook **309**.17
brothels **318**.11, 16, 22–3
brownfield land **396**.21, 27
brucella **348**.19
bruxism **389**.20
BTEC First Diploma **403**.8
BTEC qualifications **403**.8, 11, 14
Buddhism **355**.2, **358**.2–4, 9, 11, 17, 18, 31, 41
    and euthanasia **362**.17
Budget (Finance Bill) **360**.41

budget airlines **365**.6, 12
budgeting **391**.16–18, 41
    see also money; tuition fees
Buenos Aires, prostitution **318**.4–5
buffer zones **401**.1
bulimia nervosa **375**.12–13, **390**.3, 5–6, 9, 21, 27–8, 41,
   400.16, **415**.3
bullfighting **303**.5
bullies
    psychology of **380**.16–17
    self-esteem **380**.17
    stereotypes **380**.18
    unaware **380**.18, 38
bullying **356**.16, **361**.41, **369**.19, **388**.41, **409**.5, 13–14, 19, 29
    anti-bullying app **361**.27
    culture **380**.29–30
    as defence mechanism **380**.17
    and empathy **380**.18
    face-to-face **361**.10
    and gender **361**.4, 11
    help and support **316**.36
    impacts **380**.8, 11, 14, 20, 26–7, 30, 34
    indirect **380**.1–3
    intervention **361**.10
    online **371**.20
    passive **380**.30
    perceived motivations **380**.7
    physical **380**.1, 38
    prejudice-based **380**.1, 4–6
    prevention **361**.28–9
    racist **308**.36, **361**.26, 41
    reasons for **380**.16–17
    responses to **380**.9, 35–6
    sexual **361**.41
    sibling **354**.14
    in sport **411**.37
    statistics **361**.10, **380**.7–9, 10–13, 14, 21–5, 31–2
    unintentional **380**.38
    verbal **380**.1
    violent **361**.11
    at work **405**.36–7
    in the workplace **361**.14–15
    workplace **380**.18–19, 20, 29–39
    see also cyberbullying; homophobic bullying; school
      bullying; workplace bullying
bupropion **406**.33
burglary **366**.1–2, 3
Burma, religious persecution **358**.38–9
burnout **404**.8–10
burqa **358**.32–3, 41
bursaries **391**.41, **403**.18
bushmeat **402**.14–15
business
    adapting **381**.12–13
    growth **381**.2
    ideas **381**.1
    impact of Brexit **381**.5–6, 9–11
    impact of COVID-19 **381**.7–13, 20–1
    impact of economy **381**.7–9
    insurance **381**.2
    loans **391**.29
    plan **381**.3
    premises **381**.24–5
    profitability **381**.1–2
    rates **381**.2
    starting up **381**.2–3
    strategy **381**.2–3
    structure **381**.2–3
    travel **365**.1, 3–4
    viability **381**.1
butane hash oil (BHO) **301**.6
'butterflies in the stomach' **351**.1
buy-one-get-one-free (BOGOF) deals **414**.30
buy-to-let **396**.2
bystander effect **380**.25

C

Cabinet **360**.2
caddisflies **402**.37
caesarean section **394**.28, 29–30, 33
Cafcass (Children and Family Court Advisory and Support
   Service), on parental separation **316**.36, 37–8
caffeine **351**.9, 19, **389**.6, 8, 41, **394**.15, **395**.41, **410**.23–4, 28,
   41
    during pregnancy **394**.10
    and teenagers **395**.30–1
Caged North West, on dog racing **303**.16
calcium **350**.23, **394**.12
Call The Midwife **367**.38–9
calories **408**.1, 17
Cambridge Analytica **383**.11–12
cameras, on drones **317**.30
Cameron, David **356**.12
Canada **360**.39
    and animal research **303**.38, 39
    CO_2 emissions **357**.3
    and euthanasia **362**.9
    immigration statistics **359**.3–4
    waste statistics **385**.4
cancer **352**.20–1, 29–30, **378**.5, 8, 21, 35–6, **379**.20, 41,
   392.30, **406**.1, 7, 19, 30–1, 34, 38, **408**.10, 15, 17
    and alcohol **397**.8–9
    anal **309**.25
    and anxiety **351**.12
    cervical **309**.25
    cervical screening **395**.16
    Kaposi's Sarcoma **314**.6
    liquid biopsies **348**.37
    and obesity **384**.2, 5, 11, 19
    palliative care **311**.2
    reducing risk of **384**.20
    screening **392**.24
    self-check **395**.17–19
    signs and symptoms **395**.18–19
    see also breast cancer
Cancer Research UK **406**.7, 19, 30–1, 38
cannabis **301**.1–2, **373**.4, 9, 22, 23
    and academic performance **399**.18–19
    addiction **399**.3, 4, 13, 17, 21, 41
    consumption trends **301**.5, 6, 21
    cut-with substances **399**.3
    decriminalising **399**.6–7
    and driving **399**.3, 26
    duration of effects **399**.2, 15
    edibles **399**.1–2, 27
    effects of **399**.2, 4, 14–28

effects on the brain **301**.11

and emergency medical treatment **301**.7

giving up **399**.4

hangover from **399**.17

inhalation methods **399**.1–2, 27

and the law **399**.3, 6–8, 11, 13, 18

legalisation of **373**.26–7

medical benefits **373**.27

medical use **399**.5, 6–8, 15, 30–8

and mental health **399**.3, 4–5, 15, 21–5, 28

misuse **399**.11–12, 23

mixing with other drugs **399**.3

penalties for possession **301**.19, 22

and pregnancy **399**.5, 15

risks **399**.2–3, 4–5

and sleep **399**.24

smoking **399**.1, 2–3

strength of **399**.13

and suicidal thoughts **399**.23

synthetic **373**.20–1, 22, 28

synthetic cannabis alternatives **301**.6–7, 31

types of **399**.1

use by men and boys **399**.9, 23

use by teenagers and young people **399**.9–12, 18

use by women and girls **399**.9, 23

vaping **399**.2

cannabis oil **399**.1

cannabis use disorder **399**.23

cans, recycling **385**.12, 25, 28

Canterbury, pilgrimage **358**.26

capitalism **381**.41, **414**.22, 41

capital punishment, of animals **374**.4

caps, contraceptive **309**.6

car bombs **355**.3–4

carbon

footprint **357**.41

offsets **357**.41

tax **357**.5–6, 41

carbon capture and storage (CCS) **357**.36

carbon dioxide **357**.6, **413**.8, 10–12

carbon footprint **350**.2, 11, **365**.27, **385**.20

carbon neutral **357**.2

cardiovascular disease **408**.10

cardiovascular diseases **384**.2, 5, 11, 19, 20

CareConfidential, on abortion **302**.4, 18, 19

cared-for children **309**.18

career colleges **403**.41

careers advisors **403**.6–7, 13

Career Transition Partnership (CTP) **356**.37

care-experienced children **380**.5

care homes **311**.5, 30–1, **378**.26

Care Homes Reading Project **311**.30–1

Care Not Killing **362**.28

Care Quality Commission, on learning disabilities **393**.24

carers **393**.12–14

Caribbean, and abortion **302**.24, 25

car loans **391**.28

carpooling **368**.3

cars and driving

driverless vehicles **311**.27

green vehicles **368**.14

legal age **354**.1

product liability **317**.32

see also electric cars

cash flow **381**.17–18

cashless society **391**.28, 30–1, 37–9

casinos **349**.2, 9, 38, 41

caste system **308**.25–6

history of **308**.25, 26

and suicide **308**.26

and violence **308**.26

cataplexy **389**.29, 31

catfishing **361**.6, 41, **409**.41

Catholicism

and abortion **302**.12, 15, 21

and euthanasia **362**.17

and food poverty **306**.25

cats **303**.18, **374**.10–11, 13

dieting **303**.20

as meat **303**.17, 18

overweight **303**.19, 20

see also big cats

Cayman Islands, waste statistics **385**.4

CBD (cannabidiol) **399**.2, 5, 13, 30–3, 36–8, 41

CBT (cognitive behavioural therapy) *see* cognitive behavioural therapy (CBT)

CCTV (closed-circuit television) **317**.23, **383**.14–15, 20, 41

as deterrent **317**.25

and human rights **317**.25

CEASE therapy (Complete Elimination of Autism Spectrum Expression) **343**.35–6

CEDAW (Convention on the Elimination of all Forms of Discrimination against Women) **300**.2, 23

celebrity

and animal welfare **303**.10

and body image **307**.5, 12, 15, 20, 24, 25

Celiac Disease Foundation **350**.24

censorship **347**.6–7

definition **347**.40

and films **347**.26–7

internet **347**.6–7, 9

social media **347**.2, 6–7, 8, 11

and surveillance **347**.8

technology of **347**.8

world map of **347**.9–10

see also blasphemy; freedom of expression; freedom of speech; no-platforming

censorship resistance systems **347**.7

centenarians **378**.4, 41

Centers for Disease Control and Prevention (CDC), on antibiotics **343**.33

Central African Republic, and war zones **300**.20

central banks **391**.30–1

cereal products **350**.23

ceremonial mace **360**.12–13

cervical cancer **309**.25, **379**.20, 41, **395**.41

cervical screening **395**.16

chamomile **351**.38

Change4Life programme **307**.39

Channel Islands, waste statistics **385**.4

character building **307**.36–7

charities **311**.28

and fairtrade **305**.16

Charity Commission **360**.2

Chartered Trading Standards Institute (CTSI) **406**.20

cheetahs **357**.18

chemical, biological, radiological and nuclear (CBRN) **355**.4–5

chemical weapons **355**.4, **401**.41

chhaupadi **379**.10–11

Chichimeca War (1550-1590) **401**.3

chickenpox **392**.35

chickens
  and food poisoning **348**.9
  sentience of **374**.9

child and adolescent mental health services (CAMHS) **415**.14–15

Child and Social Work Act 2017 **395**.10

childbirth
  complications **348**.1
  fear of **394**.34
  labour **394**.28–9
  methods of **394**.28–30
  pain relief **394**.28
  recovery from **394**.31–3
  trauma **394**.35
  young mothers **348**.2

child brides **364**.1

childcare **353**.30, **377**.10

child exploitation **388**.41, **412**.14, 41

Child Exploitation and Online Protection Centre (CEOP) **361**.34, **409**.41

childhood experiences, and anxiety **351**.2

child labour **412**.17–27, 41

ChildLine **307**.38, **316**.36, **354**.10, 17, **369**.19, **380**.21
  on divorce **316**.36
  on exam stress **353**.15–16
  on forced marriage **316**.20–1
  on internet pornography **318**.33
  on parental separation **316**.36
  on racism **308**.1–2

child maintenance **316**.15

child marriage **388**.18, 41, **412**.14, 35–6, 41
  see also forced marriage

child poverty **306**.7, 10–11, 13–14, 16–17, 23, 29–30, 38, **377**.8, 11–13, 15, 29
  and death **306**.26
  and food poverty **306**.13, 17, 23, 25, 28, 36
  and happiness **306**.16
  and health **306**.23, 26, 30
  history of **306**.5
  and housing **306**.7
  and income **306**.13, 14, 16
  and mental health **306**.14, 15, 23
  and rich-poor gap **306**.13, 15
  and salvaging from waste dumps **306**.32
  and school costs **306**.15
  and state benefits **306**.7, 11
  and transport poverty **306**.13
  and wellbeing **306**.14–15
  and work **306**.11

child protection plan (CPP) **388**.2, 41

child protection register (CPR) **388**.2

Child Q **412**.37–8

children
  rights of **372**.3, 11–13
  rules for **361**.28–9
  screen time **371**.5–7, 18
  secure attachment **354**.12–13
  surveillance of **317**.37
  vulnerable **353**.24–7, **361**.22
  see also adolescence; babies and birth; boys and young men; education; girls and young women

Children and Family Court Advisory and Support Service (Cafcass), on parental separation **316**.36, 37–8

Children and Social Work Act 2017 **354**.9, **379**.6

Children's Charter 1908 **306**.5

Children's Society, *The*
  on child poverty **306**.11, 14–15
  on cyberbullying **361**.2
  on mental illness **306**.14
  on parental debt **353**.35
  on wellbeing **306**.14

child sexual exploitation **388**.5–7, 41

child trafficking **300**.5, **412**.17, 22, 24–5, 41
  and child exploitation **300**.4
  global prevalence **300**.7
  sex trafficking **300**.6

Chile **360**.39

China
  ageing **311**.26
  and animal welfare **303**.16–18
  censorship in **347**.26–7
  CO_2 emissions **357**.3–4, 6, 32
  drug policies **301**.28
  fertility rates **363**.30

Vol. numbers appear first (in bold) followed by page numbers; a change in volume is preceded by a semi-colon.

Vol. 305	Globalisation – Good or Bad?
Vol. 314	HIV & AIDS
Vol. 316	Marriage
Vol. 347	The Censorship Debate
Vol. 348	World Health
Vol. 349	Gambling Culture
Vol. 350	Lifestyle Diets
Vol. 351	The Anxiety Epidemic
Vol. 352	Biotech & Bioethics
Vol. 353	Education
Vol. 354	Relationships
Vol. 355	Terrorism
Vol. 356	British Armed Forces
Vol. 357	The Climate Emergency
Vol. 358	Religion Today
Vol. 359	Migration & Immigration
Vol. 360	Government
Vol. 361	Cyberbullying
Vol. 362	Euthanasia
Vol. 363	Population Change
Vol. 364	The Gender Equality Debate
Vol. 365	Tourism Today
Vol. 366	Crime in the UK
Vol. 367	Discussing Abortion
Vol. 368	Sustainable Living
Vol. 369	LGBT+ Issues
Vol. 370	Domestic Violence and Abuse
Vol. 371	The Internet and Us
Vol. 372	Our Human Rights
Vol. 373	Drug Use and Abuse
Vol. 374	Animal Rights
Vol. 375	Body Image
Vol. 376	Racism
Vol. 377	Poverty
Vol. 378	Ageing
Vol. 379	Understanding Sexual Health
Vol. 380	About Bullying
Vol. 381	Business
Vol. 382	Active Citizenship
Vol. 383	The Privacy Debate
Vol. 384	Health & Fitness
Vol. 385	Waste & Recycling Issues
Vol. 386	Sexualising Society
Vol. 387	Fertility Issues
Vol. 388	Discussing Child Abuse
Vol. 389	Sleep
Vol. 390	Eating Disorders
Vol. 391	Money
Vol. 392	National Health
Vol. 393	Disability
Vol. 394	Pregnancy
Vol. 395	Teen Self-Care
Vol. 396	UK Housing
Vol. 397	Alcohol Issues
Vol. 398	Homelessness
Vol. 399	Discussing Cannabis
Vol. 400	Suicide & Self-Harm
Vol. 401	War & Conflict
Vol. 402	Endangered Species
Vol. 403	Student Options
Vol. 404	Depression
Vol. 405	Employability
Vol. 406	Smoking
Vol. 407	Bereavement
Vol. 408	Healthy Eating
Vol. 409	Online Safety
Vol. 410	Addiction
Vol. 411	Sport
Vol. 412	Rights of the Child
Vol. 413	Energy
Vol. 414	Consumerism
Vol. 415	Mental Health

government **360**.36
healthcare **392**.16
herbal medicine **343**.4–5, 28
and HIV **314**.39
and Hong Kong **318**.4
housing **311**.2
human rights issues **372**.30
immigration statistics **359**.4
and international trade **305**.31, 32
privacy laws **383**.7
religion in **358**.3
selective abortion **367**.24
war and conflict **401**.20–1
chines liver fluke **348**.19
chlamydia **309**.5, 11, **379**.3, 14–15, 20, 24, 25, **387**.19
chocolate **412**.21–2
cholera **348**.19
cholesterol **392**.32
Christianity **358**.2–5, 8, 11, 41
Bible **358**.13, 31, 34
decline of **358**.3
holidays **358**.22–3
marriage **316**.26
rejection of **358**.6–7
theocratic states **358**.4
UK population **358**.18
US population **358**.20
youth conferences **358**.6
see also Catholicism; Church of England
Christmas
and depression **404**.11
and family arguments **354**.15
chromosomes, and biological sex **369**.1, 3
chromosome shattering **352**.29
chronic bronchitis **392**.30–1
chronic depression **404**.1
chronic fatigue syndrome **343**.5, **393**.14
chronic kidney disease (CKD) **392**.31
chronic obstructive pulmonary disease (COPD) **348**.5–6,
  406.1, 41
chronic pain **343**.22, **373**.3
chronic traumatic encephalopathy (CTE) **411**.15
churches *see* religion
Church of England
disestablishment of **358**.18
and marriage **316**.4
'Church of the Flying Spaghetti Monster' **358**.4
CIA, on surveillance **317**.21, 22, 35
cigarettes **392**.21, 23, **399**.9, 15, **406**.1, 41, **410**.4
advertising **406**.1
age restriction **406**.37
consumption trends **301**.4, 6, 21
see also e-cigarettes; tobacco
cigars **406**.8
cinema *see* film and theatre
circadian rhythms **389**.14, 16, 20, 41
circular economy **381**.41, **385**.34, 41, **414**.41
circumcision **314**.16–17
circuses
and animal welfare **374**.26
and banning wild animals **303**.10, 26–7
tricks **303**.29
cisgender **369**.1–2
cities

and green living **385**.31
and tourism **365**.4
see also urban areas
Citizens Advice Bureau **414**.6, 10
citizenship **359**.2
definition **382**.1, 41
deprivation **382**.3, 5
status **382**.1–5
see also culture and citizenship
city technology colleges **353**.4
civic duty **382**.22–4, 26, 36–7
civil liberties **372**.5
Civil Partnership Act 2004 **316**.8–9
civil partnerships **316**.3–5, 8–9, 15, **354**.3, 4–5, 7, 40, **369**.23–
  4, **380**.5
civil rights
of ethnic minorities **306**.5
and racial discrimination **308**.3
and racism **308**.29
of women **306**.5
of young people **308**.3
Civil Service **360**.3
civil solidarity pacts **316**.9
civil wars **401**.3, 4, 41
civvy street **356**.41
Clare's Law **370**.41
class *see* social class
Class B drugs **399**.3, 6–8
see also cannabis
Classmates.com **409**.1
clean air **412**.16
clean eating **350**.22–3
cleaning products **368**.15
clickbait **317**.10
climacteric **387**.8
climate action, and sport **411**.8
climate change **352**.6, **363**.22, 24, **368**.13, **372**.31, **413**.1, 3–4,
  27, 36, **415**.33–4
and air travel **365**.24–6
attitudes towards **357**.7
definition **357**.41
deniers **357**.5, 31–2
effect on animal species **357**.18–19
emergency **357**.1–2, 10
government targets **357**.1–2
and human extinction **357**.22
models **357**.41
and political instability **357**.5–6
projections **357**.8–9
refugees **357**.41
social divisions in belief **357**.7
and spirituality **358**.15
targets **357**.1–2, 36–7
Climate Change Act 2008 **357**.1, 8
climate crisis **402**.5, 8–9
impacts on health **392**.37
climate strikes **382**.17–18
clinical depression **404**.1, 41
clinically assisted nutrition and hydration (CANH) **362**.2
clocks changing **389**.12
Clomiphene citrate (Clomid) **387**.15
cloning **402**.36
closed-circuit television (CCTV) *see* CCTV (closed-circuit
  television)

Closed Party List **360**.25
close protection **383**.9
close quarter attacks **355**.4
closeted **369**.13
clothing
    age-appropriate **386**.4
    fast fashion **414**.20–1
    religious **358**.32
    and sexualisation **386**.3, 11
cloud storage **371**.30
CO₂ emissions **357**.22–3, **368**.3, 9, 24
    and agriculture **357**.24–7
    'Hothouse Earth' **357**.11–12
    per capita **357**.4
    pre-industrial revolution **357**.3
    reducing **357**.36
    and reforestation **357**.38–9
    worldwide **357**.3
    see also net zero
coal **357**.5, **413**.1, 2
    see also fossil fuels
coastal erosion **357**.9
coastlines
    see also oceans
cobalt production **413**.15
cocaethylene **397**.3
cocaine **301**.2, **373**.4–5, 9, 22, **397**.3, **399**.11, 12, 22
    classification and penalties for possession **301**.19, 22
    consumption trends **301**.7
    see also addiction; substance misuse
cocoa plant matter **413**.38–9
codeine **373**.22
coding skills **405**.3
coeliac disease **350**.24–5
coercive control **370**.2–3, 19, 41, **388**.8–10
    see also emotional abuse
coffee see caffeine
cognitive behavioural therapy (CBT) **351**.7, 24, 27, 41, **387**.7,
    400.2, 34, 41, **404**.5, 18–19, 27, 36, 41, **410**.1, 41, **415**.21,
    24–5, 41
cohabitation **316**.8, 15–20, **354**.3, 5–7, 8, 40, **363**.2
    see also living arrangements; marriage
Cohabitation Rights Bill **316**.16–17
co-housing communities **311**.37
coins **391**.1
colds **394**.7
Cold War **401**.1, 14
Collarbone Challenge **307**.19
collective privacy **383**.11–12
college
    technology **353**.4
    university technical colleges (UTCs) **353**.5
    see also university
Colombia
    employment rights **405**.33
    tobacco taxation **406**.35–6
colonialism **376**.1, 26, 38, **382**.8–9
    in sport **411**.10
colour breathing **400**.22
colouring books, for adults **351**.37
combination pill **387**.17
coming out **369**.12, 13, 17–19, 41
commercial sexual exploitation of children **386**.41
Committee on Climate Change (CCC)
    report on net zero **357**.1
    on responsible travel **365**.24
'common law marriage' **316**.15, 16, **354**.6–7, 40
    see also cohabitation
Commonwealth
    and the Armed Forces **356**.7
    veterans **356**.28
Commonwealth citizens **382**.2–3
Commonwealth Games **411**.34–5, 41
communicable diseases **348**.2, 41, **378**.5
communication **311**.12, 31
    and family life **316**.35
    reading **311**.30–1
Communications Act 2003 **361**.37
Communications Data Bill **317**.27
communism **360**.1
community **382**.18, 21–2, 25–6, 41
    see also volunteering
community energy **413**.34–5
community mental health teams (CMHTs) **351**.25, **400**.2,
    404.5
company pensions see pensions
Compare the Market, on veganism **350**.6
compassion **398**.36–7
competition, in business **381**.18, 20, 41
competitor research **381**.1
complaining **414**.8–12
Complementary and Alternative Medicine (CAM) **343**.1–2, 41
    definition **343**.1
    pregnancy and **343**.20
    types of **343**.2–17
    see also acupuncture; aromatherapy; Chinese medicine;
        herbal medicines; homeopathy
compound interest **391**.6
comprehensive schools **353**.41
compromise **354**.28
compulsive behaviour **351**.35–6, **410**.3
computers **311**.28–9
    misuse **366**.2
    and surveillance **317**.14–15
    see also internet; tablet computers
conception **394**.41
    assisted **387**.25
concussion **411**.14–16
condoms **309**.2, 3, 6, 23, **379**.3, 4, 8, 11, 13, 41
    female **309**.6
    male **309**.6
    and STIs **309**.2, 3, 9, 23, 24, **314**.4, **318**.2, 4
Confederation of British Industry (CBI) **405**.33
confidence **415**.1
    and cyberbullying **361**.9, 15, 38–9
    see also self-esteem
confidentiality **415**.23
    abortion **302**.5
    and HIV **314**.20
    sexual health **309**.17
conflict **351**.19
    see also war and conflict
Confucianism **358**.4, 10
congestion charge **392**.22
conscientious objection **367**.3
'conscious uncoupling' **316**.34
consent **354**.29–31, 40, **379**.26, 31–2, 37, **386**.3–4, 19, 31,
    34–5, 37–8

age of **354**.1, 33
conservation **365**.41, **385**.3, 41, **402**.7, 12–13, 15–23, 26, 29, 31, 33, 36–9, 41
  wild animals **374**.28–9
  see also animals; sustainable tourism; zoos
Conservative Party **360**.21–2
  peers **360**.11
constipation **394**.5, **395**.20–1
constitutional law **360**.4
constitutional monarchy **360**.1
construction industry **396**.38
construction methods **396**.1
consumer
  choice **414**.13
  definition **414**.1–3
  dispute **414**.6
  loyalty **414**.35
  rights **414**.4–7, 41
consumerism **368**.5
  avoiding **414**.14–17
  and choice **414**.13
  definition **414**.14, 20–1
  and globalisation **305**.7–8
  and mental health **414**.18
  see also consumer trends; shopping
Consumer Ombudsman **414**.6
Consumer Rights Act 2015 **414**.6
consumption
  see also consumerism
contraception **309**.6, 7–8, 15, 17, **348**.2, **354**.33, 40, **379**.2, 4, 8–9, 11–12, 41, **387**.1, 17–18, 23, 41, **394**.41
  access to **379**.8–9
  condoms **379**.3, 4, 8, 11, 13, 41
  contraceptive caps **309**.6
  contraceptive pill **379**.8–9, 12–13, 41, **392**.2
  diaphragms **309**.6
  effectiveness **379**.12–13
  emergency **379**.4, 41
  hormones **309**.6
  implants **379**.9, 12, 41
  injections **379**.9, 41
  intrauterine **309**.6–7
  methods **379**.12–13
  natural family planning **309**.7
  service cuts **309**.26
  sterilisation **309**.7
  vaginal rings **309**.7
  see also condoms
contraceptive injection **387**.18
contraceptive patch **387**.17–18
contraceptive pill **379**.8–9, 12–13, 41, **392**.2
controlling behaviour **354**.28, 36, **370**.2
Convention against Torture **300**.2, 17, 21, **372**.3
Convention on the Elimination of All Forms of Discrimination against Women (CEDAW) 1979 **300**.2, 23, **372**.1, 3
Convention on the International Trade in Endangered Species of Wild Fauna and Flora (CITES) **374**.36–7
Convention on the Rights of Persons with Disabilities (UNCRPD) 2008 **372**.3
Convention on the Rights of the Child *see* United Nations Convention on the Rights of the Child (UNCRC)
cooking club **311**.35
cooling-off period **414**.5
co-operatives and fairtrade **305**.17

COPD (chronic obstructive pulmonary disease) **392**.30–1
coral **357**.17
coral reefs **365**.34–5, **402**.10
Corbyn, Jeremy **357**.1, **360**.19, 21
coronary heart disease (CHD) **392**.31
  and aspirin **311**.14, 15
coronavirus *see* COVID-19
Coroners and Justice Act 2009 **362**.2
corporate manslaughter **366**.6
corporate social responsibility (CSR) **368**.2, 4, **381**.26, 41, **405**.21
Corpus Christi **358**.22
corticosteroids **389**.2
cortisol **404**.15, 16
cosmetics industry, and animal research **303**.38–9
cosmetic surgery **307**.20–4, **375**.8, 16, 25, 34, 41
cost of living crisis **414**.19, 32–3
Costs of War project **401**.29–31
cottage hospitals **392**.1
cotton **368**.24–5
coughs, persistent **395**.19
Council of Europe **300**.2, 30, **372**.7
councils *see* local authorities
council tax **396**.2
counselling **351**.35, **369**.8, **400**.4, **415**.21, 41
  abortion **302**.4–5, 6, 17, 18, 19, 27
  therapy **343**.6
counterfeit alcoholic drinks **397**.3
counter-terrorism **317**.26, **355**.3, 12, 30, 39, 41
  legislation **355**.12
  and surveillance **317**.26, 27
  see also Prevent
counting sheep **389**.5
'country of birth' **363**.4
countryside **385**.31
county lines **366**.10–12, 41
coursework **403**.6, 36
Court of Justice of the European Union (CJEU), international data transfer **383**.3
courts *see* justice system
cover letters **405**.9–10
COVID-19
  and access to contraception **379**.8–9
  African response **392**.18
  and animal welfare **374**.6
  Asian response **392**.16
  Australian response **392**.16–17
  and bullying **380**.10, 14
  and child labour **412**.20
  and depression **404**.6–7, 11, 27
  and the environment **368**.2
  ethnic differences **376**.8, 26
  EU response **392**.15
  Everyone-In programme **398**.17–18, 22, 32
  exercise gender gap **384**.27–9
  and food insecurity **408**.28
  health worker deaths **392**.8
  and homelessness **377**.37–8
  homeworking **383**.15–16
  and humanitarian disasters **401**.18, 33
  and human rights **372**.38–9
  impact of lockdown **370**.17, **377**.8, **414**.39
  impact on business **381**.7–13, 20–1
  impact on children **412**.4

impact on endangered species **402**.27–8

impact on exam results **403**.16

impact on health **392**.38

impact on homelessness **398**.2, 6, 8, 10–11, 17–21, 25–6, 30

impact on house sales **396**.14

impact on mental health **392**.14, 38, **400**.6, 33, **415**.12, 14

impact on NHS **392**.6–7

impact on sleep **389**.13, 24–7, 38–9

impact on smoking **406**.6, 18

impact on vaping **406**.18

impacts of (general) **391**.20–2, 25, **393**.12–15, 24

and obesity **384**.11, **408**.9

personal protective equipment (PPE) **392**.8–9

and poverty **377**.3, 35–6

and privacy **412**.8

recovery from **411**.11–13

socio-economic impacts **400**.14–15

South American response **392**.17–18

tracing apps **383**.10, 22–3

UK before **392**.35–6

UK response **392**.14

and unemployment **405**.23–5

USA response **392**.13

vaccination programme **392**.2

cows and bulls

bovine TB **303**.27–8

bullfighting **303**.5

sentience of **374**.9

and slaughter **303**.15

crabs (pubic lice) **309**.12

crack cocaine **373**.4–5, 22

cramping **394**.5, 7, 20

cravings **373**.1

creative roles **405**.2

creative therapies **415**.2

creativity

imaginary friends **354**.18

see also arts and crafts

credit **414**.14, 15, 41

credit building debt **391**.29

credit cards **391**.3, 29, 41

credit crunch see austerity

cremation **407**.41

crematoriums, as energy source **413**.39

Cretaceous mass extinction **402**.2

Crimea, annexation of **401**.18

crime and justice **317**.26

2019 statistics **366**.1

animal rights **374**.4, 5, 8

animal welfare **303**.8–9, 17, 18

arson **366**.2

burglary **366**.1–2, 3

computer misuse **366**.2

criminal damage **366**.2

definition **366**.41

forced marriage **300**.13, 14, 15–16, **316**.20–3

fraud **366**.1, 2

homicides **366**.1, 2, 6, 17

hospital admissions **366**.9, 17

men as victims of crime **364**.19

motoring offences **366**.34

petty crime **300**.6–7

and politics **366**.6–7

public order offences **366**.2, 41

reporting **366**.7

rights of children **412**.29, 31

robbery **366**.3

sexual offences **366**.3

surveillance **317**.25, 26

theft **366**.1–2, 3

victims of crime **317**.33

violent offences **366**.1, 3, 6–9

weapons offences **366**.1, 3, 6

youth crime **366**.4

see also hate crime; law; young offenders

crime rates, and overpopulation **363**.23

Crime Survey for England and Wales (CSEW) **366**.8–9, 41, **370**.25, **388**.2–4, **399**.11

2019 statistics **366**.1–3

on cyber-bullying **380**.10–13

on domestic abuse **370**.4

on elderly abuse **370**.19

criminal damage **366**.2

Criminal Justice Act 1948 **366**.31

Criminal Justice and Public Order Act 1994 **366**.36

Criminal Justice System (CJS) **318**.10, **366**.41

see also justice system

Vol. numbers appear first (in bold) followed by page numbers; a change in volume is preceded by a semi-colon.

Vol. 305	Globalisation – Good or Bad?	Vol. 368	Sustainable Living	Vol. 392	National Health
Vol. 314	HIV & AIDS	Vol. 369	LGBT+ Issues	Vol. 393	Disability
Vol. 316	Marriage	Vol. 370	Domestic Violence and Abuse	Vol. 394	Pregnancy
Vol. 347	The Censorship Debate	Vol. 371	The Internet and Us	Vol. 395	Teen Self-Care
Vol. 348	World Health	Vol. 372	Our Human Rights	Vol. 396	UK Housing
Vol. 349	Gambling Culture	Vol. 373	Drug Use and Abuse	Vol. 397	Alcohol Issues
Vol. 350	Lifestyle Diets	Vol. 374	Animal Rights	Vol. 398	Homelessness
Vol. 351	The Anxiety Epidemic	Vol. 375	Body Image	Vol. 399	Discussing Cannabis
Vol. 352	Biotech & Bioethics	Vol. 376	Racism	Vol. 400	Suicide & Self-Harm
Vol. 353	Education	Vol. 377	Poverty	Vol. 401	War & Conflict
Vol. 354	Relationships	Vol. 378	Ageing	Vol. 402	Endangered Species
Vol. 355	Terrorism	Vol. 379	Understanding Sexual Health	Vol. 403	Student Options
Vol. 356	British Armed Forces	Vol. 380	About Bullying	Vol. 404	Depression
Vol. 357	The Climate Emergency	Vol. 381	Business	Vol. 405	Employability
Vol. 358	Religion Today	Vol. 382	Active Citizenship	Vol. 406	Smoking
Vol. 359	Migration & Immigration	Vol. 383	The Privacy Debate	Vol. 407	Bereavement
Vol. 360	Government	Vol. 384	Health & Fitness	Vol. 408	Healthy Eating
Vol. 361	Cyberbullying	Vol. 385	Waste & Recycling Issues	Vol. 409	Online Safety
Vol. 362	Euthanasia	Vol. 386	Sexualising Society	Vol. 410	Addiction
Vol. 363	Population Change	Vol. 387	Fertility Issues	Vol. 411	Sport
Vol. 364	The Gender Equality Debate	Vol. 388	Discussing Child Abuse	Vol. 412	Rights of the Child
Vol. 365	Tourism Today	Vol. 389	Sleep	Vol. 413	Energy
Vol. 366	Crime in the UK	Vol. 390	Eating Disorders	Vol. 414	Consumerism
Vol. 367	Discussing Abortion	Vol. 391	Money	Vol. 415	Mental Health

criminal record **366**.34
criminal responsibility, age of **354**.1, **412**.29
Crisis, on hidden homelessness **364**.20
critical thinking **405**.2, 35
criticism **388**.8
Crohn's disease **393**.14
crops
    abiotic stress resistance **352**.3
    genetically engineered **352**.2
    pest resistant **352**.2
crowdfunding **381**.14–15, 41
Crown Prosecution Service (CPS) **388**.2
    on coercive control **370**.2–3
Cruelty Free International (CFI) **374**.20–1
cruelty-free products **374**.2, 20
    see also animal experimentation
cruelty to animals **350**.8
Crusades (1095-1291) **401**.2
cryptocurrencies **391**.30, 32–6, 41
crystallized intelligence **378**.23
crystal meth **373**.5, 22
cuckooing **366**.12, 41
cultivation hypothesis **386**.6
cultural tourism **365**.1
culture and citizenship **382**.37
    and domestic abuse **370**.28–9
    and forced marriage **316**.20–1
    and globalisation **305**.5–6
    and immigration **359**.15–17, 25–6
    and marriage **316**.26
    see also British identity; identity
currencies **391**.1, 30–1
    digital **391**.30–2
curriculum **353**.2–4, 6–7, 12, 15, 41
Curriculum for Excellence **403**.1
custody and detention **366**.41
    see also crime and justice; prison
customer
    definition **414**.1–3
    service **414**.10
customer loyalty **381**.3, 18
customisation **381**.4
cutting *see* self-harm
CV (curriculum vitae) **405**.7–8
    see also employability
cyanide **348**.19
cyber-attacks **352**.32
    see also surveillance and access
cyberbullying **354**.10, **371**.20, **380**.1, 10–13, 21, 24–5, 41, **388**.6, 41, **409**.13, 41
    adult **361**.14–15, 29–30
    and age **361**.4
    anti-bullying app **361**.27
    being negative online **361**.16–17
    catfishing **361**.6, 41
    and confidence **361**.9, 15, 38–9
    cyber stalking **361**.6, 7
    definition **361**.1–2, 41
    denigration **361**.6
    duty of care **361**.24
    exclusion **361**.6, 7, 14–15, 41
    experiences of **361**.2, 3–5, 7–10
    flaming **361**.6, 7, 41
    and gender **361**.4

    harassment **361**.6, 7, 25–6, 41
    how to help **361**.2–3
    impacts of **361**.1–2
    impersonation **361**.6, 7
    online safety legislation **361**.24–5
    outing **361**.6
    parental mediation **361**.28–9
    perpetrators **361**.19, 31
    protection from **361**.28–9, 33–4, 38–9
    recording evidence of **361**.3
    reporting **361**.9, 32–3
    in schools **361**.3, 22, 37, **380**.10–11
    and self-harm **361**.19
    signs of **361**.2
    social media **380**.19, 22–4
    in sport **361**.34–5
    statistics **361**.3–4, 7–9
    and suicide **361**.19, 23
    trickery **361**.6
    trolling **361**.5, 6, 12–13, 20–1, 36–7, 41
    types of **361**.2, 6
    in universities **361**.25–6
    in the workplace **361**.14–15, 29–30
    see also bullying
cyberflashing **386**.19–20
'cyber holiday' **361**.39
Cyber Monday **414**.24–5
cyber-predators **371**.20
cybersecurity **371**.28–9
cyber stalking **361**.6, 7
cyborgization **352**.33
cyclones **357**.13
cyclothymia **404**.1, 41
Cyprus, waste statistics **385**.3
Czech Republic, drug policies **301**.27

D

D&E (dilation and evacuation) abortion **302**.2, 3, 6–7
dab **399**.1
daily prayer **358**.28–30
dairy products **350**.23, 36
Dalai Lama **358**.15
Dangerous Dogs Act 1991 **303**.21
Dangerous Drugs Act 1920 **373**.26
dark tourism **365**.1, 22, 41
data ethics **383**.1
data privacy **352**.31–2
Data Privacy Day **317**.9
data protection *see* General Data Protection Regulation
  (GDPR); privacy **383**.11–12
    trends **383**.1–4
Data Protection Act 1998 **317**.25, 31–2
Data Protection Act 2018 **383**.41
data sovereignty **317**.32
dating online **409**.28–9
dating violence **370**.20–2
Dawkins, Richard **358**.2
'dayhab' **373**.39
D-Day landings **356**.8
death and mortality **306**.27, **311**.12
    AIDS-related **314**.3, 6, 14–15, 27
    and anxiety **351**.7

bodily processes after dying **407**.1–3
from bullfighting **303**.5
and child poverty **306**.26
cultural differences **407**.32
decline in **363**.20
defining **407**.1
in detention centres **359**.2
financial impacts **316**.15
HIV/TB-related, global statistics **314**.3
impacts of **407**.7
maternal **348**.1
near death experiences **407**.4–5
neonatal **348**.1
painless **311**.12
readiness for **311**.12
of refugees and migrants **300**.20–1
registering **407**.12
rights **316**.16
and sleep **348**.7
from smoking **406**.1, 3, 24
talking about **407**.8
thinking about **407**.6–7
see also accidents; bereavement; euthanasia; life
    expectancy; suicide
death cafe **407**.41
death certificate **407**.12
death penalty **362**.15, **366**.30
death rates **363**.3, 13–17, 41
death threats **308**.22
Death with Dignity Act 1997 **362**.13, 25, 32
debating **360**.10
debit cards **391**.3
debt **305**.38, **306**.9, **353**.35, **366**.10, **381**.11, 18–19
    and austerity **305**.33
    business loans **391**.29
    car loans **391**.28
    credit building **391**.29
    credit cards **391**.3, 29
    debt bondage **318**.23
    definition **391**.41
    and exports **305**.33
    and financial flows **305**.33
    and gambling **349**.5, 26–7
    Generation Z's attitude to **391**.26–8
    government **391**.20–2
    impact of Covid-19 **391**.20–2, 25
    mortgages **391**.28
    overdrafts **391**.25, 41
    payday loans **391**.29
    personal **391**.26–9
    student loans **391**.28–9, 41
decarbonisation **368**.8, 9, **413**.10–12, 37
decluttering **395**.39, **414**.16
decriminalisation **369**.24–8, **373**.29–30
deep vein thrombosis (DVT) **392**.31
defamation **347**.1, 14, 40
deforestation **357**.16, **402**.2, 4, 41
    see also reforestation
dehumanisation **386**.1
dehydration **395**.20–1, **408**.5
deities **358**.17
delivered goods **414**.5, 6, 39
Deloitte **356**.30–1
delusions **404**.1, **415**.4

dementia **362**.7, 28, **378**.5, 26, 29–30, 38–9, 41, **384**.22,
    389.14–15, **392**.31–2, **411**.14–15, **415**.35
    brain training **311**.20–1
demisexual **369**.2
democracy **360**.1, 28–9, 32
Democratic Republic of Congo (DRC) **357**.16
    poverty **377**.21
    war and conflict **401**.6
demographics
    definition **363**.41
    see also population
demonstration effect **393**.31
denigration **361**.6
Denmark **360**.39
    and animal welfare **303**.6
    drug policies **301**.28
    and SDGs **314**.9
    waste statistics **385**.4
dental health **395**.8, 10, 24–6
    braces and orthodontics **395**.26
dentistry **392**.1–2, 11–12
Department for Education (DfE)
    on bullying in schools **361**.11
    on cyberbullying **361**.3–4
    on school funding **353**.31
Department for Work and Pensions **360**.2
Depaul UK **398**.23
deployment **356**.29, 41
depopulation **363**.34–5, 41
    see also overpopulation
deposit return schemes **385**.5
depressants **373**.41
depression **351**.41, **354**.19, **369**.35–6, **373**.2–3, 13–14,
    378.17, 38, **380**.20, **384**.32, 36–7, **388**.31, **400**.12, 14, 20, 41,
    415.3, 5, 16, 35–6, 41
    and alcohol **397**.24
    antenatal **351**.22–3
    and the brain **404**.14–16
    and cyberbullying **361**.19
    definition **404**.41
    and dreams **389**.9
    and eating disorders **390**.2
    key facts **404**.2–3
    and physical health **351**.12
    postnatal depression (PND) **394**.36–7
    recovery from **404**.23–6
    and sleep **389**.16, 21, 27, 30
    statistics **404**.2, 6
    treatments **404**.3, 16, 18–19, 27, 36
    types **404**.1
    see also mental health
depressive episode **404**.1–2
deprivation
    and exercise **384**.16–17
    and recycling **385**.32
deradicalisation **355**.27
derealisation disorder **399**.25
descriptive stereotypes **378**.22
design and technology **403**.4, 5
destitution **377**.1
detention **359**.2
    see also custody and detention
detention centres **359**.2, 41
detox **373**.33–4, 37–8, 41, **397**.11, 15, 18, 41

developing countries
  and fertility **306**.27
  and global poverty **306**.27
  as meaningless term **306**.27–8
  and population growth **363**.24
  see also aid; country by name; globalisation; MDGs; SDGs
devolved governments **360**.2, 3, 4, 9
Devonian mass extinction **402**.1
diabetes **343**.34, **384**.2, 5, 11, 19, 20, **392**.28, 32, **408**.22–4, 41
  and animal research **303**.13
  gestational **394**.17
  and meat-free diets **350**.16–17
diabulimia **390**.4, 41
Diagnostic and Statistical Manual of Mental Disorders (DSM)
  390.6, **415**.41
dialectical behaviour therapy (DBT) **400**.34, **404**.36
diamorphine **373**.5
Diana, Princess of Wales **314**.25, **390**.27–8
diaphragms **309**.6, **379**.41
diazepam **373**.11, 22
dictatorships **360**.1
diet **378**.39, **384**.41, **390**.41, **395**.41, **408**.41
  and anxiety **351**.2
  balanced **394**.8, 11–12, **408**.8
  and constipation **395**.20
  demographics **350**.4–5, 32
  eating habits **375**.2
  Eatwell Guide **384**.12–13
  enhanced **378**.20–1
  food poverty **306**.19, 21, 31
  foods to avoid **394**.13–15
  healthy **408**.1–3
  Japanese **378**.10
  and loneliness **378**.25
  malnutrition **384**.2–3, 12–13
  meat consumption **408**.21
  Mediterranean **378**.34, **384**.9–10
  and mental health **415**.32
  and obesity **384**.2–3, 12–13
  and stress **395**.33
  sustainable **368**.5, 33–5, 41
  veganism **408**.12
  vegetarianism **408**.12
  see also dieting; eating disorders; food; healthy eating;
    nutrition
dietary inequality **408**.41
dieting **384**.38
  and body image **307**.2–3
  for pets **303**.19–20
diffusion of responsibility **380**.25
digestive system **389**.2
DigiKnow **361**.37
digital abuse **354**.40, **388**.41, **409**.41
  see also cyberbullying
digital assets **407**.11
digital bullying *see* cyberbullying
digital citizenship **361**.19
digital content **414**.4, 7
digital currency **391**.30–1
digital detox **409**.37–9, 41
digital divide **371**.3
Digital Economy Bill **318**.30
digital emancipation **412**.9–11
digital footprint **371**.25

Digital Inclusion Fund **371**.4
digital memories **407**.27–9
digital native **409**.41
digital privacy **412**.8–11
digital technology **305**.24–5, 27, 34, 37, **351**.14
  see also apps; computers; internet; mobile phones
Dignitas **362**.5, 8, 14, 34–5, 36–7, 39, 41
dignity in death **362**.32
dilation and evacuation (D&E) abortion **302**.2, 3, 6–7
  see also abortion
dinosaurs **402**.2
diphtheria **392**.1
diphtheria, tetanus and pertussis vaccine (DTP) **348**.29–30
diplomatic sanctions **305**.14
direct action **382**.17, 18–20
direct discrimination **376**.3, **393**.20
direct to consumer (D2C) commerce **381**.3
disability
  and accessibility **393**.6–8, 30–1
  attitudes to **393**.7, 16–18, 24–6
  defining **393**.1, 41
  discrimination **393**.2, 19–23
  and employment **393**.35–8
  and fashion **393**.37–9
  hate crime **393**.16–18
  history of **393**.11–12, 29
  and housing inequality **396**.5–6
  impacts of Covid-19 **393**.12–14
  medical model of **393**.1
  non-visible **393**.8–9, 14–15, 41
  and participation **393**.30–1
  and physical activity **393**.30–1
  positivity **393**.32
  and poverty **393**.2, 24
  prejudice **393**.27–8
  in the Royal Family **393**.10–11
  social model of **393**.1
  socio-economic costs of **393**.24–5
Disability Discrimination Act 1995 **372**.3
Disability History Month **393**.11–12
disabled people **388**.10
  and abortion **302**.1, 2, 22, 31
  and assisted suicide **362**.18–20, 38
  and bullying **361**.11
  and Down's syndrome **302**.36–7
  and euthanasia **362**.27
  see also disability; learning disabilities
disabling environments **393**.1
disablist bullying **380**.4, 10
disadvantaged children **412**.4–5
  and early schooling **353**.10
disasters **357**.23
discharge **394**.6–7, 20
discipline **353**.28–9
discrimination **364**.3, 17, 18, 41, **369**.13, **372**.1–3, 4, 7, 35, **377**.2, **378**.19, 41, **380**.41, **393**.41, **412**.5
  age **311**.6, 16–17
  in the Armed Forces **356**.16
  cultures of **376**.16
  direct **376**.3, **393**.20
  and disability **393**.2, 19–23
  harassment **393**.21, 22
  harrassment **376**.4, 41
  against HIV **314**.22

indirect **376**.3–4, **393**.20
racial **376**.3–4, 8–9, 11–12, 41
religious **308**.1, 3, 4, 8
same-sex **316**.11
in sport **411**.9–10, 37
victimisation **376**.4, **393**.16–17, 21
see also racial discrimination
discriminatory language **380**.4
diseases
communicable **348**.2, 41
foodborne **348**.19
noncommunicable **348**.1, 2
see also individual diseases
dismissal **405**.32
disordered eating **350**.18–20, 26, 41, **375**.17, 41, **390**.6–7, 41
see also eating disorders
displaced people *see* refugees
disposability, of products **385**.20
disposable cups **368**.11
disposable diapers **385**.12, 29
disposition **351**.33
dissociative disorders **399**.25, **400**.2, **415**.5–6
distraction **351**.14
distressed relationships **316**.29
Ditch The Label
Annual Bullying Survey 2020 **380**.7–9
on why people bully **380**.16–17
diversity
in the Armed Forces **356**.1–2, 16–18
and bullying **380**.6
in business **381**.29–32
in sport **411**.9
divorce **316**.4, 24, 30, 31, 38, 39, **354**.3, 6, 40
common reasons for **316**.30
and 'conscious uncoupling' **316**.34
emotions and feelings **316**.31, 32, 36, 38–9
and fault **316**.31–2, 34
legal steps **316**.28
online **316**.33
overseas **316**.4
and prenuptial agreements **316**.14–15
talking about **316**.36, 38–9
time factors **316**.28
Diwali **358**.25

dizziness **394**.5, 7
DNA (Deoxyribonucleic acid) **352**.1, 41
database **317**.29, **383**.41
doctors
and abortion **302**.1, 4–6, 13, 25–6, 31, 33
and sexual health **309**.17
views on euthanasia **362**.6–7, 22–6, 28–9, 31, 39
dogs **374**.10–11, 12–13
and animal experimentation **374**.18–19
dangerous **303**.8, 21
fighting **303**.8–9
hunting with **303**.27
as meat **303**.17–18
overweight **303**.19, 20
puppy farms **303**.3, 4
racing **303**.16, **349**.31
slaughter **303**.17, 18
trafficking **303**.3, 4
welfare legislation **303**.2
dolls
images **307**.13
and surveillance **317**.37
dolphins **402**.12
domestic abuse **354**.35, 37, **364**.6, 19, **366**.2, **388**.2–3, **412**.4
and abortion **302**.32
attitudes towards **370**.28–9
coercive control **370**.2–3, 19, 41
dating violence **370**.20–2
definition **370**.41
female perpetrators **370**.16
and homelessness **370**.27–8, 32–3
impact of lockdown **370**.17
impact on children **370**.9–10, 18
increase in **370**.13–14
legislation **370**.8, 18, 30–3
men as victims of **370**.10–11, 16, 24–6
myths **370**.9–11
prevention **370**.38–9
PTSD **318**.28
in Scotland **370**.6–7, 12
signs of **370**.36–7
societal acceptance of **370**.28–9
statistics **370**.3–5, 24–5
teenagers **370**.20–3, 34–6

Vol. numbers appear first (in bold) followed by page numbers; a change in volume is preceded by a semi-colon.

Vol. 305	Globalisation – Good or Bad?
Vol. 314	HIV & AIDS
Vol. 316	Marriage
Vol. 347	The Censorship Debate
Vol. 348	World Health
Vol. 349	Gambling Culture
Vol. 350	Lifestyle Diets
Vol. 351	The Anxiety Epidemic
Vol. 352	Biotech & Bioethics
Vol. 353	Education
Vol. 354	Relationships
Vol. 355	Terrorism
Vol. 356	British Armed Forces
Vol. 357	The Climate Emergency
Vol. 358	Religion Today
Vol. 359	Migration & Immigration
Vol. 360	Government
Vol. 361	Cyberbullying
Vol. 362	Euthanasia
Vol. 363	Population Change
Vol. 364	The Gender Equality Debate
Vol. 365	Tourism Today
Vol. 366	Crime in the UK
Vol. 367	Discussing Abortion
Vol. 368	Sustainable Living
Vol. 369	LGBT+ Issues
Vol. 370	Domestic Violence and Abuse
Vol. 371	The Internet and Us
Vol. 372	Our Human Rights
Vol. 373	Drug Use and Abuse
Vol. 374	Animal Rights
Vol. 375	Body Image
Vol. 376	Racism
Vol. 377	Poverty
Vol. 378	Ageing
Vol. 379	Understanding Sexual Health
Vol. 380	About Bullying
Vol. 381	Business
Vol. 382	Active Citizenship
Vol. 383	The Privacy Debate
Vol. 384	Health & Fitness
Vol. 385	Waste & Recycling Issues
Vol. 386	Sexualising Society
Vol. 387	Fertility Issues
Vol. 388	Discussing Child Abuse
Vol. 389	Sleep
Vol. 390	Eating Disorders
Vol. 391	Money
Vol. 392	National Health
Vol. 393	Disability
Vol. 394	Pregnancy
Vol. 395	Teen Self-Care
Vol. 396	UK Housing
Vol. 397	Alcohol Issues
Vol. 398	Homelessness
Vol. 399	Discussing Cannabis
Vol. 400	Suicide & Self-Harm
Vol. 401	War & Conflict
Vol. 402	Endangered Species
Vol. 403	Student Options
Vol. 404	Depression
Vol. 405	Employability
Vol. 406	Smoking
Vol. 407	Bereavement
Vol. 408	Healthy Eating
Vol. 409	Online Safety
Vol. 410	Addiction
Vol. 411	Sport
Vol. 412	Rights of the Child
Vol. 413	Energy
Vol. 414	Consumerism
Vol. 415	Mental Health

and violence **370**.9–10
  see also elder abuse
Domestic Abuse Bill **370**.8, 18, 30–3, 41
domestic extremism **355**.3, 17
domestic servitude **372**.17, 21, 41
domestic tourism **365**.1, 4
donor egg treatment **387**.15, 21, 25, 38–9
doomscrolling **404**.32–3
dopamine **373**.28, **406**.8–9, 41, **410**.6–7, 20, 41
  and gambling **349**.8
doping **411**.34–6, 41
double effect treatment **362**.41
Dove Campaign for Real Beauty **307**.18
Dove Global Beauty and Confidence Report **307**.4
downsizing **378**.18
Down's syndrome **302**.36–7, **393**.5, 25, 26–7, 32
draft legislation **360**.3, 6
Draize test **374**.16, 18
dreaming **389**.9, 41
drill and grime music **366**.27, 41
drink-driving **373**.14–15, 24–6, **397**.22–3, 27, 41
drink spiking **397**.20–1, 41
driverless vehicles **311**.27
drones **317**.30
drought **402**.9
drug addiction *see* addiction
drug driving **373**.14–15, 24–6, 41
drugs **301**.1, **373**.1–2
  among young people **301**.13, 21, 37
  and assaults **309**.27–8
  costs **309**.24–5
  criminal gangs **366**.10
  definition **301**.1, **373**.41
  and driving **301**.25
  intravenous **301**.14, 15–16, 23, **314**.1–2, 6, 15–16
  legalisation campaigns **301**.20–1, 24, 27, 29–32
  policies, global **301**.27–8, 32
  polydrug/polysubstance use **301**.5, 13
  statistics **373**.6–8
  teachers as information sources **301**.13
  UK trends **301**.5, 23–4, 23–4, 27, 29
  war on drugs **301**.23, 24, 28, 29
  and welfare benefits claims **301**.26
  see also addiction; substance misuse
drug safety testing **392**.24
drug-trafficking **373**.1
drunkenness **397**.2–3
Dutch Caribbean, and marriage **316**.5, 6
duty-free **365**.11
dying *see* death and mortality
dyslexia **393**.5
dysthymia **404**.1, 41

E

earnings *see* income; salaries; wages
ears, tissue engineering of **352**.18
earthworms **350**.13
Easter Monday **358**.22
Eastern Tropical Pacific Marine Corridor (CMAR) **402**.29
eating disorders **307**.1, **350**.18–20, 26, 41, **375**.6, 9, 12–14, 21–3, 29, 41, **386**.3, **415**.3, 6, 31, 41
  in children **390**.12–14, 26

definition **390**.1, 41
and health problems **390**.20
help for **390**.3, 11, 32–9
impact of COVID-19 **390**.12–13, 31
impacts of **390**.9–11
in men and boys **390**.9–10, 15–16, 29–30
myths and misconceptions **390**.17–18
relapse **390**.38
screening for **390**.9–11
and self-harm **400**.16–18
signs of **390**.3
statistics **390**.8–13
therapeutic treatments **390**.11, 35
types of **390**.3–5
in women and girls **390**.8, 9–10
  see also anorexia nervosa; bulimia nervosa; disordered eating
eating habits **375**.2
eating problems **390**.1–2
  see also disordered eating; eating disorders
Eatwell Guide **350**.2, **384**.12–13, **408**.36, 41
Ebola virus **348**.22, 28, 35, 37, **374**.15
e-bullying *see* cyberbullying
echinacea **343**.32
Echinococcus tapeworms **348**.19
e-cigarettes **301**.6, **373**.16–19, **406**.1, 8, 16–24, 33, 41
  see also vaping
Ecodesign for Energy-Related Products and Energy Information Regulations 2021 **414**.6
eco-friendly **368**.5, 41
  products **368**.4, 24
eco funeral **407**.41
eco-homes **396**.32–5, 41
ecological footprint **382**.37
e-commerce **414**.26, 41
  see also online shopping
ecommerce **381**.41
  trends **381**.3–4
economic gain **401**.1
economic migrants **359**.37–8, 41
economic policy **391**.15, 20–2
economics, and population ageing **378**.2
economy **306**.5, 6, 27
  impact on business **381**.7–9
  see also globalisation; poverty; see also austerity
ecosystem **402**.41
ecosystem change **402**.3–5, 10–11
ecosystems, degradation **306**.38
ecotourism **365**.1, 28–9, 41
ecstasy **373**.5, 9, 22, **399**.12
ecstasy (MDMA) **301**.2, 5, 7–8, 11, 19, 22, 31
ectopic pregnancy **387**.15, **394**.10, 22–4, 41
Ecuador **360**.36
edibles (cannabis) **399**.1–2, 27
Edinburgh, and tourism **365**.4
education
  and the Armed Forces **356**.11
  boys falling behind **364**.19
  and character building **307**.36–7
  and child labour **412**.20
  and child poverty **306**.13, 15, 30
  compulsory **353**.1–2
  and couples' stability **316**.25–6
  and feminism **308**.24

further **353**.2, 41
on human rights **412**.12
impact of COVID-19 pandemic **412**.4
and inequality **308**.5, 28
inequality of **364**.19
and poverty **306**.12, **377**.2, 8, **412**.28
pre-school **353**.4
primary **353**.4
right of girls to **364**.6
right to **412**.3, 13
secondary **353**.4
stages of **353**.4–5
and tackling racism **376**.7, 34
'whitewashed' curriculum **376**.7, 38
see also financial education; higher education; schools;
    students; universities
Education, Health and Care Plan **353**.4
Education Act 1996 **353**.1, 3–4
Education Health and Care (EHC) plan **403**.18
Education Policy Institute (EPI), on off-rolling **353**.25
eggs **408**.13
Egypt
censorship in **347**.11
and surveillance **317**.28
Eid-al-Adha **358**.25
Eid al-Fitr **358**.25
Eilish, Billie **386**.11
ejaculation **379**.4, **387**.2
elder abuse **311**.21, 22, **370**.19, 41, **378**.22, 41
elderly people *see* older people
elections **372**.4
abstaining from voting **360**.19
compulsory voting **360**.16–17
first-past-the-post **360**.9, 24, 26–7
general **360**.41
local **360**.18
mandatory voter identification **360**.18
manifesto **360**.41
right to vote **360**.20
voting systems **360**.24–5
Electoral Register, and right to vote **360**.20
electric cars **368**.2, **413**.11–12, 13–16, 27
electricians **405**.2
electricity **357**.36–7
prices **413**.7, 10–12, 37
renewable **357**.34
see also renewable energy
electrification **357**.36
electroconvulsive therapy (ECT) **404**.16, **415**.26–7
electronic cigarettes *see* e-cigarettes
electronic monitoring **366**.39
electronic waste **368**.38–9
elephants **303**.29, **357**.19, **402**.32–3
circus tricks **303**.29
poaching **303**.27
riding trips **303**.29
trophy hunting **374**.28–9
zoos **374**.33
e-liquids **406**.36, 41
elite athletes **411**.41
email **371**.2
Embassy Village **398**.33
emergency accommodation **398**.2–3, 24, 41
emergency contraception **379**.4, 41

emetophobia **351**.5
emigration **359**.4, 41, **363**.2
see also migration
emissions *see* CO$_2$ emissions
emotional abuse **354**.28, 37, **370**.1, 41, **379**.29
definition **388**.1, 4, 8, 41
impacts of **388**.10–11
misconceptions **388**.10
reporting **388**.9–10
signs of **388**.9
statistics **388**.2
types of **388**.8–9
see also coercive control
emotional self-care **395**.1
empathy **382**.28–9, **386**.6, **405**.2
and bullying **380**.18
employability
definition **405**.1
improving **405**.3–4
skills **405**.1, 2, 35
employees **381**.18
employers, and surveillance **317**.14–16
employment **308**.27, 29, **377**.1, 3, 11–12, 34
and apprenticeships **308**.38, 39
burnout **317**.16
deteriorating global conditions **317**.16
direct discrimination **311**.6
and disability **393**.35–8
equal rights at work **364**.2, 30–1
for ex-armed forces personnel **356**.30–1, 36–9
indirect discrimination **311**.6
and inequality **308**.2, 4, 12, 27, 30–1, 38–9, **311**.6
and pensions **311**.7, 8–9, 11
and racial stereotyping **308**.16
and retirement **311**.23
rights **405**.28–9, 32–4
and role models **308**.16, 27
and segregation **308**.13
self-employed **405**.29
status **405**.28–9, 33
and surveillance **317**.14–16
tribunals **311**.6
victimisation **311**.6
zero-hours contracts **405**.30–1
see also migration; recruitment and retention;
    unemployment; women in the workforce; work
Employment Relations Act 1999 **405**.32, 34
Employment Rights Act 1996 **405**.32
encryption **383**.4
endangered species
Chinese herbal medicine **343.5**
large carnivores **303**.27
End Child Poverty Coalition **377**.15
End of Life Assistance Bill (Scotland) **362**.3
end-of-life care **311**.2, 12, **362**.41, **407**.8
see also palliative care
endometriosis **387**.20, 24
energy **305**.10
decarbonising **368**.8
efficiency **317**.31, **368**.9–10, 14–15
green **368**.41
renewable **368**.3–4
saving **368**.15
see also electricity; gas

energy crisis **413**.18–19, 20–8
energy drinks **410**.25–8
energy intake **408**.1
energy management **413**.25
energy prices **413**.7, 10–12, 18–19, 20–3, 28, 37
energy savings **413**.24–5
energy suppliers **413**.22–3, 28
enforced returns **359**.2
engineers **405**.2
English
    as core subject **403**.5
    resitting **403**.3
English Baccalaureate (EBacc) **353**.19
English Bill of Rights 1689 **372**.2
enlistment **356**.10
entrepreneur **405**.3, 41
entrepreneurs **403**.21
entrepreneurship **381**.16, 22–3, 41
environment
    and addiction **373**.2–3
    impacts of tourism **365**.27–37
    plastic waste **365**.32–3
    see also ecosystems; habitat; sustainability
Environment Agency **357**.9
environmental issues *see* climate change; ecosystems;
  greenhouse gases; sustainability; waste; wildlife
environmental migrants **357**.41
Environmental Protection Agency (EPA) **374**.19
environments, disabling **393**.1
epidemics **363**.23
epidural **394**.28
epilepsy **351**.24, **392**.28, 32, **399**.31–3
Epiphany **358**.22
episiotomy **394**.31
equality **356**.17, **372**.1–3, 9–10, **377**.3, 32–3, 35
    and bullying **380**.6
    versus equity **364**.4
    and gender **379**.2
    in relationships **354**.28
    role models for **364**.23
    see also inequality
Equality Act 2010 **308**.30, **311**.6, **364**.41, **372**.3, **376**.3–4,
  380.1, 31, **393**.1, 19, **405**.32, 34, 36
    bullying **380**.4
    and religion **358**.16
equal opportunities **353**.30
equal pay **364**.9–10, 12, 15–16, **405**.32
    in sport **411**.26–7
Equal Pay (Amendment) Act 1983 **364**.12
Equal Pay Act 1970 **364**.12
equity **380**.6
erection **395**.27
eSports **411**.34–5, 41
essential oils *see* aromatherapy
estrogen **387**.8
ethanol **397**.3
ethical consumerism **368**.5, 18, 41
ethical consumption **368**.16
ethical issues **352**.4, 9, 31–9
    see also bioethics
ethical practice **381**.26–8
ethical shopping **368**.15
ethical trade **305**.28
    see also fairtrade

ethical veganism **358**.16–17
ethics, and privacy **383**.1
Ethiopia **377**.22
    and MDGs **306**.29–30
    war and conflict **401**.18–19
ethnic cleansing **401**.14
ethnicity, and bullying **380**.5, 10, 29
ethnic minorities **306**.5, **308**.3, 35, 38, **376**.41, **382**.41
    in the Armed Forces **356**.2, 18–19
    and British identity **308**.4, 5
    and dentistry **392**.12
    and diversity **308**.10–11, 13, 35
    and education **308**.28
    and employment **308**.13
    and politics **308**.4, 13–14, 32–3
    and segregation **308**.13–14
    and self-harm **400**.7
    see also Black, Asian and minority ethnic (BAME); diversity
ethno-nationalism **355**.6
etizolam **373**.11
eulogy **407**.41
Euro 2022 **411**.1–2, 31
Eurogroup for Animals **374**.26
Euromillions lottery **349**.21
Europe
    growth in tourism **365**.19
    as holiday destination **365**.6
    life expectancy **378**.5, 7
    population decline **363**.27
    population growth **363**.33
    population of **363**.32–3
    retirement age **378**.12–14, 19
    tourism statistics **365**.19–21
    see also European Union (EU)
European Convention on Human Rights (ECHR) **300**.1–2,
  372.2, 5–6
    on freedom of expression **347**.2
    on privacy **317**.3, 25
    and rights **300**.27–8
    and the UK legal system **300**.27, 29–31, 34
European Court of Human Rights **300**.2, 34, **372**.5–6, 7
    on surveillance **317**.14–15
European Economic Area (EEA) **359**.1
European Food Safety Authority (EFSA), on poultry
  inspections **348**.9
European Parliament **360**.25
European Social Survey (ESS), on acknowledging climate
  change **357**.7
European Union (EU) **382**.41
    on animal welfare **303**.7, 15–16
    citizenship **382**.2
    and globalisation **305**.4, 9, 29, 38
    healthcare **392**.14–15
    immigration to UK **359**.6–7
    and international trade **305**.10–14
    migrant workers **359**.18–19
    on migration **318**.38–9
    nationals **359**.2
    and pooled sovereignty **360**.4
    on privacy **317**.32
    on surveillance **317**.28
    see also Brexit
European Union Terrorism Situation and Trend Report 2018
  355.5

euthanasia **400**.41
    abuse of **362**.29
    and children **362**.9, 27
    countries permitting **362**.4, 8–9
    as criminal act **362**.8
    definitions **362**.1, 4, 8, 16, 39
    and dignity in death **362**.32
    doctors views on **362**.6–7, 29, 31
    and 'do no harm' **362**.6, 17
    ethical issues **362**.16–39
    history of **362**.2
    and human rights **362**.2, 15
    legislation **362**.1–5, 7, 16–17
    and malpractice **362**.7
    parental consent for **362**.9
    public view of **362**.6–7, 28, 30
    and religion **362**.17
    slippery slope argument **362**.41
    statistics **362**.5–6
    terminology **362**.4
    types of **362**.1
    see also assisted suicide; physician-assisted suicide (PAS)
Everyone-In programme **398**.17–18, 32
eviction **398**.6, 18, 38–9, 41
e-waste **368**.38–9, 41
exams **403**.6
    and age **353**.11–13
    English Baccalaureate (EBacc) **353**.19
    GCSEs **353**.14–17, 19
    gender-based results **353**.16–17
    International Baccalaureate (Ibac) **353**.41
    A-levels **353**.18–19
    revision **403**.33, 36–9
    and stress **353**.15–16, 20–1, **395**.36–7, **403**.32–5
exclusion **382**.15
    as cyberbullying **361**.6, 7, 14, 41
exclusions, from school **353**.26–7, **412**.33–4
executions **372**.33, 34–5
executive agencies **360**.2
executors **407**.9, 41
exercise and activity **307**.39, **351**.9, 39, **378**.11, 38–9, **392**.38
    aerobic **384**.22–3
    anaerobic **384**.22–3
    benefits **384**.18–19, 20–2, 32, 34–5

extreme **390**.3
    intensity **384**.21, 41
    lack of **384**.14–17
    and mental health **384**.22, 32, 36–7, **415**.32
    moderate **384**.21
    during pregnancy **394**.9
    recommendations **384**.16–18, 22, 32
    and self-esteem **307**.31, 39
    and sleep **384**.23–5, **389**.2, 6
    vigorous **384**.21
    weight-bearing **384**.22
    and wellbeing **395**.33, **415**.34–6
    see also sport and leisure activities
exoskeletons **352**.33
expat **359**.41
    see also migration
expiring content **371**.33–5
exploitation **388**.41
    see also child exploitation
explosive devices **355**.3–4
    on aircraft **355**.4
    suicide bombers **355**.2, 4, 7, 20–2
exports **305**.15, 26, 33
    live exports **303**.15–16
    and peak globalisation **305**.31
extinction **402**.1, 10
    and biotechnology **352**.25–6
    events **357**.12
    of humans **357**.22
    natural **402**.41
    preventing **357**.33, **402**.38–9
    rediscovered species **402**.37
    reversing **402**.31
    species at risk **357**.18–19, 33–5, **402**.12–13, 18–21, 32
    see also mass extinction
Extinction Rebellion **357**.2, 10–11, 31–2, 41
extracurricular activities **405**.1
extremism **355**.31, 41
    see also right-wing extremism; terrorists and terrorist groups

---

Vol. numbers appear first (in bold) followed by page numbers; a change in volume is preceded by a semi-colon.

Vol. 305	Globalisation – Good or Bad?	Vol. 368	Sustainable Living	Vol. 392	National Health
Vol. 314	HIV & AIDS	Vol. 369	LGBT+ Issues	Vol. 393	Disability
Vol. 316	Marriage	Vol. 370	Domestic Violence and Abuse	Vol. 394	Pregnancy
Vol. 347	The Censorship Debate	Vol. 371	The Internet and Us	Vol. 395	Teen Self-Care
Vol. 348	World Health	Vol. 372	Our Human Rights	Vol. 396	UK Housing
Vol. 349	Gambling Culture	Vol. 373	Drug Use and Abuse	Vol. 397	Alcohol Issues
Vol. 350	Lifestyle Diets	Vol. 374	Animal Rights	Vol. 398	Homelessness
Vol. 351	The Anxiety Epidemic	Vol. 375	Body Image	Vol. 399	Discussing Cannabis
Vol. 352	Biotech & Bioethics	Vol. 376	Racism	Vol. 400	Suicide & Self-Harm
Vol. 353	Education	Vol. 377	Poverty	Vol. 401	War & Conflict
Vol. 354	Relationships	Vol. 378	Ageing	Vol. 402	Endangered Species
Vol. 355	Terrorism	Vol. 379	Understanding Sexual Health	Vol. 403	Student Options
Vol. 356	British Armed Forces	Vol. 380	About Bullying	Vol. 404	Depression
Vol. 357	The Climate Emergency	Vol. 381	Business	Vol. 405	Employability
Vol. 358	Religion Today	Vol. 382	Active Citizenship	Vol. 406	Smoking
Vol. 359	Migration & Immigration	Vol. 383	The Privacy Debate	Vol. 407	Bereavement
Vol. 360	Government	Vol. 384	Health & Fitness	Vol. 408	Healthy Eating
Vol. 361	Cyberbullying	Vol. 385	Waste & Recycling Issues	Vol. 409	Online Safety
Vol. 362	Euthanasia	Vol. 386	Sexualising Society	Vol. 410	Addiction
Vol. 363	Population Change	Vol. 387	Fertility Issues	Vol. 411	Sport
Vol. 364	The Gender Equality Debate	Vol. 388	Discussing Child Abuse	Vol. 412	Rights of the Child
Vol. 365	Tourism Today	Vol. 389	Sleep	Vol. 413	Energy
Vol. 366	Crime in the UK	Vol. 390	Eating Disorders	Vol. 414	Consumerism
Vol. 367	Discussing Abortion	Vol. 391	Money	Vol. 415	Mental Health

F

Facebook **371**.10, 33, **381**.36, **383**.7, 11, 13, 32, **409**.2–3, 18–20, 22, 36–7
    cyberbullying on **361**.8
    and friendships **354**.17
    and online abuse **388**.23, 36
    reporting/dealing with abuse on **361**.32
    sharing childhood images without consent **317**.38
    time spent on **361**.5
    see also cyberbullying; social media; social networking
Facewatch **383**.18–20
facial recognition technology **372**.31–2, **383**.14–15, 17–22, 41
factory farming **350**.8, 41, **374**.41
fad diets **350**.26
faddy eating **390**.41
fainting **394**.7
Fairtrade **305**.16, 17, 28, 28–9
fair trade **368**.16, 41
faith
    versus belief **358**.16
    as dynamic and personal **358**.1
    popularity of **358**.2
    see also religion
faith schools **353**.2, 3, 41
fake fur **374**.32, 41
    see also fur-free
fake news **347**.18–22, 40, **409**.26
    and children **347**.21–2
fallopian tubes **387**.5, 19
    blocked **387**.1
    surgery **387**.24
falls **392**.29, 34
families
    cohabiting couples **363**.2
    definition **354**.40, **363**.2
    and distressed relationships **316**.29
    and divorce **316**.31, 32, 34–5
    living together **311**.26, 36
    marriage **316**.13
    of military personnel **356**.29
    see also parents
Family Affluence Scale **384**.17
Family Justice Young People's Board **316**.37
Family Law (Scotland) Act 2006 **316**.15–16
family planning **348**.2, **379**.11–12, **392**.2
    see also contraception; sexual health
family planning clinics **367**.1
family-related visas **359**.1
family separation **412**.14–15
fantasy football **349**.2
Farah, Mo **412**.23–5
FareShare **377**.13
farming **350**.12–13, 31, 41, **374**.9, 41, **402**.8–9
    fairtrade **305**.16–17
    see also animal welfare; food production
Faroe Islands, waste statistics **385**.3
fashion industry
    and body image **307**.16–18
    and disability **393**.37–9
    ethical shopping **368**.15
    sustainability in **368**.2–3, 26–31
fast fashion **368**.2, 11, 30–1, 41, **414**.20–1, 41
    sustainability in **368**.11

fast food litter **385**.5, 8–9
fat, adipose tissue **384**.4–5
fatalities *see* death and mortality
fathers
    and abortion **302**.37–9
    absence of **364**.20, 23
    impact on child development **388**.31
    and marriage **316**.26
    role of **354**.12–13
    talking to **354**.9–10, 16
    teenage parents **309**.20
fatigue **394**.5–6
fats **408**.1–2, 9, 10–11
faulty goods **414**.4–6
Fawcett Society, on gender stereotypes **364**.28–9
FBI, on surveillance **317**.21–2
fear **351**.21
fear of missing out (FOMO) **351**.15, 41, **410**.12
Feast of St Francis of Assisi **358**.23
Feast of the Immaculate Conception **358**.23
feelings *see* emotions and feelings
fellowship **358**.21
female condom **379**.13, 41
female genital mutilation (FGM) **300**.19, **309**.38, **358**.35–6, 41, **364**.7, 41, **372**.23–6, 41, **379**.2, **388**.14–15, 41
female sterilisation **309**.7
female terrorism **355**.18, 25–7
femicide **370**.15
Femicide Census 2018 **370**.15
feminism **364**.41
    and abortion **302**.15, 23, 27, 39
    and gender equality **364**.5–6
    men as feminists **364**.22
    and politics **360**.30–1
    and press **308**.24
    and prostitution **318**.8–9, 17–18, 20–1
ferrets **402**.36
fertile window **387**.1
fertilisers **357**.35
fertility **306**.27, **387**.41
    and eating disorders **390**.20
    female **387**.2–3, 6, 20
    lifestyle factors **387**.21–2, 28–9
    male **387**.2, 16, 19, 20
    myths **387**.14–15
    problems **387**.1
    rates **302**.25, **363**.3, 6–11, 19–21, 26–7, 30–1, **387**.2, 11–13
    testing **387**.2
    see also infertility
fetal development **394**.1
fetishisation **386**.7–8, 41
F-gases **357**.37
FGM *see* female genital mutilation (FGM)
fialuridine **374**.15
fibre **408**.9, 13
    and constipation **395**.20
fibroids **387**.20, 24
fibromyalgia **343**.22, **393**.14
fidget spinners **351**.7
fight or flight response **351**.1, 41
film and theatre
    censorship **347**.26–7
    disability representation **393**.26–8
    and gender equality **364**.2

filters **375**.29, 41
financial abuse **354**.28, **370**.1, 41
financial assets global, and trade **306**.34
financial crisis (2008)
    and globalisation **305**.32, 36
    and international trade **305**.32
financial education **306**.12, **391**.5–6
    and financial skills **306**.12
Financial Services Compensation Scheme **391**.3
financial skills **391**.5–6
financial support for students **403**.18
financial wellbeing **391**.23–4
Finnish-Soviet War (1939-1940) **401**.1
fire, smoking-related **406**.3
FIRE (Financial Independence, Retire Early) lifestyle **391**.8
firearms **355**.4, **366**.1
fire safety regulations **396**.22–3
first-past-the-post **360**.9, 24, 26–7
first-time buyers **396**.17
first-time parents **354**.1
first trimester **394**.1
fish
    and animal experimentation **374**.19
    overfishing **357**.30
    as pets **374**.10–11
fit for purpose **414**.4
fitness **311**.17, **384**.41
    see also exercise and activity; sport
fitness tracker **384**.14, 41
'five a day' **384**.13
five freedoms, of animal welfare **374**.5, 8
five stages of grief **407**.21
fixed-odds betting terminals **349**.1, 17, 26–30, 41, **392**.24
fizzy drinks **350**.22–3
flaming **361**.6, 7, 41
flexible working **392**.7, **405**.41
flexitarian diet **350**.1, 21, 30–5, 41
flirting, and assault **309**.27
flooding **402**.2, 9
flood risks **357**.9, 20
flower remedies **343**.6
Floyd, George **376**.6, 10, 13, 38
flu **394**.7
flu vaccine **395**.13
flying, phobia of **351**.4
fly-tipping **385**.41
foetal abnormality **394**.41
foetuses, unviable to term **302**.34–6
FOI (freedom of information) **317**.12
folic acid **394**.8, 13, **408**.9
folk religions **358**.2
follicle stimulating hormone (FSH) **387**.8
food
    allergies **350**.27–9, 41
    banks **306**.20, 22, 24–5, 36
    GM (genetically modified) **352**.41
    groups **350**.23
    intolerances **350**.27–9, 41
    labelling **303**.7, **350**.34
    packaging **350**.36
    poisoning **348**.9
    poverty **306**.13, 17, 19–21, 24–6, 28, 31, 36
    production **305**.11
    supplements **343**.6

    synthetic **352**.19
    see also diet; healthy eating; hunger; nutrition; veganism; vegetarianism
food banks **368**.16, **377**.4–6, 16–17, 18–19, **408**.31
food-based dietary guidelines (FBDGs) **394**.11
foodborne diseases **348**.19
food cravings **394**.4
food disorders **410**.7
food hygiene **392**.24, **394**.9
food industry **384**.3, 20
    sustainability in **368**.3
food insecurity **384**.12, **408**.28
food labelling **384**.20, **392**.23–4
food packaging **408**.15
food poisoning **394**.13
food poverty **408**.28–9, 30–1, 41
food reformulation **408**.38
Food Standards Agency (FSA)
    on food allergies **350**.27
    on poultry inspections **348**.9
food waste **368**.32, 36, **385**.13, 25, 31, 33, 38, 41
football
    injuries **411**.16
    LGBTQ issues **411**.17–18
    pools **349**.2
    prejudice **411**.1–2
    and problem gambling **349**.12–13, 37
    and racism **376**.29–30
    in schools **411**.28
    Super League **411**.38–9
    women in **411**.1–2, 21, 26–8, 31
forced labour **300**.6, **372**.4, 14–17, 21, 41
    see also slavery; trafficking
forced marriage **300**.10–11, 13–16, **316**.20–2, **364**.20, **372**.14–15, 27, 29, 41, **388**.16–18, **412**.13
Forced Marriage (Civil Protection) Act 2007 **316**.22
Forced Marriage Protection Orders **316**.21–2
forced swim test **374**.19
foreign aid see aid
foreign direct investment **381**.38
foreign travel see travel
forests **352**.26–8
    deforestation **357**.16
    rainforest **357**.6, 16
    reforestation **357**.38–9
forest schools **353**.8
Forfeiture Act 1982 **362**.14
Fortnite **349**.23
fossil fuels **348**.11, **357**.5–6, 6, 12, **402**.11, **413**.1, 2–4, 8, 18–19, 28, 36, 37, 41
    see also coal; gas; oil
fossils **402**.2
foundation degrees **403**.20
foundation schools **353**.2
Foundling Hospital, history of **306**.5
Four Paws **374**.36–7
fourth industrial revolution **405**.1
fracking **357**.2
France
    and civil solidarity pacts **316**.9
    and dark tourism **365**.22
    employment rights **405**.33
    immigration statistics **359**.3
    Islamophobia **308**.37

and palliative sedation **362**.9
refugee camps **359**.41
waste statistics **385**.2
see also Europe
FRANK website **301**.12–13
fraud **366**.1, 2, **371**.1
freedom **354**.28, 30, **372**.4
of expression **347**.2–3, 40
European Convention on Human Rights (ECHR) **347**.2
laws **347**.3
and school uniform **353**.34
and surveillance **317**.4
of information **317**.12
of the press **347**.12–17
and religion **358**.32–9
see also liberty
freedom fighters **355**.1–2
Freedom in the World 2019 **360**.32–3
Freedom of Information Act 2000 **347**.40
'free-from' groceries **350**.24, 27
freelancers **381**.41, **405**.41
free press **347**.14, 16, 40
free-range **350**.31, 41
free school meals **306**.23, **377**.8, 13, **384**.12–13
and inequality **306**.13
free schools **353**.3, 41
free speech **347**.1, **361**.18, **371**.14–15, **372**.4, 33
Free Speech University Rankings 2018 **347**.4
free sugars **408**.1, 3
see also sugars
free trade **305**.6, 11, 27, 35, **306**.28
NAFTA **305**.11
and protectionism **305**.31–2
French Revolution (1789-1799) **401**.3, 8–9
frenemies **354**.17
frequent flyers **365**.24–5
fresh water depreciation **363**.23
freshwater ecosystems **402**.4–5, 10
Fridays For Future movement **382**.17
friend requests, unwelcome **361**.5
friendships **354**.17–25
best friends **354**.19, 21
falling out **354**.23
imaginary **354**.18
importance of **354**.21–2, 25
toxic **354**.24–5
see also relationships
frontbenchers **360**.41
fruit **408**.1–2, 9
fruit machines **349**.2, 41
fuel banks **306**.8
fuel poverty **306**.8, 25, **377**.41
and bill payments **306**.8
and fuel banks **306**.8
and pre-payment meters **306**.8
fulfilment **381**.4
full-time reserve service personnel (FTRS) **356**.1, 7
functioning addicts **410**.35–6
funerals **407**.9, 11, 13–15, 34–5, 41
see also death and mortality
fur farming **303**.30–2
fur-free **374**.30–2
further education **353**.2, 41, **403**.5, 41
see also higher education

Future Homes Standard **396**.39
future jobs **405**.1–2
Future Reserves 2020 **356**.1

G

gabapentinoids **373**.13
GAD (Generalized Anxiety Disorder) *see* Generalised Anxiety Disorder (GAD)
Gaddafi, Muammar **401**.5
gagging order **347**.40
Galentine's Day **354**.21
Gambia, tobacco taxation **406**.35
GambleAware **349**.12–13, 32
gambling **391**.14, **392**.24, **410**.10, 41
addiction **349**.26–7
advertising **349**.6, 12, 17, 25, 34–5
age restrictions **349**.1–2
among sports people **349**.12–13
arcades **349**.1, 17
the 'big win' **349**.3
bingo **349**.2, 7, 41
casinos **349**.2, 9, 38, 41
and children **349**.16–17, 22–4
compulsive nature of **349**.8–9
and debt **349**.5, 26–7
definition **349**.1, 41
dependence on **349**.5
distorting reality **349**.8–9
and dopamine **349**.8
as entertainment **349**.3
Fixed-Odds Betting Terminals (FOBTs) **349**.41
gaming machines **349**.1, 2, 9
and gender **349**.7, 10
'loot boxes' **349**.22–5
lotteries **349**.2, 10, 21, 41
online **349**.4, 7, 10, 14, 15, 18–23, 41
participation statistics **349**.10–11
prevalence in UK **349**.7, 10
as a problem **349**.3, 4–7, 10, 12–13, 26–30, 32, 37–9, 41
as public health issue **349**.27, 32
reasons for **349**.3
remote **349**.41
self-help tips **349**.33
'skin gambling' **349**.18–20, 41
stopping **349**.3
and video games **349**.24
and young people **349**.5, 7, 15–20, 37
see also addiction; betting
Gambling Act 2005 **349**.1, 6, 17
Gambling Commission **349**.41
on fixed odds betting **349**.26–30
on young people gambling **349**.7
Gambling With Lives charity **349**.4, 30
gaming **307**.21–2, **371**.10, 38–9, **386**.5–6, **395**.35, **409**.30–4
gender inequalities in **364**.25–6
gaming addiction **410**.14–17
gaming machines **349**.1, 2, 9
see also arcades
gamma butyrolaction (GBL) **373**.22
gamma hydroxybutyrate (GHB) **373**.22
Gandhi, Mahatma **374**.2
on animal rights **350**.8

gang abuse **379**.30
gang grooming **388**.7, 26
gangs **366**.10, 41
gap years **403**.22, 41
gardening **368**.14
gardens
　ponds **357**.35
　wildflower lawns **357**.33
garlic **343**.31
gas
　intestinal **394**.5
　natural **413**.2, 28
　prices **413**.7, 10–12
gas and air **394**.28
gaslighting **354**.37, **370**.41, **380**.32–3, **388**.8, 10
gastrointestinal bleeding, and aspirin **311**.15
gay people **369**.2, 12, 13, 20–3, 32
　and AIDS **314**.6
　and civil partnerships **316**.9
　and private life **317**.3
　see also LGBTQIA+ community; same-sex relationships
Gaza, and war zones **300**.20
GCHQ **383**.17
GCSEs **353**.14–17, 19, 20–1, 41, **403**.1
　choosing **403**.4–9
　grade inflation **403**.16–17
　importance of **403**.2
　number grades **403**.3
　resits **403**.3
GDP (gross domestic product) **391**.41
GDPR (General Data Protection Regulation) **317**.32
gender
　and addiction **410**.3
　bias **381**.33–5
　binary **369**.2
　and blood donation **382**.30–1
　and body image **307**.1, 5, 9, 13, 15
　and bullying **361**.11, **380**.6
　and business **381**.33–5
　and child labour **412**.19
　and cyberbullying **361**.4, 11
　defining **364**.41, **369**.1–2, 3, 41
　development **369**.10
　and diet **350**.32

difference **364**.4
discrimination **364**.3, 17, 41, **372**.7
　and drug abuse **373**.7
dysphoria **369**.5–8, 37, 41
equality **364**.4–5, 8–9, 22–3, **372**.9–10, 27, 30
equal pay **364**.9–10, 15–16
equal rights at work **364**.2
and exam results **353**.16–17
and exercise **384**.15–17, 26–9, 33
and gambling **349**.7, 10
and gaming **409**.33–4
identity **369**.1–2, 4, 6, 37–9, 41
imbalance in voting **360**.36
inclusion **411**.9–10, 22–5
inequality **411**.12–13
and internet use **371**.2
and life expectancy **363**.5, 13, 15
nonconforming **369**.10–11
norms **379**.2
and obesity **384**.6–8
pay gap **364**.9–10, 15–16, 41, **368**.9
preferences **369**.5
roles **369**.3–4
and school uniform **364**.13–14
selection, and abortion **302**.30–2, 37
and smoking **406**.1
socialisation **369**.10–11
and social media **409**.5, 10, 13–14, 35
stereotypes **364**.27–39, 41, **369**.3–5, 10, **380**.6, **386**.3, 20, 27–8, 41
and unconscious bias **364**.3
variant **369**.2
and volunteering **382**.14
　see also LGBTQIA+ community; men; women; women and girls
gender gap **364**.2, 10–12
gender identity disorder (GID) **369**.5–8, 37
gender inequality **370**.13
gender pay gap **364**.9–10, 15–16, 41, **368**.9, **411**.27, 41
genderqueer **369**.1–2, 9
gender stereotypes **364**.27–39, 41, **369**.3–5, 10, **380**.6, **386**.3, 20, 27–8, 41
gene
　editing **314**.35, **348**.23, **352**.6, 9–11, 31, 36–9, 41

Vol. numbers appear first (in bold) followed by page numbers; a change in volume is preceded by a semi-colon.

Vol. 305　Globalisation – Good or Bad?
Vol. 314　HIV & AIDS
Vol. 316　Marriage
Vol. 347　The Censorship Debate
Vol. 348　World Health
Vol. 349　Gambling Culture
Vol. 350　Lifestyle Diets
Vol. 351　The Anxiety Epidemic
Vol. 352　Biotech & Bioethics
Vol. 353　Education
Vol. 354　Relationships
Vol. 355　Terrorism
Vol. 356　British Armed Forces
Vol. 357　The Climate Emergency
Vol. 358　Religion Today
Vol. 359　Migration & Immigration
Vol. 360　Government
Vol. 361　Cyberbullying
Vol. 362　Euthanasia
Vol. 363　Population Change
Vol. 364　The Gender Equality Debate
Vol. 365　Tourism Today
Vol. 366　Crime in the UK
Vol. 367　Discussing Abortion

Vol. 368　Sustainable Living
Vol. 369　LGBT+ Issues
Vol. 370　Domestic Violence and Abuse
Vol. 371　The Internet and Us
Vol. 372　Our Human Rights
Vol. 373　Drug Use and Abuse
Vol. 374　Animal Rights
Vol. 375　Body Image
Vol. 376　Racism
Vol. 377　Poverty
Vol. 378　Ageing
Vol. 379　Understanding Sexual Health
Vol. 380　About Bullying
Vol. 381　Business
Vol. 382　Active Citizenship
Vol. 383　The Privacy Debate
Vol. 384　Health & Fitness
Vol. 385　Waste & Recycling Issues
Vol. 386　Sexualising Society
Vol. 387　Fertility Issues
Vol. 388　Discussing Child Abuse
Vol. 389　Sleep
Vol. 390　Eating Disorders
Vol. 391　Money

Vol. 392　National Health
Vol. 393　Disability
Vol. 394　Pregnancy
Vol. 395　Teen Self-Care
Vol. 396　UK Housing
Vol. 397　Alcohol Issues
Vol. 398　Homelessness
Vol. 399　Discussing Cannabis
Vol. 400　Suicide & Self-Harm
Vol. 401　War & Conflict
Vol. 402　Endangered Species
Vol. 403　Student Options
Vol. 404　Depression
Vol. 405　Employability
Vol. 406　Smoking
Vol. 407　Bereavement
Vol. 408　Healthy Eating
Vol. 409　Online Safety
Vol. 410　Addiction
Vol. 411　Sport
Vol. 412　Rights of the Child
Vol. 413　Energy
Vol. 414　Consumerism
Vol. 415　Mental Health

and health **311**.19

and perceptions of ageing **311**.18

and rates of ageing **311**.18, 34

therapy **352**.4–6

general anxiety disorder **415**.3

General Data Protection Regulation (GDPR) **317**.32, **383**.2, 7, 22, 41

general elections **360**.41

Generalised Anxiety Disorder (GAD) **351**.5, 7, 24, 41, **375**.28

General Osteopathic Council (GosC) **343**.3

general practitioners (GPs) **392**.13

'Generation Me' **358**.14

Generation X **350**.4–5

Generation Y, and the Armed Forces **356**.41

Generation Z **350**.4–5

Millennium Cohort Study (MCS) **399**.9–10

and religion **358**.1

genetically altered animals **374**.24–5

genetically modified organisms (GMOs) **352**.4–6

genetic data **352**.31–2

genetic engineering

of children **352**.14–15

of crops **352**.2

genetic factors, in ageing **378**.11

genetic modification (GM) **303**.35, **352**.4–5, 41

genetics, and addiction **373**.2

genetics testing **394**.41

Geneva Conventions **401**.33, 41

genital herpes **309**.9, 11, 13, **379**.20, 24, 25

genital warts **309**.11, **379**.20, 24, 25

vaccination **309**.25

genitourinary medicine (GUM) clinic **367**.1

genocide **401**.14, 33, 36, 41

genome **408**.14

genomic medicine **352**.11–13

genomic vaccines **348**.36–7

gentrification **306**.4

GeoCities **409**.1

geoengineering **357**.23, 41

geopolitics **357**.6

geothermal energy **413**.1–2, 5, 31, 41

Germany

and animal welfare **303**.12

attitudes to Armed Forces **356**.3–4

CO_2 emissions **357**.3

immigration statistics **359**.3–4

refugee statistics **359**.34

and surveillance **317**.27–8

war guilt **356**.3–4

gestation **394**.41

gestational diabetes **394**.17

giant panda bears **357**.18

Gibraltar, and citizenship **382**.5

'giggle doctors' **343**.24

ginger **343**.31

giraffes **303**.6

girlfriends **354**.26–7

see also romantic relationships

girls and young women

and body image **307**.4

and bullying **361**.11

as child brides **364**.1

and education **314**.18

female genital mutilation (FGM) **358**.35–6, **364**.7

and gaming **409**.33–4

impact of social media **361**.1

periods **309**.30

persecution of **358**.38–9

and pink toys **364**.35–6

and pregnancy **309**.22

right to education **364**.6

and self-esteem **307**.38

and selfies **318**.35

and sex **309**.29

and sexual dysfunction **309**.16

smoking statistics **406**.1

and social media **409**.5

glass

as plastic alternative **385**.25

recycling **385**.12, 29

glass ceiling **364**.41

Global Challenges Foundation (GCF), on population growth **363**.24

Global Coalition to End Child Poverty **377**.29

global displacement **359**.34

global economic cycle **305**.4

global financial crisis (2008)

and globalisation **305**.32, 36

and international trade **305**.32

global footprint **368**.4, 41

Global Gender Gap Index 2018 **364**.2, 30

Global Gender Gap Report 2017 **364**.6

global inequalities **364**.2

globalisation **305**.1, 4–7, 20–1, 36–9, **414**.26

and aid **305**.22–3

and banks **305**.32, 38

and brain drain **305**.6

and brands **305**.7–8, 8–9

and consumer patterns **305**.7

cultural **305**.5–6

and debt **305**.33, 38

and digital technology **305**.24–5, 34, 37

and environment **305**.2, 6

and financial flows **305**.32

and global economic cycle **305**.4

history of **305**.3–5, 36, 38

impacts **305**.1–2, 9, 20–1, 24, 36–8

and inequality **305**.5, 39

and localism **305**.21

and migration **305**.4, 6, 31

political **305**.5–6, 37–9

and protectionism **305**.32–3

and regionalism **305**.29–30

and sovereignty **305**.20

see also international trade; manufacturing

global population

decline in **363**.26, 27–31, 34–5

depopulation **363**.34

growth of **363**.1–2, 6, 19, 24, 27–30, 34–6

overpopulation **363**.22–5, 30

global poverty **305**.22, 30, **306**.26–8, 35–6, 38, **377**.20–8, 30–1, 34–5

Global Terrorism Index 2018 **355**.14–16

global tourism **365**.6, 27

Global Vaccine Action Plan (GVAP) **348**.29

global warming **357**.2, 6, 20–1, 38, 41, **363**.22, **402**.1

see also climate change; energy efficiency; greenhouse gases

'glossy work' **405**.38–9
gluten **350**.23, 24, 41
gluten-free diets **350**.24–5
GM *see* genetic modification (GM)
God
    as all-powerful deity **358**.17
    belief in **358**.2, 19
    existence of **358**.19
    see also religion
gods **358**.17, 23
    see also deities; religion
Golden Rice **352**.2
goldenseal **343**.32
gonorrhoea **309**.10–11, **379**.14–15, 20, 24, 25, **387**.19
Good Childhood Report 2013, The **354**.9–10
Good Friday **358**.22
Good Friday Agreement **300**.33, 36
Good Law Project **392**.9
goods, for personal use **414**.4
Google **383**.26–7
    and deleting searches **317**.17
Go Set a Watchman **308**.9
Gove, Michael **357**.31, **359**.22
    on climate change **357**.8
government
    on AIDS **314**.27
    borrowing **391**.15, 20–2
    Cabinet **360**.2
    Civil Service **360**.3
    definition **360**.41, **382**.41
    departments **360**.2
    executive agencies **360**.2
    how it works **360**.2–3
    local **360**.3, 18
    ministers **360**.2, 4
    non-departmental public bodies (NDPBs) **360**.2
    spending **360**.4
    types of **360**.1
    see also devolved government; legislation; Parliament
Government of Wales Act 1998 **360**.9
grammar schools **353**.3, 41
grandparents
    and parental separation **316**.37–8
    time spent with grandchildren **311**.13
grasslands **402**.3–4
Great Barrier Reef **357**.17
Great British Spring Clean (GBSC) **385**.7
Greece
    and abortion **302**.14
    and tourism **365**.16
    waste statistics **385**.3
greenbelt land **396**.41
green cities **368**.9
green consumerism **368**.5
green driving **368**.14
green energy **368**.41
    see also renewable energy
green fluorescent protein (GFP) **413**.39
Green GB Week **357**.8
Green Homes Grant **413**.28
greenhouse gases (GHGs) **357**.6, 8, 12, 36, 37, 41, **368**.3, **385**.30, 35, **413**.8, 36
    see also methane emissions; see also carbon dioxide emissions

Green Papers **360**.6
Green Party **360**.21
    on climate change **357**.2
Greenpeace **365**.24
    on supermarket plastics **385**.26–7
green technology **385**.15, **396**.36
green turtles **357**.19
greenwashing **368**.41, **413**.41, **414**.21
Grenfell Tower **396**.22–3
greyhound welfare **349**.31
grief **400**.37–8, 41, **407**.16–20, 30–1, 36–7
    five stages of **407**.21
    seven stages of **407**.22–3
    see also bereavement; death and mortality
grooming **361**.34, **386**.41, **388**.6, 19–21, 26, 41
    see also sexual exploitation
gross domestic product (GDP) **381**.41
groundwater extraction **402**.4–5, 41
groups
    exclusion from **361**.6, 7
    social exclusion **361**.11
group therapy **400**.41, **410**.41, **415**.21
Guam, waste statistics **385**.4
guilt **404**.25
Gurkhas **356**.1, 7
Guru Nanak Birthday **358**.25
Guru Tegh Bahadur Sahib Martyrdom **358**.25
gynaecologist **394**.41
Gypsy communities **376**.23–4, 41, **380**.4–5

H

habeas corpus **372**.5, **374**.3
Habeas Corpus Act 1679 **372**.2
habitats **363**.22, **402**.41
habituation **349**.5
hacking **361**.6
    see also surveillance and access
haemorrhage **367**.16
Haiti **377**.22
    war and conflict **401**.22–3
Haitian Revolution (1791-1804) **401**.3
halal slaughter
    banning **303**.6
    and labelling **303**.7
Halloween **414**.23
halls of residence **403**.41
hallucinations **399**.2, 4, 15, **404**.1, **415**.4
    imaginary friends **354**.18–19
hallucinogenics **373**.4, 41
hangover **397**.2–3, 8, 19, 24, 41
    from cannabis **399**.17
Hannukah **358**.25
happiness **306**.16, **314**.37
    and ageing **378**.32
harassment **361**.6, 7, 41, **376**.4, 41, **380**.19, 31, **393**.21, 22, **409**.33–4
    age discrimination **311**.6
    racial **308**.2–3
    in universities **361**.25–6
    see also bullying
'hard' subjects **403**.6
Harlow's monkeys **374**.18

Harry, Prince (Henry of Wales), on HIV **314**.25
Harry Potter books, and censorship **347**.34–5
hash (hashish) **399**.1, 13, 41
hashtags **409**.41
hate crime **308**.8, 12, 17, 29, 34, **355**.17, **369**.30–1, 41, **376**.30, 41, **380**.6, **393**.16–18
hate mail **371**.26–7
hate speech **347**.1, 2, 3
hazardous chemicals **348**.2
headaches **394**.5
headstone **407**.41
health
    effects of cannabis **399**.15
    during pregnancy **394**.8–15
    see also mental health
Health Act 2006 **406**.41
health and social care **378**.29–30, 41
    in Japan **378**.11
health and wellbeing **311**.17
    and increasing life expectancy **311**.4
    and inequality **306**.13, **308**.6–7
    and intergenerational communities **311**.36
    new technologies **348**.36–7
    and religion **358**.21
    sleep **348**.7
    and social isolation **311**.35–6
    universal coverage **348**.2
    world health statistics **348**.1
    see also exercise and activity; mental health; wellbeing
health anxiety **351**.5
healthcare **305**.22–3, 29–30
    in Africa **392**.18
    in Asia **392**.15–16
    in Australia **392**.16–17
    cost of **392**.1, 3, 11–12
    in the European Union (EU) **392**.14–15
    inequality **392**.36
    as percentage of GDP **392**.3
    pre-Second World War **392**.1
    private **392**.11
    right to **412**.3, 13
    in South America **392**.17–18
    in the USA **392**.12–13
    see also doctors; hospitals
healthcare workers **405**.2
health inequalities **392**.21, **406**.30
    in sport **411**.10–13
health promotion data **395**.8–10
health security **392**.39
health tourism **392**.13
health tracking **383**.30–1
health workers
    Covid-19 deaths **392**.8
    staffing crisis **392**.6–8, 20
healthy eating **408**.26–7, 34–5
healthy habits **378**.35–6, 39
hearing voices **415**.6
    see also schizophrenia
heartbreak **354**.38–9
heartburn **395**.19
heart disease **348**.5–6, **378**.5, 9, 11, 21, 35, 39, **406**.1, 9, 16
    and aspirin **311**.14, 15
Heart Research Institute (HRI) **406**.12
heated tobacco products

    see also e-cigarettes
Heathrow airport, expansion **357**.2
heat pumps **413**.2, 28, 31, 41
    see also geothermal energy
heatstroke **357**.29
heatwaves **402**.5
heavy drinking see alcohol
hedgehogs **357**.34–5, **374**.13, 15
Help to Buy scheme **396**.3
hepatitis **343**.5
    A **348**.19
    B **309**.11, 13
    C **309**.13
    vaccination **309**.10–13
herbal cannabis **399**.13, 41
herbal medicine **343**.6, 8–9, 14–15, 26–8, 31–4
herd immunity **392**.41, **395**.11
hereditary peers **360**.4, 11
heredity see genes
Her Majesty's Inspectorate of Prisons **360**.2
heroin **301**.2–3, 11, 19, 22–3, 34, **373**.3, 5, 11, 22, **399**.22
heros
    Armed Forces as **356**.3–4
    see also veterans
herpes **379**.3
    genital **309**.9, 11, 13
    simplex **387**.19
heteronormative **369**.13
heterosexism **369**.13
heterosexual **369**.2, 13, 15, 41
hidden homelessness **364**.20, **398**.1, 3, 4, 7, 22, 41
high blood pressure **392**.32–3
high cholesterol **392**.32
higher education **403**.1, 41
    see also further education; graduates; students; universities; university
Higher Nationals (HNC/Ds) **403**.20
high functioning addicts **410**.35–6
high rise buildings **396**.4, 22–3, 27
hijab **353**.34, **358**.32
Hinduism **358**.2–4, 9, 11, 12–13, 41
    Ayurveda **358**.21
    caste system **308**.25–6
    gods **358**.23
    holidays **358**.23–4
    rise in **358**.18
    sacred texts **358**.31
Hippocrates **362**.23
Hippocratic Oath **362**.6, 17
hip to waist ratio **384**.4
Hitler, Adolf **401**.2, 8
HITT (high intensity interval training) **384**.41
HIV (human immunodeficiency virus) **301**.8–12, 14–16, 21–2, 23, 25, 35, 38–9, **309**.3, 12, 13, 24–5, **314**.1–5, **379**.2, 16–18, 24, 25
    and animal experimentation **374**.15
    early diagnosis **314**.5, 8, 10
    global statistics **314**.3
    and innate AIDS defence **314**.36
    key affected populations **314**.15
    late diagnosis **314**.4, 5, 7, 8
    misinformation **314**.19, 20, 23, 24
    mother to child transmission **314**.2, 29–30
    and other conditions **314**.29

paediatric and adult care **314**.18
related illness **348**.1, 17–18
risks **301**.1, **314**.4, 15, 16, 23
statistics **348**.17
and steroid injecting **301**.14, 15
stigma **314**.6, 11, 18, 20, 22–6
and testing **314**.4–5, 8, 9, 17, 21, 24–5, 28–9, 39
timeline **314**.6
treatments **343**.5, 9, 38–9
and viral loads **314**.2
see also AIDS (Acquired Immune Deficiency Syndrome)
hoarding disorder **351**.3, **415**.6
hobbies **414**.17
and self–esteem **307**.31
Holi **358**.23
holidays
countries visited **365**.5
ecotourism **365**.1, 28–9
global tourism **365**.6
length of **365**.11
popular destinations **365**.6, 12–13
religious **358**.22–5
trends **365**.3–5, 11–12
Holocaust **358**.13, **401**.14, 38–9
Holy Saturday **358**.22
home
leaving **354**.1
owning own **354**.1–2
and privacy **317**.3, 25
retirement homes **311**.17, 24, 25–7, 32–3
see also housing; living arrangements
home assistants **381**.4
home care, care transfer delays **311**.5
Homeless Link **398**.1
homelessness **364**.20, **377**.37–8, **392**.24, **396**.1, 5
among veterans **356**.32
causes of **398**.1
deaths from **398**.7
definition **398**.1, 41
and domestic abuse **370**.27–8, 32–3
and health **398**.7
and mental health **356**.33
myths about **398**.4
reducing **398**.1–2, 6–7, 30–5, 38–9

and right to vote **360**.20
at risk of **398**.3
in Scotland **398**.1, 5–7, 15, 24–6
statistics **398**.2, 6–7, 10, 16, 22
stereotypes **398**.4, 7
stigmas **398**.30
in Wales **398**.2–3, 6–7, 10–11
see also rough sleeping
Homelessness Prevention Grant **398**.38–9
Homelessness Reduction Act 2017 **398**.1, 38
homeless villages **398**.33
homeopathy **343**.6, 9–10, 19–20, 29–31, 35–6, 41
home ownership **396**.2–3, 6–7, 17, 19, 37
second homes **396**.24–6
home schooling **353**.24
homework **353**.36–9
homicides **366**.1, 2, 6, 17
domestic **370**.3, 15
see also femicide
homophobia **369**.13, 30–1, 32, 41
homophobic bullying **380**.5–6
homosexuality **369**.2, 13, 15, 41
decriminalisation of **369**.24–8
see also gay people; LGBTQIA+ community; same-sex relationships
honesty **354**.28
honey **343**.31
Hong Kong
and citizenship **382**.5, 8
and prostitution **318**.4
waste statistics **385**.3
hormone replacement therapy (HRT) **387**.7, 8, 10
hormones **309**.6
progestogen **309**.6–8
testosterone **309**.8
hormone therapy **369**.8
Hornsea 2 **413**.6
horses, welfare legislation **303**.2
hospital admissions, and violent offences **366**.9, 17
hospitals **311**.17A&E
and abortion **302**.2–4, 6
asylums **392**.2
care transfer delays **311**.5
cottage **392**.1

Vol. numbers appear first (in bold) followed by page numbers; a change in volume is preceded by a semi-colon.

Vol. 305	Globalisation – Good or Bad?	Vol. 368	Sustainable Living	Vol. 392	National Health
Vol. 314	HIV & AIDS	Vol. 369	LGBT+ Issues	Vol. 393	Disability
Vol. 316	Marriage	Vol. 370	Domestic Violence and Abuse	Vol. 394	Pregnancy
Vol. 347	The Censorship Debate	Vol. 371	The Internet and Us	Vol. 395	Teen Self-Care
Vol. 348	World Health	Vol. 372	Our Human Rights	Vol. 396	UK Housing
Vol. 349	Gambling Culture	Vol. 373	Drug Use and Abuse	Vol. 397	Alcohol Issues
Vol. 350	Lifestyle Diets	Vol. 374	Animal Rights	Vol. 398	Homelessness
Vol. 351	The Anxiety Epidemic	Vol. 375	Body Image	Vol. 399	Discussing Cannabis
Vol. 352	Biotech & Bioethics	Vol. 376	Racism	Vol. 400	Suicide & Self-Harm
Vol. 353	Education	Vol. 377	Poverty	Vol. 401	War & Conflict
Vol. 354	Relationships	Vol. 378	Ageing	Vol. 402	Endangered Species
Vol. 355	Terrorism	Vol. 379	Understanding Sexual Health	Vol. 403	Student Options
Vol. 356	British Armed Forces	Vol. 380	About Bullying	Vol. 404	Depression
Vol. 357	The Climate Emergency	Vol. 381	Business	Vol. 405	Employability
Vol. 358	Religion Today	Vol. 382	Active Citizenship	Vol. 406	Smoking
Vol. 359	Migration & Immigration	Vol. 383	The Privacy Debate	Vol. 407	Bereavement
Vol. 360	Government	Vol. 384	Health & Fitness	Vol. 408	Healthy Eating
Vol. 361	Cyberbullying	Vol. 385	Waste & Recycling Issues	Vol. 409	Online Safety
Vol. 362	Euthanasia	Vol. 386	Sexualising Society	Vol. 410	Addiction
Vol. 363	Population Change	Vol. 387	Fertility Issues	Vol. 411	Sport
Vol. 364	The Gender Equality Debate	Vol. 388	Discussing Child Abuse	Vol. 412	Rights of the Child
Vol. 365	Tourism Today	Vol. 389	Sleep	Vol. 413	Energy
Vol. 366	Crime in the UK	Vol. 390	Eating Disorders	Vol. 414	Consumerism
Vol. 367	Discussing Abortion	Vol. 391	Money	Vol. 415	Mental Health

and end-of-life care **311**.2
  history of **306**.5
  and surveillance **317**.31
  teaching **392**.1
'Hothouse Earth' **357**.11–12
housebuilding **396**.4
household
  definition **363**.2
  living alone **363**.2
household income **391**.41
household responsibilities, and gender equality **364**.9
household waste
  reducing **385**.1, 35, 38
  see also recycling
House of Commons **360**.2, 4–7, 10, 12–14
House of Commons Women and Equalities Select Committee **375**.18
House of Lords **360**.2, 4–7, 11
  bishops' bench **358**.18
  Select Committee on Medical Ethics **362**.2–3
house prices *see* property prices
housing **306**.7
  affordability **396**.1–3, 5–6, 36–7
  co-housing and friends **311**.37
  costs **306**.7, **377**.2
  crisis **396**.1–3, 5
  future of **396**.27
  inequality **396**.5
  and loneliness **378**.37–8
  new homes **396**.3–4, 28–32
  safety **396**.22–3, 39
  security **396**.5
  as social asset **396**.6–7
  supply **396**.3–4
  temporary accommodation **306**.7
Housing Act 1980 **396**.8
housing associations **396**.41
housing bubble **396**.9, 41
Howard League for Penal Reform is **366**.41
HPV (human papillomavirus) **309**.10, 11, 13, 22, 25, **379**.5–6, 20, 41
HSI (Humane Society International), on banning cosmetics tests **303**.38–9
Humane Cosmetics Act **303**.39
human embryos *see* embryos
Humane Society International (HSI) **374**.21
  on banning cosmetics tests **303**.38–9
Human Fertilisation and Embryology Act 1990 **302**.1, **367**.3
Human Genome Project 2003 **352**.11, 29
human germline editing **352**.35–6
human growth hormone (HGH) **389**.2–3
human immunodeficiency virus *see* HIV (human immunodeficiency virus)
humanism
  and abortion **367**.7–8
  and marriage **316**.6, 10
  and secularism **302**.15
humanistic therapy **404**.37–8
humanitarian
  aid **359**.32, 34
  crisis **359**.33–4, 37
  policy **359**.34
humanitarian disasters **401**.18, 33
humanitarian intervention **300**.23–4, **401**.14, 41

Humanitarian Law **401**.14, 41
humanitarian relief **306**.38
humanities **403**.4, 5, 6
human papillomavirus *see* HPV (human papillomavirus)
human papillomavirus (HPV) vaccine **392**.22, **395**.10, 15–16, 25, 41
human rights **302**.35–6, **317**.2–3, 25, **379**.2
  and being human **300**.23, 26
  breaches of **372**.7, 30–1, 33–4
  campaigns to protect **300**.21
  and civil liberties **372**.5
  countries with poor records **300**.21
  and decriminalisation **318**.3, 5–7, 13, 17
  definition **372**.1, 41
  definitions **300**.1
  gender and sexuality **369**.24–5
  global policy **318**.3
  history of **372**.2–3
  international conventions **300**.2
  and lack of choice **318**.21
  legislation **372**.2–7
  multiple abuses of **318**.3–4
  as non-binding **317**.14
  and obligations **372**.1
  obligations of the State **300**.1, 26–7
  and precedence **317**.14–15
  and proportionality **317**.24–5
  and restrictions **302**.11, 34
  sexual rights **309**.1–2
  social justice and equality **300**.38–9
  and sport **411**.8
  violations **412**.28–39
  and war zones **300**.20–1
  see also United Nations Convention on the Rights of the Child
Human Rights Act 1998 **355**.41, **372**.3, 4, 5–7, 12, 41, **405**.34
  Article 2. right to life **362**.15
  and the European Convention on Human Rights **300**.1–2, 27, 29–30
  freedom of expression **347**.2–3
  public perception **300**.39
  social benefits **300**.34–5
  and social justice **300**.38–9
Human Rights Watch, on violence against women **360**.36
human trafficking **359**.38, **364**.6, **372**.14–22, 41
  see also child trafficking; trafficking
Human Trafficking and Exploitation Act 2015 **372**.17
humour
  and belittlement **307**.27–8
  and religious ceremonies **316**.7
Hungary **360**.33
  and animal welfare **303**.3
hunger **306**.19–20, 24–6, 28, 36, **394**.6
  and food theft **306**.23, 31
hunting **402**.4, 12, 13, 15, 22, 25, 41
  with hounds **303**.27
  lions, trophy hunting **303**.27
  see also poaching; trophy hunting
Hunting Act 2004 **303**.27
hurricanes **357**.13–15
hybrid species **402**.25–6
hydration **408**.5–7
hydrocarbon fuels **357**.12
hydrocephalus **393**.12

hydrogen **357**.36–7
hydrogen power **413**.33
hydropower **413**.2, 5, 9, 31, 41
hygiene, obsession with **350**.27
hyperinflation **391**.1
hypersexualisation **386**.3, 8
hypersomnia **389**.20
hypertension **384**.20, **392**.32–3
hypnotherapy **343.6**
hypocrisy, and racism **376**.1–3
hypomania **415.6**
    see also bipolar disorder

I

IAPT (Improving Access to Psychological Therapies) **351**.7
ibuprofen **373**.13
Ice Ages **357**.11–12
Iceland, waste statistics **385**.4
ice sheets **357**.20–1
identity **382**.6–11
    and immigration **359**.25–6
IGCSE (International GCSE) **353**.41, **403**.41
'illegal immigrants' **359**.36
    see also asylum seekers
illiteracy **364**.6
    see also education
Imagery Rehearsal Therapy (IRT) **389**.10
imaginary friends **354**.18
imagination, as anxiety treatment **351**.29–30
IMF (International Monetary Fund), and globalisation **305**.37
immigrants, definition **359**.3
immigration **363**.2, **398**.5
    and assimilation **359**.26
    attitudes to **359**.15–17, 22–5
    benefits of **359**.15–17, 27–8
    controls **382**.2
    and culture **359**.15–17
    definition **382**.41
    fees **382**.3
    and identity **359**.25–6
    impacts of **359**.15–17
    leave to remain **382**.2, 4–5
    media representations of **359**.20–1
    negative outcomes of **359**.16–17
    policies **359**.13–14, 27–8
    population statistics worldwide **359**.3–5
    rates **382**.9
    see also migrants; migration
Immigration Act 1971 **382**.2
immune system **303**.34, **343**.18, 34, **389**.1, 3, 8
immunisation **348**.29, **379**.5–6, **392**.2, 28, 41
immunity **394**.7
imperialism **401**.2
impersonation **361**.6, 7
implantation bleeding **394**.3–4
imprisonment *see* prison
impulse buying **414**.28
inalienability **372**.1
inbound tourism **365**.1
incinerators **385**.16–17, 41
inclusion **381**.29–32
inclusive sport **384**.26–9, 41, **411**.9–10, 41

income **306**.1, 18, 20–1, **377**.5, 24–5
    basic **377**.35–6
    and inequality **306**.2, 3, 10, 13–14, 19, 21, 26–7, 31–2, 33
    low **306**.13, 16, 17, 20
    median **377**.3, 12
    Minimum Income Standard (MIS) **377**.1, 41
    wealth inequality **377**.32–3
    see also living standards; retirement; salaries; wages
indefinite leave to remain **382**.2, 4–5
independent monitoring boards **360**.2
Independent Press Standards Organisation (IPSO) **347**.16
independent schools **353**.4
India
    caste system **308**.25–6
    CO_2 emissions **357**.3
    data protection **383**.2
    fertility rates **363**.31
    healthcare **392**.16
    immigration statistics **359**.3
    partitioning of **358**.13
    population growth **363**.28
    selective abortion **367**.25
    see also Hinduism
indigestion **395**.19
indirect bullying **380**.1–3
indirect discrimination **376**.3–4, **393**.20
Indonesia, CO_2 emissions **357**.3
industrial action **405**.32, 34
industrial biotechnology **352**.3
Industrial Revolution **360**.15
inequality **368**.3, **370**.12–13, **376**.26–7, **377**.3, 32–3, **392**.36
    and bullying **380**.15–16
    in education **353**.30
    health and activity levels **411**.10–113
    in school **353**.28
    see also socio-economic prejudice
infanticide **366**.6, **412**.13
infant mortality **363**.41, **378**.4, 6, **379**.11, **392**.28, **394**.26–7, 41
infantry **356**.7, 11, 12
infertility **387**.20–1, 41
    assisted conception **387**.25
    myths **387**.14–15
    treatments **387**.24–5
    see also fertility
inflammation **404**.15
inflation **391**.21–2, 41
influencers **371**.10, 32, **409**.24, **414**.34
influenza
    pandemic (1918) **348**.14–15
    viruses **357**.23
InfoCircus **374**.26
Information Commissioner's Office (ICO), on cyberbullying **361**.5
infringements of children's rights **412**.28–9
inhuman treatment **372**.4
innuendo **386**.28
Insecam **383**.10
insects, as food **368**.37
insemination **387**.2
insolvency **381**.17–21
insomnia **351**.14, 17, **373**.13, **387**.9, **389**.9–10, 20, 23–7, 38–9, 41
Instagram **371**.10, 33, **409**.2–3, 25, 36–7

bullying language **380**.19
  cyberbullying on **361**.15
  reporting/dealing with abuse on **361**.32
Institute for European Environmental Policy (IEEP) **368**.8
Institute for Fiscal Studies (IFS)
  on relative poverty **356**.33
  on school spending **353**.31–2
Institute of Customer Service (ICS) **414**.10
institutional racism **376**.15–19, 24–5
insurance **381**.2
integrated healthcare **343**.2
intelligence **378**.23
  and gene editing **352**.9–11
intelligence analysts **356**.5
intensive farming **350**.12–13, 41, **363**.23, **374**.6, 41
interest **391**.6, 39, 41
  rates **396**.10–11
Intergovernmental Panel on Climate Change (IPCC) **357**.2, 6,
  20, 39, 41, **402**.5
Intergovernmental Science-Policy Platform on Biodiversity
  and Ecosystem Services (IPBES) **402**.3, 10
internally displaced persons **359**.31, 38, 41
International Baccalaureate (Ibac) **353**.41
International Bill of Human Rights **300**.26
International Conference on Population and Development
  (ICPD) **372**.9, **379**.2
International Convention on the Elimination of All Forms of
  Racial Discrimination (CERD)1965 **372**.1–2
International Covenant on Civil and Political Rights (ICCPR)
  300.2, 26
International Covenant on Economic, Social and Cultural
  Rights (ICESCR) 1976 **300**.26, **372**.2
International Criminal Court **401**.33
international data transfer **383**.3
International Energy Agency (IEA) **413**.30–1, 37
International Guiding Principles for Biomedical Research
  Involving Animals **374**.17
International Humanitarian Law (IHL) **359**.41
International Labour Organisation (ILO) **412**.23, 41
International Men's Day **364**.18
International Monetary Fund (IMF), and globalisation **305**.37
International Renewable Energy Agency (IRENA) **413**.36
international terrorism **355**.3
international tourism **365**.1
international trade **305**.4–5, 14–15, 18–19, 21–7, 29–32
  see also European Union (EU); fairtrade; free trade;
    manufacturing
International Union for the Conservation of Nature (IUCN)
  402.4, 18
  Red List of Threatened Species **402**.41
International Women's Day **364**.1, 8, 22
internet **317**.10, **409**.41
  access **371**.1–2
  censorship **347**.6, 9
  clickbait **317**.10
  gaming **371**.10
  impacts of **371**.8–10, 12–13
  as information source **409**.10–12, 26
  pornography **318**.30–6, 34–5
  risks **371**.4, 9–10, 12–14, 14, 18–24
  safety **371**.12–17, 22–7, **409**.10–17
  time spent on **361**.5
  use **371**.1–5
  see also digital footprint; social media

Internet connection records (ICRs) **317**.6–8
Internet of things (IoT) **317**.31–2, **371**.28–9, **383**.10–11, 24–6
  and personal data **317**.33
  and product liability **317**.32
  safety risks **317**.32
internet safety **380**.21
  see also cyber-bullying
internet service providers (ISPs), and internet pornography
  318.30
Internet Watch Foundation (IWF), on revenge porn **361**.26
internships **403**.21, **405**.1
interoception-directed therapy **351**.28–9
intersectionality **378**.22, **380**.5
intersex people **369**.1, 2, 3
interventionism **401**.14
interviews **405**.3, 4, 13–17
intimidation **354**.28, **388**.8
intoxication **397**.2, 21, 41
intrauterine devices (IUDs) **309**.6–7
intrauterine insemination (IUI) **387**.25
intrauterine systems (IUSs) **309**.7
intra-vas devices (IVDs) **309**.8
invasive species **402**.2, 3, 7, 10, 13, 38, 41
Investigatory Powers Act 2016 **317**.4–8, 19–20, **383**.17
investment **381**.7, 10–11, 14–15, 25, 33, 38, 41
'invisible homelessness' see hidden homelessness
in vitro fertilisation (IVF) **387**.14–15, 21, 25–33, 41, **394**.41
in vitro meat **352**.41
involuntary smoking see passive smoking
iodine **350**.38–9
IoT see internet of things
IPPR (Institute for Public Policy Research), on benefit reforms
  377.7
Iran
  censorship in **347**.11, 36
  CO_2 emissions **357**.3
  war and conflict **401**.5, 8, 10–11, 18, 21
Iraq **356**.14, 24, 39
  censorship in **347**.11
  conflict **300**.20
  war and conflict **401**.3, 7, 10, 17, 29, 31
Iraqi Conflict (2003-2021) **401**.3, 10
Ireland
  and abortion **302**.34
  abortion laws **367**.18–19
  and animal welfare **303**.3–4
  prostitution **318**.10
  waste statistics **385**.2
  see also Northern Ireland
Irish Republican Army (IRA) **355**.2, 3–4, 7
  ceasefire **355**.12
iron **350**.38–9, **394**.12
iron deficiency anaemia **394**.17
irregular menstrual cycle **387**.1, 20
irreligiosity (no religion) **358**.1–2, 6–7, 18–20
  see also non-religious population
ISIS (Islamic State of Iraq and al–Sham) **300**.20, 23
Islam **355**.41, **358**.2–5, 8, 11, 41
  burqa **358**.32–3
  and euthanasia **362**.17
  and halal slaughter **303**.6–7
  hijab **358**.32
  holidays **358**.25
  and LGBT **369**.32–3

Muhammad, prophet **358**.8, 25
pilgrimage **358**.27
Quran **358**.8, 25, 31
radical Muslims **355**.2, 17
see also Muslims
Islamic State **401**.24
Islamic State (IS) **355**.3, 4, 5, 14–15, 41
Islamic theocratic states **358**.3
Islamophobia **308**.4, 15, 34, 37, **358**.1, **376**.30–1, 41
Isle of Man, and civil partnerships **316**.9
isolation **354**.28, 36, **388**.9
ISPs (internet service providers), and internet pornography **318**.30
Isra and Mi'raj **358**.25
Israel **358**.4, 8
war and conflict **401**.4, 21, 21–2, 37
waste statistics **385**.3
Israelites **358**.13
IT *see* information technology
Italy
and food poverty **306**.31
immigration statistics **359**.3–4
and surveillance **317**.27–8
IUDs (intrauterine devices) **309**.6–7, **387**.17
IUSs (intrauterine systems) **309**.7
IVDs (intra-vas devices) **309**.8
ivory trade **303**.27, **402**.24
see also wildlife trade

J

jail *see* prison
Jainism **358**.2, 4, 9–10, 31
Janmashtami **358**.23
Japan
ageing **311**.27
and animal research **303**.38–9
CO_2 emissions **357**.3
drug policies **301**.27–8
government **360**.39
health and social care **378**.11
and international trade **305**.13
life expectancy **378**.10

religion in **358**.9
retirement age **378**.14
Jedi Knights, as alternative religion **358**.4–5
jellyfish **413**.39
Jesus Christ **358**.8
and Christian holidays **358**.22
see also Christianity
jihadist attacks **355**.5, 6
job market **405**.1–2, 24
job roles **405**.2
job search **405**.5–6
cover letters **405**.9–10
CV writing **405**.7–8
interviews **405**.3, 4, 13–17
Johnson, Boris **360**.11
on child poverty **377**.15
on immigration **359**.13–14
Joint Committee on Statutory Instruments (JCSI) **360**.8
jokes and banter, racist **308**.2
Joseph Rowntree Foundation (JRF)
on austerity policies **377**.14
defining poverty **377**.1
Minimum Income Standard (MIS) **377**.1
on poverty **306**.6
poverty in working households **377**.11–12
journalism
freedom of speech **347**.1
and internet **317**.10
and surveillance **317**.4–5
violence against **347**.17
see also press
journalling **361**.3
Journal of Adolescent Health **379**.2
Judaism **358**.2–5, 8, 11, 13, 41
anti-Semitism **376**.12
and euthanasia **362**.17
food poverty **306**.20
holidays **358**.24–5
Holocaust **358**.13
kosher slaughter **303**.6–7
rise in **358**.18
Rosh Hashanah **358**.20
sacred texts **358**.31
Talmud **358**.31

Vol. numbers appear first (in bold) followed by page numbers; a change in volume is preceded by a semi-colon.

Vol. 305	Globalisation – Good or Bad?	Vol. 368	Sustainable Living
Vol. 314	HIV & AIDS	Vol. 369	LGBT+ Issues
Vol. 316	Marriage	Vol. 370	Domestic Violence and Abuse
Vol. 347	The Censorship Debate	Vol. 371	The Internet and Us
Vol. 348	World Health	Vol. 372	Our Human Rights
Vol. 349	Gambling Culture	Vol. 373	Drug Use and Abuse
Vol. 350	Lifestyle Diets	Vol. 374	Animal Rights
Vol. 351	The Anxiety Epidemic	Vol. 375	Body Image
Vol. 352	Biotech & Bioethics	Vol. 376	Racism
Vol. 353	Education	Vol. 377	Poverty
Vol. 354	Relationships	Vol. 378	Ageing
Vol. 355	Terrorism	Vol. 379	Understanding Sexual Health
Vol. 356	British Armed Forces	Vol. 380	About Bullying
Vol. 357	The Climate Emergency	Vol. 381	Business
Vol. 358	Religion Today	Vol. 382	Active Citizenship
Vol. 359	Migration & Immigration	Vol. 383	The Privacy Debate
Vol. 360	Government	Vol. 384	Health & Fitness
Vol. 361	Cyberbullying	Vol. 385	Waste & Recycling Issues
Vol. 362	Euthanasia	Vol. 386	Sexualising Society
Vol. 363	Population Change	Vol. 387	Fertility Issues
Vol. 364	The Gender Equality Debate	Vol. 388	Discussing Child Abuse
Vol. 365	Tourism Today	Vol. 389	Sleep
Vol. 366	Crime in the UK	Vol. 390	Eating Disorders
Vol. 367	Discussing Abortion	Vol. 391	Money

Vol. 392	National Health
Vol. 393	Disability
Vol. 394	Pregnancy
Vol. 395	Teen Self-Care
Vol. 396	UK Housing
Vol. 397	Alcohol Issues
Vol. 398	Homelessness
Vol. 399	Discussing Cannabis
Vol. 400	Suicide & Self-Harm
Vol. 401	War & Conflict
Vol. 402	Endangered Species
Vol. 403	Student Options
Vol. 404	Depression
Vol. 405	Employability
Vol. 406	Smoking
Vol. 407	Bereavement
Vol. 408	Healthy Eating
Vol. 409	Online Safety
Vol. 410	Addiction
Vol. 411	Sport
Vol. 412	Rights of the Child
Vol. 413	Energy
Vol. 414	Consumerism
Vol. 415	Mental Health

Tanakh **358**.13, 31
Torah **358**.25
jungle camps **359**.37, 41
junk food **350**.16, 19, 41, **392**.24, **395**.41, **408**.20, 25, 35, 41
jury duty **382**.2–3
justice system **366**.30–9
    2018 statistics **366**.32–4
    on divorce **316**.28, 33
    on forced marriage **316**.22–3
    global criminal justice response to trafficking **300**.7
    and human rights **300**.38–9
    on parental separation **316**.36–8
    on prenuptial agreements **316**.14
    prison **366**.30–1, 35
    prosecutions and convictions **366**.32–3
    on prostitution **318**.2, 16
    and protection of civilians in war zones **300**.21
    remand **366**.33
    sentencing **366**.34
    sovereignty of UK courts **300**.28, 31, 33, 36
    for torture survivors **300**.18
    see also crime and justice

K

Kaposi's Sarcoma **314**.6
karo-jisatsu **378**.11
karoshi **378**.11
Keep Britain Tidy, on littering **385**.5–7
Keep Doing Good programme **382**.21
keeping fit see exercise and activity; fitness
Kefir **343**.37–8
Kellogg's, and free meals **306**.17
Kenya, and child poverty **306**.32
ketamine **373**.5, 9, 22, **404**.28–9
    classification and penalties for possession **301**.19, 22
    effects on the brain **301**.11
Key Stage 3 **403**.1
Key Stage 4 **403**.1, 5
key workers **396**.1–2
khat **301**.22, **373**.22, 23
Kickstart jobs **403**.21
kidfluencers **412**.27, 41
kidnappings **355**.4
KidsRights Index **412**.41
    on global pandemic **412**.4–6
kill chain **401**.7
kinetic energy floors **413**.38
King, Martin Luther **372**.3
Kissinger, Henry **359**.39
kit houses **396**.39
Klarna **391**.26–8
knife crime **366**.1, 17–29, 41
    and community work **366**.25–6
    drill and grime music **366**.27
    effects of **366**.18
    increase in **366**.4–6, 22, 24
    in rural areas **366**.23
    statistics **366**.17, 22–4
    see also weapons offences
Kopimism **358**.4
Korean War (1950-1953) **401**.3
kosher slaughter

banning **303**.6
    and labelling **303**.7
Krishna **358**.23
Kübler-Ross, E. **407**.21
Kunis, Mila **359**.38
Kuwait
    CO_2 emissions **357**.4
    immigration statistics **359**.3
Kyrgyzstan **377**.23

L

labelling
    black people as white **308**.31
    clothing label sizes **305**.8–9
    fairtrade labels **305**.16, 28
    of food **350**.34
    gender and sexuality **369**.17
    by multiracial and biracial people **308**.20–1
    see also food labelling
labels **397**.2
labiaplasty **386**.36
laboratory animals see animal experimentation
labour exploitation **398**.28–9
labour market **405**.41
    see also job market
Labour Party **360**.21–2
    on climate change **357**.1
    peers **360**.11
    racism and sexism in **376**.22
lacto-vegetarians **350**.21
Lag B'Omer **358**.24
landfills **368**.3, 19, **385**.1, 12–15, 28, 30, 34–5, 41
language
    and equality **364**.23
    offensive **361**.5, 6
Latin America
    and abortion **302**.15, 24–5
    population decline **363**.27
    population growth **363**.20
    women's political representation **360**.34–5
Latvia, and tourism **365**.16
laughing gas **343**.24, **373**.23
lavender **351**.32, 37–8
law see justice system; legislation
Law of Property Act 1922 **364**.12
Lawrence, Stephen **376**.16–18
Laylat al-Qadr (Night of Destiny) **358**.25
League Against Cruel Sports, on dog fighting **303**.8–9
Learning and Skills Act 2000 **353**.5
learning difficulties **393**.5
learning disabilities **393**.5, 12, 24, 41
    and bullying **361**.11
    and mental health **415**.17
    and poverty **306**.9
leave to remain **382**.2, 4–5
leaving home **354**.1, **363**.2
Lebanese Civil War (1975-1990) **401**.2
left brain **403**.6
left-wing extremism **355**.6
legal age of adulthood **354**.1
legal highs **301**.9, 17–18, 31–2
    alcohol substitutes **301**.31

and emergency medical treatment **301**.6–7
health risks of **301**.18, 23, 31–2
impact on homeless communities **301**.9
incidents involving **301**.17–18
laws against **301**.30–1
phenethylamines **301**.31
synthetic cannabis **301**.6–7, 31
use by young adults **301**.5
see also nitrous oxide; Novel Psychoactive Substances (NPS)
legislation
alcohol **397**.4, 26–7
for cannabis worldwide **399**.6, 8, 13, 18, 26
Class B drugs **399**.3, 6–8
leisure *see* sport and leisure activities
leisure travel **365**.1
see also holidays
lemon balm **351**.39
Lent **358**.22
lesbian **369**.2, 12, 13, 20–3
lesbian, gay, bisexual and transgender *see* LGBTQIA+ community
Lesotho, and HIV **314**.25
less developed countries (LDCs) **377**.20, 34, 41
lethal force **401**.6–7
lethargy, and cannabis use **399**.2
'levelling up' **392**.36
levelling up **396**.27, **398**.32, **408**.32–3
Leveson Inquiry **347**.16
Lewinsky, Monica, on trolling **361**.20–1
Lewis, Martin **413**.26
LGBTQ+ **369**.2, 12, 14, 20, 41
in the Armed Forces **356**.17
and asylum applications **359**.2
attitudes to **392**.2
and body image **375**.10–11, 18–19, 34
bullying **380**.5
and HIV **314**.1–2, 4–5
and homelessness **398**.15
human rights **372**.6, 36
and mental health **415**.16
relationship abuse **379**.30
and religion **358**.1
rights **369**.24–5, 28
in sport **411**.17–18
see also gay people; non-binary people; same-sex relationships; sexual orientation; transgender people
LHA (Local Housing Allowance) **396**.2, 41
libel **347**.15, 40
Liberal Democrat Party, peers **360**.11
liberalisation of trade *see* free trade
Liberty **383**.17
liberty
civil liberties **372**.5
right to **372**.1, 4
Liberty, on surveillance **317**.5
Libya
and surveillance **317**.28
war and conflict **401**.4, 5, 13, 30–1
lice, pubic **309**.12
licensed family entertainment centres (FECs) **349**.1
life expectancy **311**.4, **352**.33–4, **363**.5, 13–18, 23, **378**.1–8, 10, 11, 34, 38–9, 39, **392**.35–6, **406**.1
gap **368**.9

history of **311**.4
improving **378**.35–6, 38–9
measuring **378**.6
men **378**.1–3, 8, 36
and pensions **311**.4, 9
and quality of life **378**.6, 9
women **378**.1–3, 8, 36
life situation **351**.2
light bulbs **368**.15
limited company **381**.2–3
LinkedIn **405**.5–6, **409**.2–3
lions **374**.26, **402**.32
as endangered status **303**.27
hunting **303**.27
liquid biopsies **348**.37
listeria **348**.19
listeriosis **394**.9, 13
literature, and reading **311**.30–1
Lithuania, and animal welfare **303**.3
littering **365**.30, **385**.5, 8–9, 41
of beaches **385**.6, 10–11
costs of **385**.7
grades of litter **385**.6
types of litter **385**.7
liver disease **397**.6
living alone **363**.2
living arrangements **354**.7
and age **354**.1–2
see also cohabitation
living funeral **407**.41
living standards **377**.3
see also income
living together **311**.26, 36
see also cohabitation; relationships
lizard venom, and blood clots **348**.34
loans **391**.3, 15, 29, 41
see also debt
local authorities **353**.1–4
on ageing **311**.17
on animal welfare **303**.1–2
on contraception **309**.26
on crime **317**.26
local developments **396**.31
local government **360**.3, 18
localism **305**.21, 27
lockdown **392**.38, 41, **393**.13–14
impact on body image **375**.18
see also COVID-19
locked-in syndrome **362**.6
'Lodgers for Codgers' **378**.27–8
logo registration **381**.2
London
and dark tourism **365**.22
and tourism **365**.4
London Assembly **360**.25
London Living Wage **306**.7
London-only Combined Homelessness and Information Network (CHAIN) **398**.6, 34
London Pride **356**.17
loneliness **354**.9, **378**.21, 24–6, 37–8, 41, **415**.6–7
see also social isolation
lone-parent families **364**.20, 23
see also single parenthood
long-acting reversible contraception (LARC) **379**.8–9

Long-Term International Migration (LTIM) **363**.3–4
looked-after children **380**.5
looked after children **412**.30–1
'loot boxes' **349**.15, 18–19, 22–5, 41, **371**.10, **391**.13
Lose Hate, Not Weight campaign **307**.18
lotteries **349**.2, 10, 21, 41
Love Island **354**.37, **375**.9, 25, **386**.18
Love Your Body campaign **307**.18
low-density polyethylene (LDPE) **385**.29
LSD (acid) **301**.3, **373**.4, 9, 22
    classification and penalties for possession **301**.19, 22
    effects on the brain **301**.11
lucid dreaming **389**.10
Lucy's Law **374**.28
lung cancer **348**.5–6
lungs, effects of cannabis **399**.15
luteinising hormone (LH) **387**.8
Luxembourg
    and euthanasia **362**.9
    immigration statistics **359**.4
    waste statistics **385**.3
lyocell fabric **368**.28–9

M

Macao, immigration statistics **359**.4
Macau, waste statistics **385**.3
mace, ceremonial **360**.12–13
Macron, Emmanuel **357**.6
Madonna-Whore Complex **386**.9
magazines
    and body image **307**.16, 18, 25
    see also media
Maggie Oliver Foundation **388**.7
magic mushrooms **373**.4, 22
Magna Carta **360**.4, 14, **372**.2, 5
Maha Shivaratri **358**.23
maintained schools **353**.2
major depressive disorder (MDD) **404**.14
malaria **348**.1, 41, **352**.7
    gene-editing **348**.23
    in the UK **348**.24–6
    using drones to fight **348**.26–7
Malaysia, and tourism **365**.16
Maldives, and divorce **316**.24
male pill **309**.8
male sterilisation **309**.7
malnutrition **306**.31, **348**.1, 3, **350**.23, **384**.2–3, 12–13, 41, **390**.4, 12–13, 41, **408**.28, **412**.13
malpractice **362**.7
Malta, waste statistics **385**.4
malware **371**.21
mammals, at risk of extinction **402**.18–20, 36
Manchester **311**.27
    and tourism **365**.4
mandatory voter identification **360**.18
Mandela, Nelson **355**.2
mania **415**.6
manic depression **404**.1
    see also bipolar disorder
manifesto **360**.41
Man-Portable Air Defence System (MANPADS) **355**.4
manslaughter **366**.6

manual therapy **343**.4, 6, 41
    see also osteopathy; physiotherapy
manufacturing **305**.1, 10
    and exports **305**.33
    see also international trade
manure, as energy source **413**.19
Marburg virus **374**.15
Marie Stopes UK **302**.6, **367**.1
marijuana *see* cannabis **373**.4
Marine Conservation Society's (MCS) **385**.6
marine life **402**.28, 29
marine plastic pollution **402**.6
Marines *see* Royal Marines
marital rape **364**.12
marketing
    and surveillance **317**.17–18
    see also advertising
market research **381**.1, 2–3
Markle, Meghan **376**.2, **400**.28
Marmot Review of 2010 **392**.21
marriage **316**.3–4, 9, 12, 17–18, 25–6, **354**.40, **369**.23–4, 29
    adolescents **379**.2
    alternatives as equal **316**.8–9, 12
    arranged **316**.21, **388**.16
    average age for **354**.1–2
    child **388**.18, 41, **412**.35–6, 41
    child marriage **372**.27–9
    cultural factors **316**.26
    definition **354**.4
    financial and legal implications **354**.3
    forced **388**.16–18
    and happiness **316**.27
    health benefits of **354**.8
    humanist **316**.6, 10
    and legal age **354**.1
    for millenials **354**.4–5
    overseas **316**.3
    and prenuptial agreements **316**.14
    refusals for **316**.8
    registration costs **316**.4
    religious ceremonies **316**.4–7, 11
    separation and divorce **354**.3, 6, 40
    and tradition **316**.8, 13
    see also civil partnerships; cohabitation; forced marriage
Marriage (Same Sex Couples) Act 2013 **316**.11
Marriage of British Subjects Facilities Acts **316**.3
Martyrdom of Guru Arjan Dev Sahib **358**.25
Marx, Karl **360**.29
mass extinctions **402**.1–2, 41
materialism **358**.14–15
    see also consumerism
materials, strength fibres **352**.3
maternal leave **354**.13
maternal mortality **348**.1
maternal smoking **406**.28–9
Maternity and Parental Leave Regulations 1999 **405**.32
maternity leave **394**.41
maternity rights **405**.32, 41
maths
    as core subject **403**.5
    resitting **403**.3
mature students **403**.5, 7
Maundy Thursday **358**.22
Mawlid (Prophet's Birthday) **358**.25

May, Theresa **360**.19, 21–2
    on online safety legislation **361**.24
MDMA powder **373**.9, 28
    see also ecstasy
meals, skipping **351**.19, 39
mealtimes, and communication **316**.35
measles, mumps and rubella (MMR) vaccine **395**.10, 11, 13
meat
    benefits of **350**.1
    consumption **350**.32, **368**.17, **408**.21
    'human steak' **352**.20
    lab grown **352**.19–20
    production **303**.16–18
    risks to health **350**.2
    substitutes **350**.31, 41
    in vitro **352**.41
meat-free diets **350**.1–2, 31
    costs of **350**.3–5
    growth in **350**.3–5
    health risks of **350**.16–17
    reasons for **350**.1
    regional variations **350**.5
    see also pescatarian diet; veganism; vegetarianism
Mecca **358**.27
media
    and alcohol **397**.33, 35
    and body image **307**.1, 4, 15, **375**.19, 22, 30, 32–3
        and racial stereotyping **308**.7
    fake news **347**.18–22
    freedom of speech **347**.1
    see also films; internet; journalists; magazines; press; radio
media intrusion **411**.32–3
media literacy **409**.9–12
median age **363**.27, 29, **378**.1
median income **377**.3, 12
mediation **380**.36
medical abortion **367**.2, 15
medical biotechnology **352**.1–2
Medically Assisted Reproduction (MAR) **387**.21
medical model of disability **393**.1
Medical Research Modernization Committee (MRMC) **374**.15
medical treatment
    emergency treatment **301**.6–8, 21
    see also complementary and alternative medicine; end-of-

life care; healthcare; hospitals
medication **404**.3, 5, 13, 16, 27–30
    for addiction **410**.8, 19, 41
medications **415**.21
medicinal cannabis **399**.5, 6–8, 15, 30–8, 41
medicine **351**.2, 18–19, 24–5, 41
    antidepressants **351**.24
    beta-blockers **351**.24
    dependence on **373**.13–14
    habit forming **373**.3
    herbal **343**.6, 8–9, 14–15, 26–8, 31–4
    misuse of **301**.13
    pain relief **373**.3, 13–14
    prescription **343**.26–7, 31, 32–3
    tranquillisers **351**.24
    viral suppression **314**.8–11, 24, 26, 35
    see also antibiotics; antidepressants; drugs; herbal medicines; pain relief
Medicines and Healthcare Products Regulatory Agency (MHRA) **406**.24
meditation **343**.6, 22
Mediterranean diet **350**.2, 23, **378**.34, **384**.9–10, **408**.21
meltwater **357**.20
memory **378**.33, **404**.12
    and anxiety **351**.34
men
    body image issues **307**.20, 22–3, 28, **375**.4–5, 7–10, 12–15, 28–9
    discrimination of **364**.18
    and domestic violence **364**.19
    as fathers **364**.20
    as feminists **364**.22
    gay community **364**.19–20
    gender equality for **364**.5
    and gender stereotyping **364**.28–9
    and homelessness **364**.20
    International Men's Day **364**.18
    life expectancy **311**.4, **378**.1–3, 8, 36
    male role models **364**.18–19
    male sex chromosome **369**.1
    mental health of **364**.18, 39
    physical health of **364**.18–19
    and prostitution **318**.8–9
    and rape **318**.36

Vol. numbers appear first (in bold) followed by page numbers; a change in volume is preceded by a semi-colon.

Vol. 305	Globalisation – Good or Bad?	
Vol. 314	HIV & AIDS	
Vol. 316	Marriage	
Vol. 347	The Censorship Debate	
Vol. 348	World Health	
Vol. 349	Gambling Culture	
Vol. 350	Lifestyle Diets	
Vol. 351	The Anxiety Epidemic	
Vol. 352	Biotech & Bioethics	
Vol. 353	Education	
Vol. 354	Relationships	
Vol. 355	Terrorism	
Vol. 356	British Armed Forces	
Vol. 357	The Climate Emergency	
Vol. 358	Religion Today	
Vol. 359	Migration & Immigration	
Vol. 360	Government	
Vol. 361	Cyberbullying	
Vol. 362	Euthanasia	
Vol. 363	Population Change	
Vol. 364	The Gender Equality Debate	
Vol. 365	Tourism Today	
Vol. 366	Crime in the UK	
Vol. 367	Discussing Abortion	
Vol. 368	Sustainable Living
Vol. 369	LGBT+ Issues
Vol. 370	Domestic Violence and Abuse
Vol. 371	The Internet and Us
Vol. 372	Our Human Rights
Vol. 373	Drug Use and Abuse
Vol. 374	Animal Rights
Vol. 375	Body Image
Vol. 376	Racism
Vol. 377	Poverty
Vol. 378	Ageing
Vol. 379	Understanding Sexual Health
Vol. 380	About Bullying
Vol. 381	Business
Vol. 382	Active Citizenship
Vol. 383	The Privacy Debate
Vol. 384	Health & Fitness
Vol. 385	Waste & Recycling Issues
Vol. 386	Sexualising Society
Vol. 387	Fertility Issues
Vol. 388	Discussing Child Abuse
Vol. 389	Sleep
Vol. 390	Eating Disorders
Vol. 391	Money
Vol. 392	National Health
Vol. 393	Disability
Vol. 394	Pregnancy
Vol. 395	Teen Self-Care
Vol. 396	UK Housing
Vol. 397	Alcohol Issues
Vol. 398	Homelessness
Vol. 399	Discussing Cannabis
Vol. 400	Suicide & Self-Harm
Vol. 401	War & Conflict
Vol. 402	Endangered Species
Vol. 403	Student Options
Vol. 404	Depression
Vol. 405	Employability
Vol. 406	Smoking
Vol. 407	Bereavement
Vol. 408	Healthy Eating
Vol. 409	Online Safety
Vol. 410	Addiction
Vol. 411	Sport
Vol. 412	Rights of the Child
Vol. 413	Energy
Vol. 414	Consumerism
Vol. 415	Mental Health

toxic masculinity **364**.34, 38–9, 41
as victims of crime **364**.19
as victims of domestic abuse **370**.10–11, 16, 24–6
see also boys and young men; fathers
MenACWY vaccine **395**.10
menopause **387**.2, 7–10, 41
menstrual cycle **387**.2, 4–5
irregular **387**.1, 20
menstruation **309**.30, **379**.2, 10–11, **387**.4, 41, **395**.27
after childbirth **394**.32
in Nepal **379**.10–11
mental health **371**.7, 23, 27, **373**.2–3, 6, 27, 30, 32, **378**.16,
21, 25–6, 30, **388**.27–9, 31, **392**.38, **395**.4–5
and abortion **302**.1, 4, 27
and alcohol **356**.26
and alcohol misuse **397**.17, 24
anxiety **395**.36, 41
apps **400**.34–5
in the Armed Forces **356**.11, 21–6, 33, 41
attitudes to **392**.2
birth trauma **394**.35
and body image **375**.1–3, 6, 28
campaigns **392**.24
and cannabis use **399**.3, 4–5, 15, 21–5, 28
and child poverty **306**.23
of children **412**.4, 15
and commercial sexual exploitation, multiple impacts
318.29
and cyberbullying **361**.1–2, 20
definition **415**.41
and eating disorders **390**.2, 6, 27–8
economic costs **415**.18
and exams **353**.15–16
and exercise **384**.22, 32, 36–7
existing problems **351**.2
and fertility **387**.23
gender and sexuality **369**.35–6
and homelessness **398**.7, 22–3, 26–8, 34, 41
impact of bullying **380**.20, 22–4, 29–30
impact of COVID-19 **400**.6
impact of Covid-19 **392**.14
impacts of war **401**.25–6
of men **364**.18, 39
as non-visible disability **393**.8
and obesity **384**.5
and physical health **415**.32, 34–6
postnatal depression (PND) **394**.36–7
post-traumatic stress disorder (PTSD) **356**.11, 22, 24–5, 35,
41
in pregnancy **394**.16, 19
referrals **395**.8
seeking help **415**.22–3, 37, 39
and self-care **395**.33
and self-harm **400**.2, 6, 14–15, 34–5
services **318**.28
and sleep **384**.24–5
and smoking **406**.25–7
and sport **411**.10, 14–15
and starting school **353**.9
statistics **415**.10–11
suicidal thoughts **375**.16
and suicide **356**.23–4, **400**.27–9
talking about **415**.37
treatments **343**.5, **415**.2, 21

types of disorders **415**.3–9
of women **351**.17–18
of young mothers **351**.22–3
see also anxiety; body image; disordered eating; self-
esteem; self-harm; stress; suicide; wellbeing
Mental Health Act 1983 **415**.41
Mental Health Awareness Week **369**.36
Mental Health Million Project **384**.25, **415**.12
mentoring, relationships **351**.31
Mercury, Freddie **359**.38
metabolic syndrome **377**.8
metaldehyde **402**.9
metallic taste **394**.6
metaverse **409**.18–23
methadone **373**.11, 22
methamphetamine (crystal meth) **301**.3, **373**.5, 22
effects on the brain **301**.11–12
methane **413**.39
methanol **397**.3
methionine **408**.14
'MeToo' movement **360**.31
Mexican-American War (1846-1848) **401**.1
Mexico
border crisis **359**.33, 37
CO_2 emissions **357**.3
disappearances **300**.21
and global poverty **306**.27
and international trade **305**.11
migration **359**.5
torture **300**.18
MI5 **355**.3, 12
surveillance data **383**.17
mice, cloned **303**.35
microaggressions **376**.20–1, 28
microcephaly **302**.24
microcrime **366**.15–16
microfinancing **377**.35
micro homes **396**.20–1, 41, **398**.35
microplastics **385**.18, 21, 41
Mid Piacenzian Warm Period **357**.12
Mid Staffordshire NHS Foundation Trust scandal **311**.2
midwives, and abortion **302**.12, 20–1, 27–9
migraine **343**.25–6, **394**.5
migrants, and homelessness **398**.5, 18
migrant workers **359**.18–19
migration **305**.4, 6, 31, **363**.3–4, 20
and death **300**.20–1
desired destinations **359**.11–13
from European Union (EU) **359**.6–7
and HIV **314**.7
impacts **305**.38–9
impacts of **359**.29
long-term **359**.7
population statistics worldwide **359**.4–5
and sending money home **359**.5
and sex trafficking **318**.38–9
from United Kingdom (UK) **359**.8–10
see also citizenship; ethnic minorities; immigration;
refugees
milestones **354**.1
military
ethos **356**.41
housing **356**.29
partners **356**.29

strength **356**.1

training **356**.11, 14

see also Armed Forces; war and conflict

military lawyers **401**.6–7

milk **408**.13, 14

millenials

and the Armed Forces **356**.8, 41

as ethical consumers **368**.5, 18

and marriage **354**.4–5

and meat-free diets **350**.4–5

and religion **358**.14

Millennium Cohort Study (MCS) **399**.9–10

mindful consumerism

see also ethical consumerism

mindful eating **350**.30–1

mindfulness **307**.32, **343**.6–7, **351**.38, 41, **389**.7, 39, **395**.4, 33, 41, **410**.7, **415**.31, 38, 41

mind mapping **403**.37

minerals **350**.38–9, **408**.9

minimalism **414**.17

minimally conscious state (MCS) **362**.2

Minimum Income Standard (MIS) **377**.1, 41

minimum service period **356**.10–11

minimum unit pricing (MUP) **392**.22

minimum viable product **381**.2

minimum wage **377**.11, 34

see also National Minimum Wage

mini pill **387**.17

ministers **360**.2, 4

Ministry of Defence **360**.2

on location of personnel **356**.2

recruitment approaches **356**.5

on transition to civilian life **356**.30–1

on women in Armed Forces **356**.12–13

minority ethnic groups *see* ethnic minorities

miscarriage **394**.19–21, 25–6, 41

mis-gendering **380**.6

misinformation online **409**.11–12

misogynoir **411**.31

misogyny **386**.12, **411**.31

missed miscarriage **394**.21

see also miscarriage

Misuse of Drugs Act 1971 **301**.19, 24, 30, 31, **373**.41, **399**.41

mixed-race couples **354**.7

mixers **397**.2

mobile phones **351**.14, **409**.9, 36–7

as anti–racist tools **308**.37

and surveillance **317**.6, 11, 21–4

see also apps; internet

mocking **380**.2

modelling *see* fashion industry

modern foreign languages **403**.4, 5

Modern Methods of Construction (MMC) **396**.39

modern monetary theory (MMT) **391**.21–2

modern slavery **372**.14–22

and homelessness **398**.28–9

Modern Slavery Act 2015 **372**.17

modular building **396**.39

moles, changes to **395**.19

Molluscum contagiosum **309**.12

Monaco

immigration statistics **359**.4

waste statistics **385**.4

monarchy (UK)

governments **360**.1

role of **360**.38–9

Royal Assent **360**.6

royal prerogative **360**.4

money

and anxiety **351**.10–11

attitudes towards **391**.8–9

future of **391**.30

management **391**.5–6, 23–4

as medium of exchange **391**.1

origins of **391**.2, 4, 15

too much **391**.18–19

value of **391**.1

worries **351**.19, **391**.23–4

see also spending money

Money Bills **360**.8

MoneySavingExpert **413**.26

monkeys

and animal experimentation **374**.15, 18

and self-consciousness **374**.3

monotheistic religions **358**.8–9, 41

mood

disorders **404**.2–3

swings **394**.4

morality, and censorship **347**.1, 9

moral judgments, and animals **374**.3–4

moral values, and irreligiosity (no religion) **358**.19

more developed countries (MDCs) **377**.20, 34, 41

morning after pill **379**.4

morning sickness **394**.6

Morocco, torture **300**.18

morphine **373**.3, 11, **374**.15

mortality *see* death and mortality

mortgage lending **391**.28, 41, **396**.10, 17, 41

repossessions **396**.16, 41

Moses **358**.13, 24

mosquitoes **348**.23

Mos-Shogbamimu, Shola **376**.2–3

mothers

and abortion **302**.10

and HIV **314**.2, 29–30

and marriage **316**.26

talking to **354**.9–10, 16

teenage parents **309**.18, 20

motions **360**.41

motivation **403**.38, **415**.32

motoring *see* cars and driving

motoring offences **366**.34

motor neurone disease **362**.6, 10–12, 34–6, **392**.33

mourning *see* bereavement; grieving

mouth piercings **395**.25

mouth ulcers **395**.19

movies *see* film and theatre

Mozambique **377**.21

MPs (Members of Parliament) **360**.4, 41

debating **360**.10

see also elections; Parliament

Muhammad, prophet **358**.8, 25

Muharram **358**.25

multiculturalism **376**.41

multiple sclerosis (MS) **362**.6, **392**.33–4, **399**.5, 15, 34, 41

multiracial and biracial people **308**.20–2

labelling by **308**.20–1

and privacy **308**.21

and skin whitening **308**.22–3

see also Black, Asian and minority ethnic (BAME)

multitasking **371**.8

mumps, and infertility **387**.20

municipal solid waste (MSW), by country **385**.2–4

murder *see* homicide; homicides **366**.6

muscle dysmorphic disorder (bigorexia) **307**.9, 13, **375**.14–15

muscle mass **384**.4, 22

musculoskeletal disorders **384**.2, 22

music, therapy **343**.7

Muslims

and British identity **308**.5

and Islamophobia **308**.4, 37

and marriage **316**.26

UK population of **358**.18

see also Islam

Muslim women **308**.8

and clothing **308**.8

and feminism **308**.24

and hate crime **308**.8

and healthcare **308**.24

and inequality **308**.8

and Islamophobia **308**.15, 34

and Twitter **308**.8

see also Islam

Myanmar, war and conflict **401**.23–4

mycotoxin **408**.17

My Death, My Decision (MDMD) **362**.28

'mystery chests' **349**.18–19

N

NAFTA (North American Free Trade Agreement) **305**.11

name-calling **361**.11, **388**.8–9

see also bullying

nano-technology **352**.41

nappies **385**.12, 29

napping **389**.4, 6

narcissism **307**.6

narco-capitalism **301**.29

narcolepsy **389**.20, 28–31, 41

National Assembly for Wales **360**.25

National Association for People Abused in Childhood (NAPAC) **388**.2

National Audit Office (NAO), on military personnel **356**.5, 7

National Cancer Act 1971 **374**.15

National Centre for Social Research, on assisted suicide **362**.6

National Child Measurement Programme for England (NCMP) **384**.7–8

National Citizen Service (NCS) **382**.14

Keep Doing Good programme **382**.21

National Crime Agency (NCA), on online child abuse **388**.23–4, 36

national curriculum **353**.2, 4, 6, 41, **403**.41

National Day of Prayer **358**.28

National Diet and Nutrition Survey **408**.8

National Food Strategy **408**.36

National Health Service (NHS)

on abortion **302**.2–4, 11, 16, 21

on aspirin **311**.14–15

attitudes to **392**.4–5

care transfer delays **311**.5

on commercial sexual exploitation **318**.29

on contraception **309**.6–8

history of **392**.1–2

on HIV **314**.24, 28–30, 33

on homeopathy **343**.29

impact of Covid-19 **392**.6–7

overview **392**.13

on social isolation **311**.28–9

staffing crisis **392**.6–8, 20

on STIs **309**.11–12, 24–5

world ranking **392**.10

see also doctors; hospitals; social care

National Health Service Act 1948 **392**.41

National Institute for Health and Care Excellence (NICE)

on back pain **343**.2, 4

on fertility **387**.1

on homeopathy **343**.10

National Insurance **354**.3

nationalism **382**.6, 41, **401**.2–3

nationality, definition **382**.1

National Living Wage **381**.41, **405**.26–7, 32, 41

National Lottery **349**.10

National Minimum Wage **405**.26, 33, 34, 41

National Pet Month **374**.10–11

National Secular Society **358**.18

national security **347**.1, 2

National Society for the Prevention of Cruelty to Children (NSPCC) **409**.22

National Transport Survey 2018 **365**.24

National Union of Students *see* NUS

National Unplanned Pregnancy Advisory Service (NUPAS) **367**.1

National Youth Social Action survey **382**.14, 19–20

Nato (North Atlantic Treaty Organization) **401**.9, 18

natural birth **394**.28

natural disasters **348**.3, **357**.23

natural extinction **402**.41

natural family planning **309**.7

natural gas *see* gas

naturalisation **382**.2, 4–5

natural light **389**.6

natural medicine **351**.37–9

see also complementary and alternative medicine; herbal medicines

natural resources

depletion of **363**.22, 25

exploitation of **402**.4–5

Naturewatch Foundation **374**.21

nausea **394**.6

Navaratri **358**.23

Navy *see* Royal Navy

near death experiences **407**.4–5

needle and syringe programmes **301**.15–16

needle exchange **373**.29, 41

needle sharing, and HIV **314**.1–2, 6, 15–16

negative thinking **351**.19, 22, 35

neglect **377**.2

definition **388**.1, 4–5, 12

signs of **388**.12

statistics **388**.2

types of **388**.12

see also abuse

negotiation **354**.28

neonatal mortality **348**.1, **394**.27

Netanyahu, Benjamin **401**.22
netball **411**.19–20
Netherlands
    and abortion **302**.14
    burqa ban **358**.33
    care home volunteering **311**.30
    and dark tourism **365**.22
    drug policies **301**.27
    and euthanasia **362**.8–9, 26–7, 39
    immigration statistics **359**.4
    and SDGs **314**.9
    waste statistics **385**.2
'netiquette' **361**.29
net migration **363**.3–4, 6
net zero **357**.1–2, 36, 41, **365**.24, **413**.8–9, 19, 23, 25, 38
new homes **396**.3–4, 28–32
newspapers see press
new technology, and health **348**.36–7
New Testament **358**.21
    see also Bible
New Zealand **360**.39
    drug policies **301**.32
    and prostitution **318**.9, 21
    and voluntary euthanasia **362**.9
NHS (National Health Service) see National Health Service
    (NHS)
NHS Volunteer Responders **382**.26, 34
Nicaragua **360**.33
nicotine **406**.8–11, 17, 41, **410**.41
    see also cigarette addiction
nicotine addiction
    see also e-cigarettes
nicotine replacement therapies (NRT) **406**.18, 28, 32–3, 41
Niger, war and conflict **401**.25
Nigeria
    religious persecution **358**.38–9
    torture **300**.18
    and war zones **300**.20
night eating syndrome **390**.5
nightmares **389**.5, 10
night shelters see hostels for homeless people
night sweats **395**.18
night terrors **389**.32

Nike, accessible footwear **393**.38–9
NIMBY (Not In My Back Yard) **396**.4, 9, 28–9, 37, 41
nitrogen **402**.5–7
nitrous oxide **373**.23
    consumption trends **301**.8, 17
    festival bans of **301**.17
    and the law **301**.30
    physical numbness/tingling **301**.8
Nobel Peace Prize **355**.2
No Fault Divorce Bill **316**.32, 34
noise pollution **365**.30
No Kill Advocacy Center **374**.39
non-binary **369**.2, 6, 9, 39, 41
non-coeliac gluten sensitivity **350**.25
noncommunicable diseases **378**.5
noncommunicable diseases (NCDs) **408**.1–2
nonconforming **369**.10–11
non-contact abuse **386**.34
non-departmental public bodies (NDPBs) **360**.2
non-discrimination **372**.1
non-EEA (European Economic Area) nationals **359**.1
non-EU (European Union) nationals **359**.2
non-ministerial departments **360**.2
non-rapid eye movement (nREM) sleep **389**.1, 9, 19, 28
non-recent abuse **388**.32
non-religious population **358**.18
non-reproductive cloning see therapeutic cloning
non-verbal abuse **361**.41
nonviolent protest **374**.2
non-visible disabilities **393**.8–9, 14–15, 41
non-voluntary euthanasia **362**.1, 16, 41
no-platforming **347**.2, 5, 31
Nordic countries
    prostitution policy **318**.8–9, 14–15, 18, 20–1
    women's political representation **360**.35
North America
    life expectancy **378**.5, 7
    population growth **363**.28
    retirement age **378**.13–14
North American Free Trade Agreement (NAFTA) **305**.11
Northern Ireland
    and abortion **302**.11–12, 14, **367**.3, 10, 19–20
    car bombs **355**.3–4
    devolved government **360**.2, 3, 9

Vol. numbers appear first (in bold) followed by page numbers; a change in volume is preceded by a semi-colon.

Vol. 305 Globalisation – Good or Bad?	Vol. 368 Sustainable Living	Vol. 392 National Health
Vol. 314 HIV & AIDS	Vol. 369 LGBT+ Issues	Vol. 393 Disability
Vol. 316 Marriage	Vol. 370 Domestic Violence and Abuse	Vol. 394 Pregnancy
Vol. 347 The Censorship Debate	Vol. 371 The Internet and Us	Vol. 395 Teen Self-Care
Vol. 348 World Health	Vol. 372 Our Human Rights	Vol. 396 UK Housing
Vol. 349 Gambling Culture	Vol. 373 Drug Use and Abuse	Vol. 397 Alcohol Issues
Vol. 350 Lifestyle Diets	Vol. 374 Animal Rights	Vol. 398 Homelessness
Vol. 351 The Anxiety Epidemic	Vol. 375 Body Image	Vol. 399 Discussing Cannabis
Vol. 352 Biotech & Bioethics	Vol. 376 Racism	Vol. 400 Suicide & Self-Harm
Vol. 353 Education	Vol. 377 Poverty	Vol. 401 War & Conflict
Vol. 354 Relationships	Vol. 378 Ageing	Vol. 402 Endangered Species
Vol. 355 Terrorism	Vol. 379 Understanding Sexual Health	Vol. 403 Student Options
Vol. 356 British Armed Forces	Vol. 380 About Bullying	Vol. 404 Depression
Vol. 357 The Climate Emergency	Vol. 381 Business	Vol. 405 Employability
Vol. 358 Religion Today	Vol. 382 Active Citizenship	Vol. 406 Smoking
Vol. 359 Migration & Immigration	Vol. 383 The Privacy Debate	Vol. 407 Bereavement
Vol. 360 Government	Vol. 384 Health & Fitness	Vol. 408 Healthy Eating
Vol. 361 Cyberbullying	Vol. 385 Waste & Recycling Issues	Vol. 409 Online Safety
Vol. 362 Euthanasia	Vol. 386 Sexualising Society	Vol. 410 Addiction
Vol. 363 Population Change	Vol. 387 Fertility Issues	Vol. 411 Sport
Vol. 364 The Gender Equality Debate	Vol. 388 Discussing Child Abuse	Vol. 412 Rights of the Child
Vol. 365 Tourism Today	Vol. 389 Sleep	Vol. 413 Energy
Vol. 366 Crime in the UK	Vol. 390 Eating Disorders	Vol. 414 Consumerism
Vol. 367 Discussing Abortion	Vol. 391 Money	Vol. 415 Mental Health

natural change in population **363**.3
population growth **363**.2
teenage parents **309**.20
and terrorism **355**.2, 3, 7
see also Ireland
Northern Ireland Act 1998 **360**.9
Northern Ireland Assembly **360**.25
Northern Ireland Executive **360**.9
North Korea
censorship in **347**.27
and international trade **305**.14
North London Cares **311**.35
Norway
and HIV **314**.34
and prostitution **318**.4, 14
NOVA classification system **408**.19–20
Novel Psychoactive Substances (NPS) **373**.9, 27–8
NSPCC (National Society for the Prevention of Cruelty to
Children) **370**.18
on cyber-bullying **380**.21
on internet pornography **318**.30, 32–6
on online privacy **317**.35
on pornography **318**.32–3
on sex **309**.29
on sexting **318**.35
on SRE **309**.33
nuclear power **413**.29, 41
nuclear weapons **355**.5, **401**.8, 18, 20, 41
nude images **354**.30
nudity **386**.17
numeracy **364**.6
see also education
nursing and care homes
care transfer delays **311**.5
and HIV **314**.26
staffing crisis **392**.20
volunteering by young people **311**.30–1
NUS (National Union of Students), on prostitution **318**.19
nutrient supplementation **352**.2
nutrigenomics **408**.14–15, 41
nutrition **348**.4, **384**.12–13, 19–20, 41, **408**.41
African region **348**.4
malnutrition **348**.1, 4
see also diet; healthy eating; malnutrition
nuts **408**.12

O

Obama, Barack **360**.17
on bullying prevention **361**.28
on multiracial and biracial people **308**.20
and UK-US 'special relationship' **317**.27
Obamacare **392**.13
obesity **377**.8, **378**.9–10 39, **390**.8, **392**.25–6, 36, **408**.25,
38–9, 41
and addiction **410**.4
causes **384**.2, 5, 11, 19
in children **392**.28
definition **384**.1, 4, 41
and exercise **307**.39, **384**.19–20
health consequences **384**.2
and meat-free diets **350**.16–17
and mental health **384**.5

pets **303**.19–20
prevalence by age **384**.7
prevalence by country **384**.9–10
prevalence by region **384**.6
preventing **384**.3, 19–20
risks of **384**.5, 11
statistics **384**.1–2, 6–10, 39
see also diet; nutrition
objectification **375**.41, **386**.1, 17–19, 27–9, 41
Obscene Publications Act 1959 & 1964 **361**.37
obsessive-compulsive disorder (OCD) **351**.3, 7, 35–6, **375**.28
obsessive compulsive disorder (OCD) **380**.20
obsessive-compulsive disorder (OCD) **390**.2, **404**.33, 37
obsessive compulsive disorder (OCD) **415**.3, 5, 7
obstetrician **394**.41
occupational pensions *see* pensions
oceans
coastal erosion **357**.9
coastal flooding **357**.20
Great Barrier Reef **357**.17
impacts of tourism **365**.34–5
overfishing **357**.30
plastic pollution **385**.21, 27
sea levels **357**.8, 20–1
see also marine environments
OCR Cambridge Nationals **403**.8
oestrogen **395**.27
Ofcom **347**.40, **414**.10, 11–12, 41
on cyberbullying **361**.5
on fake news **347**.22
on TV streaming **347**.28–9
Offences Against the Person Act 1861 **302**.13, 25–6
offenders
previous convictions **366**.34
see also justice system; prison; young offenders
offensive language **361**.5, 6
Office for Health Improvement and Disparities (OHID) **406**.24
Office for National Statistics, on depression **404**.22
Office for National Statistics (ONS)
on birth rates **363**.7
on coercive control **370**.3
Crime Survey for England and Wales **399**.11
on death rates **363**.15
on debt **391**.20
on domestic abuse **370**.4, 24–5
on fertility rates **363**.30, **387**.11–13
on gender pay gap **364**.15–16
on homicides **366**.6
on lone-parent families **364**.20
on money management stress **391**.24
on non-religious population **358**.18
on personal and economic well-being **351**.10–11
on population growth **363**.6
on rough sleeping **398**.22
on UK tourism **365**.6
on violent crime **364**.19
on youth crime **366**.13–14
Office for Product Safety and Standards (OPSS) **406**.20
Office for Statistics Regulation (OSR) **377**.15
officer training **356**.14
offline ecommerce **381**.3
off-rolling **353**.24–7
offshore wind farms **413**.5, 6, 28, 31, 33, 41
'off the grid' children **353**.24–5

Ofgem **413**.7, 20, 22, **414**.10
Ogallala aquifer **402**.4
OGTT (oral glucose tolerance test) **394**.17
oil, crude **413**.2, 33
old age care
    cost of **378**.29–31
    see also health and social care
old-age dependency ratio (OADR) **363**.5
older people **392**.29–35
    and animal welfare **303**.11
    and aspirin **311**.14–15
    and body image **307**.5
    body image issues **375**.5
    brain training **311**.20–1
    citizenship **311**.32
    elder abuse **311**.21–2
    and employment **308**.39
    and food poverty **306**.18
    and globalisation **305**.7
    and HIV **314**.15, 26
    and housing **311**.32–3
    and poverty **306**.18
    and sleep **389**.5
    and social isolation **311**.28–9, 32
    and STIs **309**.21
    urban areas **311**.32
    and volunteering **306**.18
    see also ageing; retirement
olive leaf **343**.33–4
olive oil **408**.10–11
Olympic Games **411**.3–6, 41
    see also Paralympic Games
Oman
    immigration statistics **359**.3
    tobacco taxation **406**.36
ombudsman **414**.6, 7, 10
Omega 3 **351**.38
one-child policy **363**.36–7
onions, and antibiotic resistance **348**.30–1
online abuse **371**.14–15, 26–7
online access **409**.9
online activism **371**.10
online advertising **371**.4
online brain training **311**.20–1
online bullying *see* cyber-bullying
online child abuse **388**.23–4, 36, 38
online communities
    see also social networking
online dating **379**.32–4
online disinhibition effect **361**.18
online divorce **316**.33
online gambling **349**.4, 7, 10, 14, 15, 18–23, 41
online grooming
    see also sexual exploitation
Online Harms White Paper **361**.24–5
online hate crime **393**.17–18
online pornography *see* internet pornography
online privacy **317**.13, 32–3, 35
    and absolute privacy **317**.21
    and data sovereignty **317**.32
    deleting searches **317**.17
    as differently viewed by adults **317**.35–6
    and increased age **317**.13
    lack of consent **317**.38

    as permanent images **317**.39
    private and public arenas **317**.35–6, 39
    risks **317**.10
    safety risks **317**.39
    sharing childhood images **317**.39
    see also surveillance and access
online racism **308**.37
online safety **386**.19–20, **400**.12, 29, **409**.10–17
    see also social media
online security **383**.5–6
online shopping **414**.29, 31, 36, 38
online socialising *see* social networking
online spending **391**.13
opiods **373**.3, 13–14, 30, 41
optimism **351**.33
Ora, Rita **359**.39
Ordovician-Silurian mass extinction **402**.1
oregano **343**.32
organ donation **382**.32–3, 41, **407**.8
organ harvesting **300**.4, **372**.21–2, 41
Organization for Economic Cooperation and Development
    (OECD) **377**.24
    on superbugs **348**.31
organs-on-a-chip **348**.36, **352**.16
orthorexia nervosa **350**.18–20, 26, 41, **390**.19, 41
osprey **402**.34–5
osteoarthritis **392**.29
osteopathy **343**.2–4
osteoporosis **378**.39, **390**.20, **392**.34
other specified feeding or eating disorder (OSFED) **390**.3, 5, 6
outbound tourism **365**.1, 12–13
    see also holidays
outing **361**.6, **369**.14
ovaries **387**.2, 4–5, 20
over-abstraction **402**.9
overconsumption **414**.18
    see also consumerism
overdose **373**.1–2, **400**.10, 20, 22, 41
overdrafts **391**.25, 41
overeating **410**.18–19
overfishing **357**.30
overpopulation **363**.22–5, 30–1, 41
    see also depopulation
overseas civil partnerships **316**.3
overseas divorces **316**.4
overseas forced marriage **316**.21
overseas prenuptial agreements, and UK agreements
    316.14–15
overseas residence, and UK marriage **316**.3
overstayer **359**.41
overtourism **365**.8, 17–18
overweight
    causes **384**.2
    definition **384**.1, 41
    preventing **384**.3
    risks of **384**.5
    statistics **384**.1–2, 6–7
    see also obesity
ovo-vegetarian diet **350**.21
ovulation *see* fertility **387**.1, 2, 4–5, **394**.4–5
owning own home **354**.1–2
Oxfam
    Even It Up campaign **377**.32
    on global poverty **306**.33

on refugee resettlement **359**.34
Oxford Internet Survey (OxIS) **371**.3

P

packaging **350**.36, **368**.11–12, 14–15, 20–2
  cigarettes **406**.30
pain
  abortion **302**.3, 7
  back **343**.2–4, 11
  chronic **343**.22
  management **343**.23
  medication **373**.3, 13, 22
  relief **301**.10, 13, **394**.28
Pakistan **360**.36
  and abortion **302**.22
  censorship in **347**.6
  and education **308**.24
  and feminism **308**.24
  healthcare **308**.24
  refugee statistics **359**.34
  religious persecution **358**.38–9
  war and conflict **401**.31
Palermo Protocol **372**.17
Palestine, war and conflict **401**.4, 21–2
palliative care **311**.2, **362**.1, 41
  choice and compassion **311**.2
palliative sedation **362**.4, 41
palm oil **357**.16
Palm Sunday **358**.22
panda bears **357**.18
pandas **402**.28
pandemic **348**.41, **392**.41
  see also Covid-19
pandemics **357**.23, **363**.23
pangolins **402**.24, 32–3
panic attacks **351**.4, 36–7, 41, **380**.20, **415**.4, 5, 7, 41
panic disorder (PD) **351**.4, **375**.28
Pankhurst, Christabel **364**.12
pansexual **369**.2, 14
paper bags **368**.24–5
paper bills *see* banknotes
paper recycling **385**.12, 28
Papua New Guinea, and prostitution **318**.4
paracetemol **373**.13
Paralympic Games **393**.30–1, 39, 41, **411**.7, 36, 41
paranoia **415**.7
  and cannabis use **399**.2
parasites **348**.19
parasomnia **389**.20
parental controls **409**.14, 41
parental responsibility **354**.3
parental separation **316**.2, 25
  emotions and feelings **316**.36–8
  help and support **316**.36–8
  and maintenance **316**.15
  talking about **316**.36–8
parents
  and abortion **302**.5
  and contraception **309**.15
  and divorce **316**.30, 36
  ethnic minorities **308**.35
  and HIV **314**.18
  and internet pornography **318**.30, 32
  and marriage **316**.2, 26–7
  older parents cared for by children **311**.13
  and online privacy **317**.13, 38–9
  and sexual health **309**.15
  and SRE **309**.32, 38
  and STIs **309**.15
  talking to **354**.9–10, 16
  teenage parents **309**.18, 20
  see also adoption; families; fathers; mothers; single-parent families
Parent Zone, on 'skin gambling' **349**.19–20
Paris 2024 Olympic Games **411**.3
Paris Agreement **357**.5–6, 11, 21, 41, **413**.1, 5
Parkinson's disease **373**.28, **392**.34
Parliament **360**.2, 3, 41
  Acts of **360**.3, 6–8, 41
  Bills **360**.6–8, 41
  ceremonial mace **360**.12–13
  composition of **360**.4
  and constitutional law **360**.4
  debating **360**.10
  Draft Bills **360**.3, 6
  functions of **360**.4
  House of Commons **360**.2, 4–7, 10, 12–14
  House of Lords **360**.2, 4–7, 11
  motions **360**.41
  MPs (Members of Parliament) **360**.4
  sovereignty **360**.4, 38–9
  two-House system **360**.5
  women in **360**.34–5
Parliament Act 1911 **360**.8
Parliament Act 1949 **360**.8
participation **393**.30–1
passenger arrivals, to UK **359**.1
passive bullying **380**.30
passive euthanasia **362**.1, 5, 16, 41
passive vaping **406**.17
Passover **358**.24
passports **382**.1, 4–5
passwords **317**.11, 34, **371**.31, **383**.11
Pastafarianism **358**.4
Patel, Priti **380**.29, 37–9
patents **381**.2
paternal leave **354**.13
paternity rights **405**.32, 41
pathogens **352**.1–2
patriotism **382**.6, 41
payday loans **391**.29
peacekeeping **401**.4, 12, 22, 34–6, 41
PEACH (Preventing Domestic Abuse for Children) **354**.37
peak globalisation **305**.31–2
peer pressure **397**.16, 36
peer support **415**.2
peer-to-peer (P2P) platforms **381**.4
pelvic floor **394**.9–10, 31
pelvic inflammatory disease (PID) **379**.3, **387**.19
penguins **357**.19
penicillin **374**.15
pensions **311**.8–10, **378**.2, 18, 41, **391**.6, 41, **405**.25, 29–30, 41
  costs **311**.7
  delays **311**.7, 11
  history of **311**.8–10

and increasing life expectancy **311**.4, 9–11
and inequality **311**.9
and marriage **354**.3
risks **316**.18
state pension **378**.1, 15–17
State Pension age **378**.1
unprotected **311**.9
Pensions Act 2011 **391**.41
Pentecost **358**.22
Pentitentiary Act 1799 **366**.31
People for the Ethical Treatment of Animals (Peta)
on animal experimentation **374**.19, 21
on animal rights **374**.1–2
people of colour
and homelessness **398**.5
and self-harm **400**.7
People's Dispensary for Sick Animals (PDSA) **303**.19–20,
374.38
people smuggling **412**.41
people trafficking *see* trafficking
PE provision **384**.30–1, 34–5
'perfect' body **375**.30, 33
performance, censorship of **347**.36–9
performance-enhancing substances **301**.14
perimenopause **387**.7–8, 41
periodic limb movement disorder (PLMD) **389**.20
period pain **343**.21
periods **387**.5
after childbirth **394**.32
see also menstrual cycle
Permian mass extinction **402**.1
Permian Period **357**.12
permitted development rights **396**.35–6
perpetrator programmes **370**.38–9, 41
perpetrators, of cyberbullying **361**.19, 31
persecution, religious **358**.38–9, 41
perseverance **351**.33
persistent vegetative state (PVS) **362**.2
personal, social, health and economic education (PSHE)
395.10
personal data **317**.2, 33
see also privacy
personal development **403**.6
Personal Finance Society (PFS) **391**.5

personality, and anxiety **351**.33
personality disorders **415**.4, 5, 7, 41
personal protective equipment (PPE) **392**.41
Covid-19 **392**.8–9
personal statement **403**.26–8
person-borne improvised explosive devices (PBIEDs) **355**.4
see also suicide bombers
personhood **374**.41
Peru and animal welfare **303**.26, 28
and MDGs **306**.29–30
pescatarian diet **350**.3, 21, 32, 35, 41
costs of **350**.4–5
pesticides **352**.2, **357**.35, **402**.9
pest resistant crops **352**.2
PETA *see* People for the Ethical Treatment of Animals (Peta)
Pet Animals Act 1951 (1983) **303**.1–2
Pet Census 2018 (Petplan) **374**.10–11
Pet Fit Club **303**.19–20
pethidine **394**.28
pet industry **402**.14
pets **407**.11
abuse of **374**.38
banning primates as **303**.11, 28
dieting **303**.19–20
ethical issues **374**.38
exercise **303**.19
history of **374**.12
overweight **303**.19–20
by popularity and region **374**.10–11
puppy farming **374**.28
puppy farms **303**.3–4
trafficking **303**.3–4
welfare legislation **303**.1–2
welfare of **374**.5, 8, 12–13
petting zoos **303**.22
petty crime, and trafficking **300**.6–7
pharmaceutical drugs **352**.1
biohacking **352**.21–2
see also medicines
phenethylamines **301**.31
philanthropy **365**.41, **382**.27
Philippines, 'Sin Tax' **406**.36
Philippines, torture **300**.18
Phillips, Jess **370**.8

Vol. numbers appear first (in bold) followed by page numbers; a change in volume is preceded by a semi-colon.

Vol. 305	Globalisation – Good or Bad?	Vol. 368	Sustainable Living	Vol. 392	National Health
Vol. 314	HIV & AIDS	Vol. 369	LGBT+ Issues	Vol. 393	Disability
Vol. 316	Marriage	Vol. 370	Domestic Violence and Abuse	Vol. 394	Pregnancy
Vol. 347	The Censorship Debate	Vol. 371	The Internet and Us	Vol. 395	Teen Self-Care
Vol. 348	World Health	Vol. 372	Our Human Rights	Vol. 396	UK Housing
Vol. 349	Gambling Culture	Vol. 373	Drug Use and Abuse	Vol. 397	Alcohol Issues
Vol. 350	Lifestyle Diets	Vol. 374	Animal Rights	Vol. 398	Homelessness
Vol. 351	The Anxiety Epidemic	Vol. 375	Body Image	Vol. 399	Discussing Cannabis
Vol. 352	Biotech & Bioethics	Vol. 376	Racism	Vol. 400	Suicide & Self-Harm
Vol. 353	Education	Vol. 377	Poverty	Vol. 401	War & Conflict
Vol. 354	Relationships	Vol. 378	Ageing	Vol. 402	Endangered Species
Vol. 355	Terrorism	Vol. 379	Understanding Sexual Health	Vol. 403	Student Options
Vol. 356	British Armed Forces	Vol. 380	About Bullying	Vol. 404	Depression
Vol. 357	The Climate Emergency	Vol. 381	Business	Vol. 405	Employability
Vol. 358	Religion Today	Vol. 382	Active Citizenship	Vol. 406	Smoking
Vol. 359	Migration & Immigration	Vol. 383	The Privacy Debate	Vol. 407	Bereavement
Vol. 360	Government	Vol. 384	Health & Fitness	Vol. 408	Healthy Eating
Vol. 361	Cyberbullying	Vol. 385	Waste & Recycling Issues	Vol. 409	Online Safety
Vol. 362	Euthanasia	Vol. 386	Sexualising Society	Vol. 410	Addiction
Vol. 363	Population Change	Vol. 387	Fertility Issues	Vol. 411	Sport
Vol. 364	The Gender Equality Debate	Vol. 388	Discussing Child Abuse	Vol. 412	Rights of the Child
Vol. 365	Tourism Today	Vol. 389	Sleep	Vol. 413	Energy
Vol. 366	Crime in the UK	Vol. 390	Eating Disorders	Vol. 414	Consumerism
Vol. 367	Discussing Abortion	Vol. 391	Money	Vol. 415	Mental Health

philosophical beliefs, as protected characteristics **358**.16

philosophy, and animal rights **374**.1, 3

phishing **371**.21

phobias **351**.4, 41, **390**.2, **415**.3, 7
   see also individual phobias

phone hacking **347**.16

phone tapping **372**.8

Photoshop **375**.2, 29, 32, 39, 41

Phunky Foods study **307**.3

physical abuse **354**.28, **370**.41, **379**.29, **393**.17
   definition **388**.1, 5, 13, 41
   impacts of **388**.13
   signs of **388**.13
   smacking **388**.35
   statistics **388**.2

physical activity *see* exercise and activity

physical addiction **410**.1, 2
   see also addiction

physical bullying **380**.1

physical self-care **395**.1

physician-assisted suicide (PAS) **362**.8, 22–5, 39, 41
   see also assisted suicide

pica **390**.4, 41

piercings, mouth **395**.25

piles **394**.31

pilgrimage **358**.26–7

pill, contraceptive
   see also contraceptive pill

'pink tax' **364**.24, 41

Pinterest **371**.10

pipe bombs **355**.4

piperazines (BZP) **373**.22

piracy, software **347**.9

placebo **343**.4, 16–17, 29, 31, 41

placenta **394**.27

placental abruption **394**.10, 27

planning system **396**.35
   local developments **396**.31
   permitted development rights **396**.35–6
   see also building of new homes

plant-based eating **350**.2, 9, 15, 36–9, 38, 41, **368**.5, 33–4
   see also vegan diet; vegetarian diet

plastic bags **368**.11, 24
   theft of **366**.15

plastic packaging **368**.11–12, 14–15, 20–2

plastics **357**.35, **402**.8

plastic surgery
   see also cosmetic surgery

plastic waste **365**.32–3, **385**.1, 20, 24
   bottles **385**.5
   exports **385**.22–3
   facts and statistics **385**.18–19
   holistic approach to **385**.20
   in landfills **385**.12
   microplastics **385**.18, 21, 41
   in the ocean **385**.21, 27
   plastic resin ID code, **385**.29
   recycling **385**.1, 5, 29–30
   reducing **385**.36–7, 39
   role of supermarkets **385**.26–7
   sustainable alternatives **385**.20, 24–5

plumbers **405**.2

pneumonia **348**.6

poaching **402**.27, 28, 33, 41

elephants **303**.27

pocket money **391**.6, 10–12

podcasts, for sleep **389**.17–19

Poland
   and abortion **302**.14, 23–4, **367**.21–2
   and animal welfare **303**.3
   and immigration **363**.4
   impacts of migration **359**.29

polar bears **357**.19

police
   and elder abuse **311**.22
   officer numbers **366**.5, 39
   and prostitution **318**.4–5, 8–9, 14–16, 21, 22–3
   and racial discrimination **308**.36
   and surveillance **317**.6
   and violence **308**.37–8
   see also crime and justice

Police and Criminal Evidence Act 1984, **366**.36

polio **392**.2

political correctness, in universities **347**.4–5

political divides, and attitudes to Armed Forces **356**.4

political media, censorship **347**.9–10

politics and government (UK)
   and diversity **308**.32–3
   and employment **308**.4
   and segregation **308**.13–14
   and voting **300**.30–1
   see also Brexit; government; Parliament

pollotarian diet **350**.21

pollution **348**.2, **357**.35, **365**.30, **368**.2–3, 25, 41, **385**.41, **402**.2, 5–7, **412**.16, **413**.15, 37
   air **348**.3, 5, 6, 10, 11–12, 41, **385**.16–17
   in oceans **385**.21
   and vegan diets **350**.9
   see also emissions; waste

polycarbonate (PC) **385**.29

polycystic ovary syndrome (PCOS) **387**.24

polydrug/polysubstance use **301**.5, 13

polypropylene (PP) **385**.29

polytheism **358**.41

polyvinyl chloride (PVC) **385**.29

ponds **357**.35

pool betting **349**.2, 41

pool frog **402**.31

Poor Law Acts **306**.5

population
   decline **363**.26, 27–31, 34–5
   as global risk **363**.24
   growth **363**.1–2, 6, 19, 24, 27–30, 34–6, 41
   see also ageing population; global population;
    overpopulation

pop-up shops **381**.3, **414**.36

pork tapeworm **348**.19

pornification **386**.41

pornography **354**.34, **370**.10, **379**.4, 38–9, **386**.2, 30–9, **409**.16–17
   addiction to **386**.31, 34
   and blocking **318**.33
   censorship **347**.6
   damage from **386**.30, 34–5
   effects on the brain **318**.32
   extreme **318**.33
   and rape culture **386**.34–6
   revenge porn **354**.39

and sexual expectations **309**.29
talking about **386**.37–8
and violence **386**.30, 33
see also internet pornography
Portugal
and abortion **302**.14
and drugs **301**.27, 29
waste statistics **385**.2
Portuguese Restoration War (1640-1668) **401**.3
positive action **376**.4
Positive Regard Teaching school **353**.26–7
possession of drugs **373**.22–3, 29–30
post-18 options **403**.18
postal explosive devices **355**.4
post-Christianity **358**.6
post-concussion syndrome **411**.14–16
posting online **409**.27
postmenopause **387**.8
post-mortem **407**.41
postnatal depression **394**.36–7, **404**.1, 4–5, 41, **415**.7
postnatal psychosis **404**.5
post-traumatic stress disorder (PTSD) **351**.3, 41, **356**.11, 22, 24–5, 35, 41, **380**.20, **389**.10, **398**.34, **401**.7, 25, 41, **404**.37, **415**.3, 8
complex **318**.27
early trauma **318**.27
mental health services **318**.28
occupational risks **318**.27–8
post-abortion **302**.17–18
stigma **318**.28
potassium **408**.2–3, 13
poultry, and food poisoning **348**.9
poverty **306**.1, 4, 6, 9–11, 18, 23, **318**.2, **356**.33, **368**.16, **372**.28, **392**.28
and abortion **367**.31–2
absolute **377**.1, 3, 41
and anxiety **351**.17–18
and banks **306**.9, 12, 37
and bill payments **306**.12
causes of **377**.2, 9–10, 14, 18–19, 27
and child labour **412**.18
children and young people **377**.8, 11–13, 15, 29
consequences of **377**.2
and debt **306**.9
defining **377**.1, 18, 41
and depression **404**.21–2
and deprivation **306**.1, 3–4, 10
and disability **393**.2, 24
and education **412**.28
and financial education **306**.12
and financial skills **306**.12
and forced marriage **300**.10
and fuel poverty **306**.8, 25
and gentrification **306**.4
global **377**.20–8, 30–1, 34–5
and health **306**.13
history of **306**.5
and housing **306**.7, 10
impact of lockdown **377**.8
and income **306**.1–3, 10, 18, 21
levels of **377**.1
measuring **377**.1
and mental health **415**.13, 17
poverty lines **306**.2, 10

regional variations **377**.12
relative **377**.1, 3, 18, 41
in retirement **378**.21, 41
and self-harm **400**.14–15
and smoking **406**.4–5, 7, 30
solutions for **377**.30–1
and state benefits **306**.5, 7, 9
and unemployment **306**.7
and wages **306**.7
and wellbeing **306**.1
and work **306**.5, 7, 10
in working households **377**.11–12
see also food poverty; global poverty; rich-poor gap; see also child poverty
poverty premium **377**.2
poverty tourism **365**.41
Powell, Enoch, and racism **308**.10
power
and bullying **380**.18, 33
and gender equality **364**.6
in relationships **354**.28
PPE *see* personal protective equipment (PPE)
prairies **402**.3–4
prayer **358**.28–30
pre-eclampsia **394**.27
pregabalin **351**.24
pregnancy **309**.3, **412**.13, 14
antenatal checks **394**.17–18
and broken abstinence pledges **309**.22
and cannabis use **399**.5, 15
chances of **387**.1
complementary therapies for **343**.20
fetal development **394**.1
FGM risks **300**.12
healthy **394**.8–15
and HIV **314**.2, 29–30
impacts **300**.10
loss **394**.19–21, 25–7
risk of **379**.4
and smoking **406**.28–9
symptoms **394**.3–7
teenage **309**.19–20
tests **394**.3
unwanted **379**.9
and Zika virus **348**.21
see also abortion; babies and birth; contraception; maternity rights
pre-implantation genetic diagnosis (PGD) **394**.41
prejudice **374**.2
and bullying **380**.4
and disability **393**.27–8
in football **411**.1–2
gender and sexuality **369**.13
against women **364**.3
see also discrimination
prejudice-based bullying **380**.1, 4–6
premature aging, babies **302**.26
premature birth **394**.19
premenstrual dysphoric disorder (PMDD) **387**.5, **415**.8
premenstrual syndrome (PMS) **387**.5, **415**.8
prenatal depression **404**.1
prenuptial agreements **316**.14–15, **354**.3
pre-school education **353**.4, 30
Preschool Implicit Association Text (PSIAT) **307**.33

prescriptions **392**.2
    see also antibiotics; medicines
prescriptive stereotypes **378**.22
preservatives **408**.17
press **308**.24
    free **347**.14, 16, 40
    freedom of **347**.12–17
    Independent Press Standards Organisation (IPSO) **347**.16
    Leveson Inquiry **347**.16
    phone hacking **347**.16
    and racial stereotyping **308**.7
    Reporters Without Borders **347**.12
    World Press Freedom Index 2018 **347**.12, 14, 16
    see also journalism; media; political media
Press Complaints Commission (PCC) **347**.40
pressure groups **360**.4, 6
Prevention of Crime Act 1908 **366**.31
Prevent strategy (counter–terrorism) **308**.13–14, **355**.24,
   31–5
Pride **369**.14, 19
Primark **414**.27
primary schools **353**.2, 4, 36–7
primates (apes and monkeys) **303**.24–5, 37–8
    banning as pets **303**.11, 28
    and personhood **303**.22–5
    and SIV **314**.35–6
Prime Minister **360**.2
priority need **398**.1, 10, 16, 22, 38, 41
prison **308**.7, **366**.30–1, 35
    and increased terms **311**.22
    and inequality **308**.7
    and rights **300**.32
    right to vote **300**.30–1
    see also custody and detention
Prison Act 1898 **366**.31
prisoners, rights of **372**.7–8
privacy **317**.1, 9, 31–2, 35, **361**.18, 33–4, **371**.21, 26, 30–1,
   372.4
    and absolute privacy **317**.21
    collective **383**.11–12
    as commodity **383**.8
    culture **383**.1
    global rights **317**.2
    human rights **317**.2–3, 25
    and invasion of **308**.21
    legislation **383**.2, 7, 17, 21–2, 41
    as luxury **383**.7–9
    policies **383**.13, 32
    and rights **317**.1
    right to **383**.5–6, 8, 41, **412**.8–11
    trends **383**.1–4
    as utility **383**.8
    see also online privacy; surveillance and access
privacy paradox **383**.10–11
Privacy Shield **383**.3
private healthcare **392**.11
private label brands **381**.3
private rental sector **396**.1–2
    see also rented accommodation
private sector **381**.12, 32, 41
privilege **382**.37
problem drinking *see* alcohol
problem gambling **349**.3, 4–7, 10, 12–13, 26–30, 32, 37–9, 41
    self-help tips **349**.33

    tackling **349**.32, 33
processed foods **350**.22, **408**.16–17, 19–20
pro-choice abortion movements **302**.16
procrastination **403**.38
producing drugs **373**.22–3
productivity, and lack of sleep **389**.36–7
products
    customisation **381**.4
    minimum viable product **381**.2
    purpose of **381**.1
    second-hand **381**.4
profiling, racist **308**.15
profiteering **401**.10–11
profound and multiple learning disability (PMLD) **393**.5
progesterone **394**.7, **395**.27
progestogen **309**.6, 8
progestogen-only pill (mini pill) **309**.7
project management **405**.2
pro-life abortion movements **302**.8–9, 12, 16, 23, 32
    and gender selection **302**.31–2
    and late abortion **302**.28, 32
    and travel abroad for abortion **302**.32–3
    and unviable foetuses to term **302**.35–6
pro-life movement **367**.9–10, 23, 33–8
propaganda **355**.5
property, protection of **372**.4
property prices **396**.1, 3, 8–15, 18
proportional representation **360**.41
prostitution **318**.1, 4–6, 10–12, 14–15, 20, 22, 26
    and abuses of power **318**.7–9
    and austerity **318**.2
    average age **318**.2
    and basic expenses **318**.19
    and condoms **318**.2, 4
    and debt **318**.23
    and decriminalisation **318**.2, 5, 8–9, 13, 17, 20–1
    global data **318**.12, 26
    and healthcare **318**.5
    history of **318**.11
    human rights **318**.3–4, 5–7, 13, 17, 21
    and inequality **318**.18, 21
    and invisibility **318**.22–3
    lack of choice **318**.1, 20, 21, 23
    legal steps **318**.2, 16
    and pastoral support **318**.19
    PTSD **318**.27–8
    rape **318**.21
    and rights **318**.6, 11–12
    safety risks **318**.12, 16–17
    and sex tourism **318**.10
    and sex trafficking **300**.3, 8, **318**.1, 5
    street prostitution **318**.14
    and support to exit **318**.15, 17–18
    and union representation **318**.24–5
    and violence **318**.2, 4–7, 9
protected characteristics **376**.3, **380**.1
    children and young people **380**.4
    of religion **358**.16
protection, right to **412**.3, 13
protectionism **305**.31–3
Protection of Freedoms Act 2012 **383**.41
protein **350**.1, 11, 24, 36, 41
    deficiency **350**.16
protein biscuits **378**.20–1

protest

  nonviolent **374**.2

  right to **372**.33

Protestantism, and euthanasia **362**.17

Protestants **358**.2

Provisional IRA **355**.3

proxy wars **401**.1, 18

prussic acid **374**.15

PSIAT (Preschool Implicit Association Text) **307**.33

psychiatric problems *see* mental health

psychiatrist **415**.26–7, 41

psychoactive drugs **399**.41

Psychoactive Drugs Act 2016 **373**.27, 41

psychoactive substances **373**.23

psychodynamic therapy **404**.36–7

psychological abuse **370**.1

  see also emotional abuse

psychological addiction **373**.1, **410**.1, 2

psychology of shopping **414**.27–31

psychosis **354**.19, **399**.21, 22, 30, 41, **400**.41, **404**.1, **415**.8, 41

psychotherapy **404**.16

  see also talking therapies

psychotic depression **404**.1

psychotic illnesses **399**.4–5, 13, 21–2, 31

PTSD *see* post-traumatic stress disorder (PTSD)

puberty **369**.6, 37, 39, **379**.6–7

  boys **395**.27, 29

  girls **395**.27–8

  hormonal changes **395**.27

  mood changes **395**.29

  physical development **395**.28

pubic lice (crabs) **309**.12, **379**.24, 25

Public Accounts Committee **360**.4

public bodies **360**.2

public events **351**.20

Public Health Act 1848 **392**.21, 41

Public Health England (PHE)

  on antibiotic resistance **348**.32

  on HIV **314**.4–5

  on sexually transmitted infections (STIs) **379**.14

public liability insurance **381**.2

public order **347**.1

public order offences **366**.2, 41

public services, impacts **305**.11–12

public spaces, and homelessness **398**.30–1

public transport **311**.25, 27, 29

  see also bus travel; railways; taxis

pupil premium **353**.32

puppy farming **303**.3–4, **374**.28, 41

Purdy, Debbie **362**.6

purging disorder **390**.5

Purim **358**.24

Putin, Vladimir **401**.15, 18

pygmy owl **402**.12

Q

Qatar

  CO_2 emissions **357**.4

  immigration statistics **359**.3

  waste statistics **385**.3

qi gong **343**.7

qualifications **405**.1

  vocational **353**.4

quality of life **363**.23, **378**.6, 9

quantitative easing (QE) **391**.15, 41

quantitative structure-activity relationships (QSARs) **374**.18

Queen, role of **360**.38–9

Queen's Speech **360**.6

queer **369**.2, 14

  see also LGBTQ+

queerbaiting **386**.22

questioning **369**.14

quitting smoking **406**.3, 17–18, 25–31, 37–9

Quorn products **350**.7, 41

Quran **358**.8, 25, 31

R

rabbits, and animal experimentation **374**.16, 18, 19, 20

race

  and housing inequality **396**.5

  stop and search statistics **366**.37–8

racecourse betting **349**.2

Race Relations Act 1965 **372**.2

Race Relations Act 1976 **308**.2, 30, 36, **372**.2, **376**.41

Vol. numbers appear first (in bold) followed by page numbers; a change in volume is preceded by a semi-colon.

Vol. 305	Globalisation – Good or Bad?	Vol. 368	Sustainable Living	Vol. 392	National Health
Vol. 314	HIV & AIDS	Vol. 369	LGBT+ Issues	Vol. 393	Disability
Vol. 316	Marriage	Vol. 370	Domestic Violence and Abuse	Vol. 394	Pregnancy
Vol. 347	The Censorship Debate	Vol. 371	The Internet and Us	Vol. 395	Teen Self-Care
Vol. 348	World Health	Vol. 372	Our Human Rights	Vol. 396	UK Housing
Vol. 349	Gambling Culture	Vol. 373	Drug Use and Abuse	Vol. 397	Alcohol Issues
Vol. 350	Lifestyle Diets	Vol. 374	Animal Rights	Vol. 398	Homelessness
Vol. 351	The Anxiety Epidemic	Vol. 375	Body Image	Vol. 399	Discussing Cannabis
Vol. 352	Biotech & Bioethics	Vol. 376	Racism	Vol. 400	Suicide & Self-Harm
Vol. 353	Education	Vol. 377	Poverty	Vol. 401	War & Conflict
Vol. 354	Relationships	Vol. 378	Ageing	Vol. 402	Endangered Species
Vol. 355	Terrorism	Vol. 379	Understanding Sexual Health	Vol. 403	Student Options
Vol. 356	British Armed Forces	Vol. 380	About Bullying	Vol. 404	Depression
Vol. 357	The Climate Emergency	Vol. 381	Business	Vol. 405	Employability
Vol. 358	Religion Today	Vol. 382	Active Citizenship	Vol. 406	Smoking
Vol. 359	Migration & Immigration	Vol. 383	The Privacy Debate	Vol. 407	Bereavement
Vol. 360	Government	Vol. 384	Health & Fitness	Vol. 408	Healthy Eating
Vol. 361	Cyberbullying	Vol. 385	Waste & Recycling Issues	Vol. 409	Online Safety
Vol. 362	Euthanasia	Vol. 386	Sexualising Society	Vol. 410	Addiction
Vol. 363	Population Change	Vol. 387	Fertility Issues	Vol. 411	Sport
Vol. 364	The Gender Equality Debate	Vol. 388	Discussing Child Abuse	Vol. 412	Rights of the Child
Vol. 365	Tourism Today	Vol. 389	Sleep	Vol. 413	Energy
Vol. 366	Crime in the UK	Vol. 390	Eating Disorders	Vol. 414	Consumerism
Vol. 367	Discussing Abortion	Vol. 391	Money	Vol. 415	Mental Health

racial bullying **380**.5, 41
racial discrimination **308**.1–4, 30–1, 36
   direct discrimination **308**.2
   and employment **308**.2, 30–1, 38–9
   history of **308**.30
   and housing **308**.30
   indirect discrimination **308**.2
   racial harassment **308**.2–3
   racial victimisation **308**.2
   racist bullying **308**.36
   see also racism; *individual ethnic groups*
racial harassment **308**.2–3
racial slurs **308**.14
racial stereotyping **308**.1–2, 7, 16, 31–2
racial victimisation **308**.2
racing, dogs **303**.16
racism **308**.1, 3–4, 9–10, 12, 17, 18–19, 29, 34, **386**.7–8, **401**.2, **409**.34
   anti-racist **376**.39
   and apps **308**.37
   in the Armed Forces **356**.16
   in Britain **376**.1–3, 4–8
   covert **376**.20
   definition **376**.41
   and employment **308**.4, 29
   experiences of **376**.4–7, 13–14
   in football **376**.29–30
   and hate crime **308**.17, 29
   history of **308**.3, 19
   impacts of **376**.26
   institutional **376**.15–19, 24–5
   microaggressions **376**.20–1, 28
   and mobile phones **308**.37
   online **308**.37
   overt **376**.20
   in politics **376**.22
   racial stereotyping **308**.1–2
   racist beliefs **376**.8
   racist jokes **308**.2
   and religion **308**.1, 3–4, 8, 17
   reverse **376**.12, 41
   in sport **411**.10, 31
   systemic **376**.15–16, 41
   tackling **376**.26–8, 32–4, 36–7, 38–9
   and Twitter **308**.14, 37
   in universities **376**.24–5
   see also discrimination; racial discrimination; *individual ethnic groups*
racist bullying **308**.36, **361**.26, 41
   and schools **308**.36
racist jokes **308**.2
racist profiling **308**.15
radicalisation **355**.4–5, 13, 19–29, 41
   of children **355**.28–9
radio, and body image **307**.27–8
radiological weapons **355**.4
rainfall **357**.8
rainforests **350**.9, **357**.6, 16, **363**.22
   see also forests
raised participation age **353**.4
Raksha Bandhan **358**.23
Ramadan **358**.25, **408**.18
ransomware **371**.29
rape **300**.24, **309**.29, **318**.21, **354**.31–2, 34, 40, **370**.12,

   372.37, **386**.34, **388**.41
   and abortion **302**.15, 31
   and blame **309**.27–8
   and consent **309**.27
   lack of consent **318**.36
   marital rape **364**.12
   of men **364**.19–20
   SRE **309**.39
   see also consent
Rape Crisis, on male rape **364**.19–20
rape culture **386**.19–20, 35–7, 41
'rape myths' **386**.6
rapid eye movement (REM) sleep **389**.1, 8–9, 28, 41
Rashford, Marcus **377**.13
raw materials **368**.11
reactive depression **404**.1, 41
real fur **374**.30–2
reality TV **375**.41
   and body image **375**.25
recession **377**.3, 9, 38, 41, **414**.41
reclassification **399**.41
recommerce **381**.4
recovery, from addiction **410**.38–9
recruitment **405**.1, 13, 21, 41
   in the Armed Forces **356**.5–7, 9–11, 16
recurrent depressive disorder **404**.1, 41
recycling **368**.11–12, 18, 38–9, 41
   business waste **385**.15
   common materials **385**.28–9
   definition **385**.41
   demographics **385**.31–2
   difficult materials **385**.29, 33
   glass **385**.12
   household waste **385**.1
   importance of **385**.28–30
   of litter **385**.11
   paper waste **385**.12
   plastic waste **385**.1, 5, 29–30
   three Rs of **385**.41
   tips **385**.30
Red List of Threatened Species **402**.12, 21, 41
redundancy **405**.28–30, 32, 41
reflexology **343**.7
reforestation **357**.38–9
Reform Act 1832 **360**.14–15
Refuge **370**.14
refugee camps **359**.31, 41
refugees **359**.30–1, **401**.5–6, 41, **415**.17
   deaths of **300**.20–1
   definition **359**.31, 35–6, 41
   famous **359**.38–9
   forced displacement **359**.33–4
   see also asylum; asylum seekers
refuges **370**.32–3, 41
   see also homelessness
refunds **414**.4–5
refusing treatment **362**.5
regional inequality **381**.8
regionalism **305**.29–30
   and global poverty **305**.30
   and healthcare **305**.29–30
   and tax safeguards **305**.29
Register of Chinese Herbal Medicine (RCHM) **343**.4–5
register offices **316**.4

and religious ceremonies **316**.5–6
time factors **316**.3
Regulation of Investigative Powers Act (RIPA) 2000 **317**.26
rehabilitation **373**.12, 33, 35–9, 41
reiki **343**.12–13
relationship contracts **316**.12
relationship education **370**.35–6
relationships **379**.26–30
abuse in **379**.29–30
arguments **379**.27
and body image **307**.7, 10–11
break ups **379**.28
and child poverty **306**.15–16
distressed **316**.29
education in schools **354**.9
emotions and feelings **316**.12
ending **354**.38–9
health benefits of **354**.8
healthy **354**.28
and internet pornography **318**.32–3, 35–6
and money **391**.8–9
online dating **379**.32–4
personal **316**.1, 12
romance **379**.27
romantic **354**.26–39
safety in **354**.36–7
and self-esteem **307**.31, 33–5
sexting **379**.35–6
unhealthy **354**.28
see also civil partnerships; cohabitation; consent; families;
marriage; same-sex relationships
relative poverty **377**.1, 3, 18, 41
relaxation **343**.7, **389**.7
religion
and abortion **302**.8–9, **367**.13, 31–2
anti-Semitism **376**.12, 41
and the Armed Forces **356**.2
benefits of **358**.21
blasphemy **358**.36–7
and bullying **380**.6
characteristics of **358**.16–17
and clothing **308**.1
clothing **358**.32
death and dying **407**.32
defining **358**.41
and divorce **316**.24
and euthanasia **362**.17
fellowship **358**.21
and food poverty **306**.20
and freedom **358**.32–9
and geography **358**.2–3
growth of **358**.3
and hate crime **308**.17
holidays **358**.22–5
impact of **358**.5, 20
irreligiosity (no religion) **358**.1–2, 6–7, 18–20
Islamaphobia **376**.30–1, 41
and LGBT **369**.32–3
and marriage **316**.4–7, 11, 26
minorities **358**.2
monotheistic **358**.8–9, 41
new **358**.4
'nonverts' **358**.7
and persecution **358**.38–9, 41

pick and mix approach to **358**.1
rejection of **358**.6–7
religious discrimination **308**.3–4, 8
religious slaughter **303**.6–7
sacred texts **358**.31
and school uniform **353**.34
and science **358**.2, 14
slaughter of animals **358**.41
timeline **358**.4–5
and Western culture **358**.14–15
world demographics **358**.2–5, 11
see also spirituality; *individual religions*
religious discrimination **372**.34
religious festivals **408**.18
religious tourism **365**.1
religious wars **401**.2, 4, 37
relocation, of businesses **381**.24–5
remand **366**.33
remote gambling (online) **349**.41
remote working **383**.4, **392**.7
renewable energy **413**.1, 8–9, 19, 36–7
rented accommodation **306**.7, 10, **396**.1–2, 5, 18, 37
eviction **306**.7
see also tenants
reporters *see* journalism
repossessions **396**.16, 41
representation, in sport **411**.9
Representation of the People Act 1918 **360**.15, **364**.10
Representation of the People Act 1983 **382**.2
reproductive health *see* fertility; pregnancy
reproductive rights **379**.2
republic governments **360**.1
repurposing **368**.11
Research Defence Society (RDS) **374**.14–16
reserve personnel *see* full-time reserve service personnel
(FTRS)
resettlement **359**.2
see also asylum; settlement applications
residence permit **359**.36, 41
residency **382**.4–5
resilience **381**.23
resits **403**.3, 20
respect **354**.28, 29
of environment **368**.10
respiratory diseases **408**.10
respiratory tract infections (RTIs) **348**.38
responsible tourism **365**.18–39, 41
responsible travel **365**.24
rest **394**.10
restless legs syndrome (RLS) **389**.20
resuscitation **407**.1
retirement **378**.41, **391**.6
affording **378**.18
age **378**.1, 12–17, 19
state pension **378**.15–17
working beyond **378**.19
retirement delays **311**.23
retirement homes **311**.17, 24–7
and community **311**.26–7
and social isolation **311**.32–3
technology **311**.24
and transport **311**.26
reusing **368**.11, **385**.15, 29
revenge porn **354**.39, **361**.26, **364**.20, **371**.14

revenge wars **401**.3

'reverse anorexia' **375**.14–15

reverse racism **376**.12, 41

reversible inhibition of sperm under guidance (RISUG) **309**.8

re-victimisation **388**.23, 27–8, 32

revision **403**.33, 36–9

revolutionary wars **401**.3

reward systems (brain) **373**.1, 28

rewilding **357**.38

rhesus status **394**.17

rheumatoid arthritis **392**.29

rhinoceros **402**.20, 32

rich-poor gap **306**.3, 7, 13

    and income **306**.2, 33

    and marriage status **316**.2

    and mental illness **306**.15

Riding Establishments Acts **303**.2

right brain **403**.6

right of abode **382**.2, 4

rights

    and duties **374**.3–4

    see also human rights

right to buy **396**.2

right to die **362**.1

    see also assisted suicide; euthanasia

right to life **362**.15, **372**.4, 6, **412**.13

Right to Live UK **362**.20

right to repair **414**.6

right to vote **360**.20

right-wing extremism **355**.3, 6, 17

rigor mortis **407**.2–3

RIPA (Regulation of Investigative Powers Act) 2000 **317**.26

risk **391**.6

risky behaviour **354**.40

Ritalin **373**.22

rivers **402**.9

road traffic accidents **348**.2

    see also cars and driving

robbery **366**.3

robotic process automation (RPA) **383**.26

robots

    in care homes **378**.26

    as citizens **382**.12

Roma communities **376**.23–4, 41, **380**.5

Roman Catholicism **358**.2

    holidays **358**.23

    see also Catholicism

romance **379**.27

Roman Empire **358**.8

Romania and animal welfare **303**.3

    and surveillance **317**.14–15

romantic relationships **354**.26–39

Rome, pilgrimage **358**.26

Rosh Hashana **358**.20, 24

rough sleeping **398**.1, 2, 4, 12–13, 16–18, 22, 32–3, 41

    among veterans **356**.32

    see also hidden homelessness

Royal Air Force (RAF) **356**.1, 11, 18–19, 33

Royal Assent **360**.6, 41

Royal British Legion **356**.31

    on Commonwealth veterans **356**.28

Royal College of Physicians (RCP), on euthanasia **362**.6, 11, 22, 25–6, 28, 31

Royal Engineers **356**.14

royal jelly **408**.14

Royal Marines **356**.1–2, 7, 8, 17, 18–19

Royal Navy **356**.1, 2, 5, 7, 17, 18–19, 20

royal prerogative **360**.4

RSPCA (Royal Society for the Prevention of Cruelty to Animals) **374**.41

    on animal experimentation **374**.20

    on breed-specific legislation **303**.21

    on dog trafficking **303**.3–4

    on puppy farming **374**.28

    on puppy farms **303**.3

rubbish *see* waste

rugby scrum **411**.41

rugby union

    injuries **411**.14–16

    women in **411**.24–5

rumour **380**.18

runners **366**.41

    see also county lines

rural development programmes **377**.30–1

rural environments, and green living **385**.31

rural tourism **365**.1

Russell Group **353**.19

Russia

    and abortion **302**.14

    annexation of Crimea **401**.18

    CO_2 emissions **357**.3

    Cold War **401**.1, 14

    immigration statistics **359**.3

    Soviet Union **401**.1, 4, 15

    and Ukraine **401**.8, 15–16, 18

    waste statistics **385**.3

Russian Civil War (1917-1923) **401**.3

Rutland Osprey Project **402**.34–5

Rwanda **360**.34, **377**.30–1

S

Sachs, Andrew **359**.39

sacred texts **358**.31

sadfishing **380**.21

sadness, excessive **400**.20

safari parks **374**.35

safe houses *see* refuges

Safer Internet Day **371**.18

safe sex **354**.40, **379**.17, 41

    see also contraception

safety, of buildings **396**.22–3, 39

safety and the internet **361**.33–4

    see also cyberbullying; online privacy

safety behaviours **351**.22

Safety Pin campaign **308**.34

salaries **356**.14, **391**.6, **405**.22

Salford **368**.9

saliva **394**.7

salmonella **394**.9

salt **408**.1–3, 9, 37

Salt Awareness Week **408**.37

Salvation Army, on rough sleeping **398**.16

salvia **301**.30

Samaritans, on suicide **364**.18

same-sex relationships **354**.4, 7

    and civil partnerships **316**.3–5, 8–9, 15

and marriage **316**.3–5, 11, **372**.36–7, **380**.5
and sex **309**.4
and STIs **309**.25
see also civil partnerships; gay people; LGBTQ+
Samsung, on surveillance **317**.13, 34–5
sanctions
  aid **305**.14
  diplomatic **305**.14
  targeted **305**.14
sanctity of life **362**.41, **400**.41
sand-powered batteries **413**.32
Sangraand **358**.25
Santa Claus, belief in **358**.16
Sarah's Law **388**.41
SATs **353**.41
  see also exams
saturated fats **408**.1–2, 9, 11, 17
Saudi Arabia **360**.36
  abuse of human rights **300**.22–3
  censorship in **347**.7, 36
  CO$_2$ emissions **357**.3
  discrimination against women **300**.22–3
  global standing **300**.22
  human rights issues **372**.30, 33–5
  immigration statistics **359**.3
  waste statistics **385**.3
Save the Children, on child refugees **359**.34
savings **391**.6, 16–18
  and ageing **311**.17
scabies **309**.12
scams **371**.21, **391**.5, 33, **409**.16–17, **414**.41
Scandinavia
  housing experiment **378**.37–8
  life expectancy **378**.4, 7
  retirement age **378**.13–14
scapegoating **369**.30–1
schizoaffective disorder **415**.8
schizophrenia **399**.4–5, 21–2, 28, 31, 41, **415**.3, 8, 41
school leaver schemes **403**.18, 19–20
schools **308**.5, 36
  academies **353**.2–3, 5–6
  attendance **353**.22–3
  bullying in **361**.11
  and child poverty **306**.13, 15, 17, 23, 36

closures **380**.14
compulsory age **353**.1–2, 7–8
and cyberbullying **361**.3, 22, 37, **380**.10–11
and employment **308**.16
excluding children **308**.5, **412**.33–4
faith **353**.2, 3, 41
foundation **353**.2
free **353**.3, 41
free school meals **306**.13, 23
funding **353**.31–3
grammar **353**.3, 41
and HIV/AIDS **314**.19–20
independent **353**.4
leaving **353**.1
and Local Authority **353**.1–4
maintained **353**.2
and mental health **415**.29–31
PE provision **384**.30–1, 34–5
policies **308**.36
primary **353**.2, 4, 36–7
right to eduction **412**.3
role in drug education **301**.4, 12–13
secondary **353**.2
and segregation **308**.13
specialist **353**.3
spending **353**.31–3
starting **353**.1, 7–10
state **353**.2, 41
teachers as information sources on drugs **301**.13
trust **353**.2
types of **353**.2
uniform **353**.34
voluntary aided **353**.2
see also education; primary schools; secondary schools
school skirts **386**.12–13
school uniforms, gender-neutral **364**.13–14
science
  GCSE & A-levels **403**.5, 7
  and religion **358**.2, 14
Science-Based Targets initiative (SBTi) **357**.2
Scientology **358**.17
SCOFF screening test **390**.9
scopolamine **374**.15
'Scores on the Doors' **392**.24

Vol. numbers appear first (in bold) followed by page numbers; a change in volume is preceded by a semi-colon.

Vol. 305	Globalisation – Good or Bad?	Vol. 368	Sustainable Living	Vol. 392	National Health
Vol. 314	HIV & AIDS	Vol. 369	LGBT+ Issues	Vol. 393	Disability
Vol. 316	Marriage	Vol. 370	Domestic Violence and Abuse	Vol. 394	Pregnancy
Vol. 347	The Censorship Debate	Vol. 371	The Internet and Us	Vol. 395	Teen Self-Care
Vol. 348	World Health	Vol. 372	Our Human Rights	Vol. 396	UK Housing
Vol. 349	Gambling Culture	Vol. 373	Drug Use and Abuse	Vol. 397	Alcohol Issues
Vol. 350	Lifestyle Diets	Vol. 374	Animal Rights	Vol. 398	Homelessness
Vol. 351	The Anxiety Epidemic	Vol. 375	Body Image	Vol. 399	Discussing Cannabis
Vol. 352	Biotech & Bioethics	Vol. 376	Racism	Vol. 400	Suicide & Self-Harm
Vol. 353	Education	Vol. 377	Poverty	Vol. 401	War & Conflict
Vol. 354	Relationships	Vol. 378	Ageing	Vol. 402	Endangered Species
Vol. 355	Terrorism	Vol. 379	Understanding Sexual Health	Vol. 403	Student Options
Vol. 356	British Armed Forces	Vol. 380	About Bullying	Vol. 404	Depression
Vol. 357	The Climate Emergency	Vol. 381	Business	Vol. 405	Employability
Vol. 358	Religion Today	Vol. 382	Active Citizenship	Vol. 406	Smoking
Vol. 359	Migration & Immigration	Vol. 383	The Privacy Debate	Vol. 407	Bereavement
Vol. 360	Government	Vol. 384	Health & Fitness	Vol. 408	Healthy Eating
Vol. 361	Cyberbullying	Vol. 385	Waste & Recycling Issues	Vol. 409	Online Safety
Vol. 362	Euthanasia	Vol. 386	Sexualising Society	Vol. 410	Addiction
Vol. 363	Population Change	Vol. 387	Fertility Issues	Vol. 411	Sport
Vol. 364	The Gender Equality Debate	Vol. 388	Discussing Child Abuse	Vol. 412	Rights of the Child
Vol. 365	Tourism Today	Vol. 389	Sleep	Vol. 413	Energy
Vol. 366	Crime in the UK	Vol. 390	Eating Disorders	Vol. 414	Consumerism
Vol. 367	Discussing Abortion	Vol. 391	Money	Vol. 415	Mental Health

Scotland **377**.38–9
    and abortion **302**.2, 11–12, 21, 32–3, 39
    and animal welfare **303**.26
    and assisted suicide **362**.30, 33
    and child poverty **306**.23
    and cohabitation **316**.15–16
    and commercial sexual exploitation **318**.29
    devolved government **360**.2, 3, 9
    domestic abuse **370**.6–7, 12–13
    gender inequality **370**.13
    identity **382**.7
    and marriage **316**.6, 10
    natural change in population **363**.3
    population growth **363**.2
    and poverty **306**.23
    and prostitution **318**.10
    secondary eduction **403**.1, 12
    and social networking **307**.38
Scotland Act 1998 **360**.9
Scottish Highers **403**.12
Scottish National Party **360**.9
Scottish Parliament **360**.25
Scottish rainforest **402**.6
Scottish Schools Adolescent Lifestyle and Substance Use
    Survey (SALSUS) **373**.8–9
Scottish Wildlife Trust **402**.34–5
Scrap the Puppy Trade campaign **303**.3
screen time **371**.5–7, 18, **384**.14, **395**.38, 41, **409**.6–8, 35–6,
    41
screen use, and sleep problems **389**.15
seabirds **402**.13
seahorse **402**.16
sea levels **357**.8, 20–1
seas *see* marine environments
seasonal affective disorder (SAD) **389**.21, **404**.1, 41, **415**.8–9,
    33
seaweed **413**.39
secondary eduction **403**.1
secondary infertility **387**.15
secondary legislation **360**.8
secondary loss **407**.16
secondary school **353**.2, 4
second-hand products **381**.4
second-hand smoke **406**.14–15, 17, 41
    see also passive smoking
second home ownership **396**.24–6
secondment **405**.41
Second Sudanese Civil War (1983-2005) **401**.2
second trimester **394**.1–2
Secretaries of State **360**.2
sectarianism **380**.6
secularism **358**.18–20
    see also irreligiosity (no religion)
secure attachment **354**.12–13
security **355**.33
    of data **383**.24–5
    and life expectancy **378**.6
    see also counter-terrorism; data protection
security cameras **383**.10, 14–15
Select Committee on Medical Ethics **362**.2–3
selective abortion **367**.24
selective breeding **352**.41
selective serotonin reuptake inhibitors (SSRIs) **351**.24, **404**.3,
    13, 29, 41

self-care **415**.1, 21
    arts and crafts **395**.35
    on a budget **395**.38
    definition **395**.1–2
    and mental health **395**.33
    mundane acts of **395**.4–6
    vs. self-love **395**.2–3
    and wellbeing **395**.6–7
    work-life balance **395**.33
self-confidence **380**.20
self-consciousness **351**.21, 36
    of animals **374**.3
self-determination **372**.1
self-driving vehicles **311**.27
self-esteem **307**.1, 29–31, 33–4, 37, **379**.1, **380**.20, **382**.38,
    386.4, **390**.2, 19, **395**.1, 29, 39, 41, **400**.4, **415**.9, 35
    and body image **375**.7–8, 10, 14, 17, 22, 29–31, 34, 35, 41
    of bullies **380**.17
    and bullying **380**.18
    destructive behaviours **307**.30
    and emotions **307**.33–4
    exercise campaigns **307**.39
    getting help **307**.35, 38
    and goals **307**.31, 35
    in–group preferences **307**.34
    and mindfulness **307**.32
    PSIAT **307**.33
    recording **307**.31–2, 34–5
    and safety **307**.34
    self-help **307**.30–2, 35
    social pressure **307**.38
    and work **307**.30
    see also body image
self-harm **353**.15–16, **356**.9, **361**.19, 31, 41, **369**.35, **375**.16,
    380.20, 41, **390**.2, **415**.4, 9, 17, 31
    age of onset **400**.5
    apps for **400**.34–5
    in children **400**.6
    and eating disorders **400**.16
    facts and statistics **400**.5
    forms of **400**.2, 4
    and gender **400**.2
    growing out of **400**.8
    in men and boys **400**.5, 10–11, 14
    myths about **400**.1, 5
    and poverty **400**.14–15
    preventing **400**.9, 30
    reasons for **400**.1, 2
    relapsing **400**.33
    at-risk adolescents **400**.9
    and social media **400**.11–13, 26, 29
    stopping **400**.3, 4, 30
    support for **400**.1, 2–3, 4, 31–2, 34–5, 39
    telling parents **400**.32
    triggers **400**.1
    in women and girls **400**.2, 5, 10–11, 14–15
    see also suicide
self-help **351**.24
    groups **343**.7
self-help box **400**.21–2
selfies **365**.41, **375**.34, 41
    and body image **307**.6–7, 10–12, 17–19
    and friendship **307**.7
    and safety **307**.7

and sexting **307**.6, **317**.35, **318**.35
self-image **400**.16
   see also body image
self-inflicted violence *see* self-harm
selfisolation **380**.20
self-love **395**.2–3
self-mastery **358**.15
self-objectification **375**.39, 41
self-service shopping **414**.37–9
self-transformation **358**.15
self-worth **361**.1
selling **381**.2
sentencing **366**.34
   see also crime and justice; justice system
sentience, of animals **374**.9
separation **316**.15–16, **354**.3
   and cohabitation agreements **316**.15–16, 16–20
   and 'conscious uncoupling' **316**.34
   and rights **316**.17
   see also divorce; parental separation
separatism **355**.6
sepsis **348**.8
September 11th attacks **401**.3, 5, 29–31
Serbia **360**.33
Serbo-Bulgarian War (1885-1886) **401**.1
Sergeant at Arms **360**.12
Serious Crime Bill **302**.31
serotonin **408**.14
serotonin syndrome **406**.33
service industry **381**.41
services **414**.4, 5
settled status **359**.13–14, 41, **382**.5
settlement applications **359**.2
seven stages of grief **407**.22
sex **309**.4
   assigned at birth **369**.1, 3, 38
   biological **369**.2, 3
   chromosomes **369**.1, 3
   coercion **309**.5, 29
   and consent **354**.29–31
   myths **379**.4
   and pornography **309**.29
   readiness for **354**.33–4
   sexual images **309**.29
   stigma **379**.19
   unprotected **379**.4
   see also gender; rape; sexual abuse; sexual assault
sex addiction **410**.6
sex and relationships education (SRE) **309**.16, 20, 22, 29,
   31–8
   and consent **309**.38–9
   discomfort about **309**.34–5
   and gender education **309**.33
   and HIV/AIDS **314**.24
   and knowledge **309**.38–9
   LBGT-inclusive **309**.34–5
   non-statutory **309**.36, 39
   as out of touch **309**.35–6
   and sexuality **309**.35, 38
   vocabulary **309**.37
Sex Discrimination Act 1975 **308**.30, **364**.12, **372**.2
Sex Discrimination Removal Act 1919 **364**.12
sex education **379**.6, **386**.19–20, 36
sexism **376**.22, **386**.6, **409**.33–4

and bullying **380**.6
   in business **381**.33–5
   and sport **411**.29–31
sexting **307**.6, **318**.35, **371**.36–7, **379**.35–6
   and online privacy **317**.35
sex tourism **318**.10
sex trafficking **300**.3–4, 6–7, **318**.37–9
   and freedom of movement **318**.39
   and misidentification **318**.38–9
   and prostitution **300**.3, 8, **318**.1, 5
   and safe migration routes **318**.39
   safety risks **318**.37–8
   violence risks **318**.37
   see also trafficking
sexual abuse **306**.6, 32, **354**.28, **364**.41, **370**.1, 41, **379**.29–30,
   386.34–5, **412**.14
   definition **388**.1, 5, 41
   forms of **388**.6–7
   online **388**.23–4, 36, 38
   reporting **388**.38
   signs of **388**.7
   in sport **388**.22, 34, **411**.9
   and SRE **309**.39
   statistics **388**.2
   survivor's story **388**.33
   women during wars **300**.24
   see also grooming; prostitution; see also pornography; sex
     trafficking
sexual assault **309**.29, **379**.37, **386**.34–7, **412**.13
   and blame **309**.27–8
   and SRE **309**.37–9
sexual bullying **354**.40, **361**.41, **388**.6–7
   see also homophobic bullying
sexual competence **354**.33–4
sexual development **379**.6–7
sexual dysfunction **309**.16
sexual exploitation **354**.36, **372**.15–18, 21
   see also commercial sexual exploitation
sexual fluidity **369**.16
sexual harassment **364**.41, **380**.19, 31, 41, **386**.19–20
sexual health **309**.1, 5, 15, 17, **348**.2, 21
   complaints **309**.17
   and confidentiality **309**.17
   definition **379**.1, 41
   definitions **309**.1
   and medical records **309**.17
   myths **379**.3
   physical **379**.1
   services **379**.8–9, 21, 23–5
   sexuality **309**.1
   sexual rights **309**.1–2
   see also contraception; pregnancy
sexual images **361**.25–6
sexualisation
   and advertising **386**.21–5, 27–8
   of celebrities **386**.9–11
   and clothing **386**.3, 11
   definition **386**.1, 41
   in gaming **386**.5–6
   of men and boys **386**.3, 17–19
   and skin colour **386**.7–8
   in sport **386**.26
   of teenagers **386**.2–4, 12–14
   and violence **386**.1, 3, 6

of women and girls **386**.3, 12–14, 18
of young children **386**.2–3
see also see also pornography
sexuality **369**.2, 12, 41, **379**.1
and housing inequality **396**.5
and human rights **372**.6, 7
as a spectrum **369**.15
and technology **352**.34
sexually transmitted infections (STIs) *see* STIs (sexually transmitted infections) **387**.19, 21, 41
sexual misconduct **364**.9–10
sexual offences **366**.3, **370**.12, 24
sexual orientation **369**.12–13, 14, 16, 41
and asylum applications **359**.2
and bullying **380**.5
UK statistics **369**.20–3
see also gay people; LGBTQ+; transgender people
sexual rights, definition **309**.1–2
sexual violence **354**.31–2, 34, **386**.19–20
sex workers **318**.2, 7
and HIV **314**.16
see also prostitution
shadow economy **381**.41
shame **404**.25
shaming **386**.12–13, 20
Shared Accommodation Rate (SAR) exemption **398**.1–2
'sharenting' **383**.35
Shavuot **358**.24
'shell shock' **356**.41
see also post-traumatic stress disorder (PTSD)
Shelter, on the housing emergency **396**.5–6
shiatsu **343**.7
shingles **392**.35
Shintoism **358**.4, 9, 31
shipping **357**.37
Shmini Atzeret **358**.25
shootings **355**.4
see also terror attacks
shoppable TV **381**.4
shopping **414**.31
bargains and discounts **414**.24–6
history of retail **414**.36–9
online **414**.29, 36, 38
psychology of **414**.27–31
self-service **414**.37–9
see also consumerism; consumers; online shopping; retail industry; supermarkets
shopping addiction **410**.29–31
showering **395**.32
shrinkflation **414**.32–3, 41
'shrooms' *see* magic mushrooms
Shrove Tuesday **358**.22
sibling bullying **354**.14
siblings and parental separation **316**.37–8
sickness **394**.6
Sierra Leone, and global poverty **306**.32
Sikhism **358**.2, 10, 18, 41
holidays **358**.25
sacred texts **358**.31
silk **352**.3
Simchat Torah **358**.25
simian immunodeficiency virus (SIV)
antibody trials **314**.35
defence **314**.36

Singapore
healthcare **392**.15–16
immigration statistics **359**.4
social housing **396**.7
waste statistics **385**.4
single-issue extremism **355**.6
single mothers, and housing inequality **396**.5–6
single-parent families **354**.11–12, 40, **377**.11–12
divorce **316**.36, 38–9
and domestic abuse **354**.35
parental separation **316**.36–8
see also lone-parent families
Single Transferable Vote (STV) **360**.25
single-use plastics **368**.22, 24
see also plastic packaging
SixDegrees **409**.1
sixth form **353**.2, 41
sixth mass extinction **402**.2
size-zero **390**.41
skin
acne **395**.22–3
self-check **395**.19
skin colour **386**.7–8
'skin gambling' **349**.18–20, 41
skin whitening **308**.22–3
skunk **399**.1, 41
Skype **371**.38
slander **347**.40
slaughter of animals, religious **358**.41
slavery **372**.4, 14–22, 41, **376**.1, 26, 38, **386**.7
of children **412**.17, 21, 41
economic value **300**.9
global prevalence **300**.9, 24
human trafficking **359**.38
Modern Slavery Act **300**.37
treatment of Yazidi women as **300**.23–4
see also forced labour; trafficking
sleep **389**.20, 22, 41, **395**.4, 33, 38, **404**.35
apnoea **406**.12–13
apps and technology **389**.10–11, 13
benefits of **389**.1–3
and cannabis use **399**.24
cycles **389**.1–2
and depression **404**.16–17
deprivation **389**.1, 14–15, 21, 36–8
disorders **389**.20–2
dyregulation **351**.14
and exercise **384**.23–5
hygiene **389**.6–7, 39, 41
and mental health **384**.24–5
monitoring **389**.10–11
myths **389**.4
optimum amount of **389**.3
paralysis **389**.28
problems **389**.15, **415**.9
quality **351**.35
and resilience **380**.22–4
routine **389**.6, 10
and self–esteem **307**.31
stages **389**.7–8, 19
and teenagers **389**.15, 35–6
too much **348**.7
see also insomnia
sleep disturbance **388**.31

sleeping pills **373**.13

sleeping rough *see* rough sleeping

sleepwalking **389**.5, 32–4, 41

slippery slope argument **362**.41

slot machines **349**.2

slurs **386**.12–14, 20

smacking **388**.35, **412**.32

small claims court **414**.7, 10

Smart, Ninian **358**.17

smart cars

    and product liability **317**.32

    safety risks **317**.32

smart devices **371**.28–9

smart homes **383**.25

smart meters **317**.31

    and surveillance **317**.31

smartphones **371**.1–2, 5–6, 11

    and body image **375**.31

    ownership **400**.11

    see also mobile phones

smart solar flowers **413**.16–17

smart speakers **371**.10–11, **381**.4, **383**.7, 25, 26–31

smart TV, and surveillance **317**.13, 34–5

smell, sense of **394**.6

SMEs (small and medium-sized enterprises) *see* small and medium-sized enterprises **381**.41

smog **348**.12, 41

smoke-free targets **406**.30–1, 34

smoking **354**.1, **373**.16–19, **378**.9, **397**.9, **415**.32

    and addiction **406**.8–10

    and animal experimentation **374**.15

    ban **392**.21

    bans **406**.14, 30, 34, 41

    cannabis **399**.2–3

    costs of **406**.2–3, 25

    deaths from **406**.1, 3, 24

    and dental health **395**.25

    and infertility **387**.21–2, 29

    and mental health **406**.25–7

    during pregnancy **394**.10

    quitting **406**.3, 17–18, 25–31, 37–9

    rise in **406**.6

    second-hand smoke **406**.14–15, 17, 41

    see also cannabis; cigarette addiction; cigarettes;

e-cigarettes; passive smoking; tobacco; vaping

Snapchat **371**.10, 33

    anonymous messages **361**.18

    cyberbullying on **361**.8

    reporting/dealing with abuse on **361**.32–3

'snowflake' generation **382**.18

'snowflake generation' **356**.8

snuff **406**.8

social action **382**.14, 18–21, 41

social anxiety disorder (SAD) **351**.4, 21–2, 41, **415**.3

social care **378**.29–30, 41, **393**.33–5, 41

    and abortion **302**.19

    and fostering **302**.19

    see also care provision for older people

social class **380**.26–7

    see also social mobility

social cohesion **378**.11

social comparison **351**.15

social events **351**.19

social exclusion **361**.11

    see also exclusion

Social Exclusion Unit (SEU) **306**.5

social housing **396**.6–7, 37, 41

social inequality **357**.6

social infrastructure **398**.30–1

social isolation **311**.28–9, 32–3, 35–6, **378**.21, 24, 39, 41

    and charity **311**.28

    and community **311**.28–9, 32–3

    and computers **311**.28–9

    cooking club **311**.35

    intergenerational **311**.35–6

    and phoning **311**.28

    and public transport **311**.29

    and self-esteem **307**.30

    and volunteering **311**.29

    see also loneliness

social media **354**.40, **361**.41, **371**.9, 10, 14, 25–7, 30, 32, **375**.41, **404**.32–4, **409**.41, **410**.11–13, **412**.8–11, 27

    addiction **409**.35, 41, **410**.41

    and alcohol **397**.33

    anonymous apps **361**.18–19

    and anxiety **351**.6, 15–16

    and bereavement **407**.27–9

    and body image **375**.2–3, 19, 22–4, 28–9, 34–9

Vol. numbers appear first (in bold) followed by page numbers; a change in volume is preceded by a semi-colon.

Vol. 305	Globalisation – Good or Bad?	Vol. 368	Sustainable Living	Vol. 392	National Health
Vol. 314	HIV & AIDS	Vol. 369	LGBT+ Issues	Vol. 393	Disability
Vol. 316	Marriage	Vol. 370	Domestic Violence and Abuse	Vol. 394	Pregnancy
Vol. 347	The Censorship Debate	Vol. 371	The Internet and Us	Vol. 395	Teen Self-Care
Vol. 348	World Health	Vol. 372	Our Human Rights	Vol. 396	UK Housing
Vol. 349	Gambling Culture	Vol. 373	Drug Use and Abuse	Vol. 397	Alcohol Issues
Vol. 350	Lifestyle Diets	Vol. 374	Animal Rights	Vol. 398	Homelessness
Vol. 351	The Anxiety Epidemic	Vol. 375	Body Image	Vol. 399	Discussing Cannabis
Vol. 352	Biotech & Bioethics	Vol. 376	Racism	Vol. 400	Suicide & Self-Harm
Vol. 353	Education	Vol. 377	Poverty	Vol. 401	War & Conflict
Vol. 354	Relationships	Vol. 378	Ageing	Vol. 402	Endangered Species
Vol. 355	Terrorism	Vol. 379	Understanding Sexual Health	Vol. 403	Student Options
Vol. 356	British Armed Forces	Vol. 380	About Bullying	Vol. 404	Depression
Vol. 357	The Climate Emergency	Vol. 381	Business	Vol. 405	Employability
Vol. 358	Religion Today	Vol. 382	Active Citizenship	Vol. 406	Smoking
Vol. 359	Migration & Immigration	Vol. 383	The Privacy Debate	Vol. 407	Bereavement
Vol. 360	Government	Vol. 384	Health & Fitness	Vol. 408	Healthy Eating
Vol. 361	Cyberbullying	Vol. 385	Waste & Recycling Issues	Vol. 409	Online Safety
Vol. 362	Euthanasia	Vol. 386	Sexualising Society	Vol. 410	Addiction
Vol. 363	Population Change	Vol. 387	Fertility Issues	Vol. 411	Sport
Vol. 364	The Gender Equality Debate	Vol. 388	Discussing Child Abuse	Vol. 412	Rights of the Child
Vol. 365	Tourism Today	Vol. 389	Sleep	Vol. 413	Energy
Vol. 366	Crime in the UK	Vol. 390	Eating Disorders	Vol. 414	Consumerism
Vol. 367	Discussing Abortion	Vol. 391	Money	Vol. 415	Mental Health

and bullying **380**.19, 22–4, 41
censorship **347**.2, 6–7, 8, 11
and children **354**.10
cyberbullying on **361**.8, 15, 18–19, 23, 25–6, 32
digital detox **409**.37–9, 41
duty of care **361**.24
fake news **347**.19, 22
fake profiles **409**.12–13
and friendships **354**.20
and gender **409**.5, 10, 13–14, 35
hacking **361**.6
and hate content **355**.35–6
history of **409**.1
impact of **361**.1
influencers **409**.24, **414**.34
and mental health **415**.13
and online abuse **388**.23–4, 36
online safety legislation **361**.24–5
and privacy **383**.5–6
profiles **405**.3
and radicalisation **355**.5
and self-harm **400**.11–13, 26, 29
and sexualisation **386**.3
'sharenting' **383**.35–9
and sleep **389**.16, 35–6
spending triggers **391**.18
and suicide **400**.26, 29
time spent on **361**.1, 5
usage **409**.35–7
and wellbeing **400**.12, **409**.5, 35–7
see also digital footprint; social networking; *individual platforms*
social mobility
see also diversity
social model of disability **393**.1
social movements **374**.2
social networking **309**.19
and body image **307**.15, 17–22
and online privacy **317**.13, 38
and self–esteem **307**.38
and selfies **307**.6–7
see also blogging; cyberbullying; Facebook; online communities; social media; Twitter
social phobia **380**.20
social safety net **382**.3
social security benefits **393**.25
see also state benefits
social services *see* local authorities
social transitioning **369**.37
social welfare *see* state benefits
socio-economic prejudice **380**.6, 15–16
socio-economics, and the Armed Forces **356**.10, 11
socio-economic status, and housing inequality **396**.5
sodium **408**.2–3
see also salt
sofa surfing **398**.1, 3, 41
see also rough sleeping
Soft Drinks Industry Levy (SDIL) **392**.21
soft skills **405**.1, 2, 35
soft subjects **403**.6
software developers **405**.2
solar panels **368**.2
solar power **413**.2, 5, 9, 11–12, 16–17, 30–1, 34, 34–5, 37, 41
solar roads **413**.39

sole trader **381**.2–3
solvent abuse **301**.11, 19, **373**.5
Soul Survivor **358**.6
South Africa
    CO_2 emissions **357**.3
    and HIV **314**.17, 32, 36
    immigration statistics **359**.3
    and prostitution **318**.17–18
South America
    and globalisation **305**.30
    retirement age **378**.13–14
Southern African Development Community (SADC) **401**.24
South Korea
    and animal research **303**.38
    and body image **307**.23–4
    CO_2 emissions **357**.3
South Sudan, and war zones **300**.20
Soviet Union **401**.1, 4, 15
    see also Russia
soya **350**.12, 31, 38, 41
soy products **408**.12
Spain
    and abortion **302**.14
    and animal welfare **303**.5
    immigration statistics **359**.3–4
    life expectancy **378**.34
    Mediterranean diet **378**.34
    and tourism **365**.5, 16
    waste statistics **385**.2
    see also Europe
spam comments **409**.16–17
spamming **371**.26–7
Spanish Civil War (1936-1939) **401**.3
Speaker, of the Commons **360**.10, 12–14
Spears, Britney **386**.9–10
Special Educational Needs (SEN)
    schools for **353**.3–4
    statement **353**.4
Special Educational Needs and Disabilities (SEND) **353**.24
specialist schools **353**.3
speciesism **374**.2
Species Threat Abatement and Restoration (STAR) metric **402**.12–13
specific phobia of vomit (SPOV) **351**.5
speech, freedom of *see* freedom of speech
speed (amphetamine) **373**.5
    classification and penalties for possession **301**.19, 22
    effects on the brain **301**.11–12
spending money
    bad habits **391**.18
    and happiness **391**.7–8
    online **391**.13
    versus saving **391**.6, 16–18
sperm **387**.2
    count **387**.14, 16
    donation **387**.25, 38–9
    quality **387**.1, 16
    surgery **387**.24–5
Spice **373**.20–1, 28
    see also synthetic cannabis
spiders, phobia of **351**.4
spider webs **352**.3
spiking of drinks **397**.20–1, 41
spirits **397**.2

spiritual beliefs *see* religion
spirituality **358**.1–2, 14
  benefits of **358**.21
spiritual self-care **395**.1
spliffs (joints) **399**.1
sport and leisure activities
  blood sports **303**.5, 8–9, 27
  and cyberbullying **361**.34–5
  equality in **364**.20–1
  and gender **384**.26–9, 33
  inclusive **384**.26–9, 41
  injuries **343**.2
  PE provision **384**.30–1
  sexual abuse in **388**.22, 34
  sexualisation in **386**.26
  see also Olympic Games; Paralympic Games; *individual sport*
spots **394**.7
squatting **398**.41
squishy **351**.7
Sri Lanka, tobacco taxation **406**.35
SSAFA (Armed Forces Charity) **356**.20, 34–5
SSRIs (selective serotonin reuptake inhibitors) **351**.41
  see also antidepressants
staffing crisis **392**.6–8
stalking **370**.5, 9, 15, 20–1, 24, 41, **371**.26–7
Stamp Duty Land Tax (SDLT) **396**.13–14, 38, 41
standards, of goods **414**.4
standoffs **401**.18
Staphylococcus aureus **348**.16
STAR approach **405**.3
starting school **353**.1, 7–10
state benefits
  benefit cuts **306**.7, 9, 11
  and health **306**.25
  impacts **306**.7, 20, 24–5
statelessness **359**.41, **382**.3, 41
statement of Special Educational Needs **353**.4
State of Child Health 2020 **392**.27–8
state pension **378**.1, 15–17, **391**.41
state schools **353**.2, 41, **403**.41
  see also schools
Statutory Instruments (SIs) **360**.8
staycation **365**.41
Steiner school **353**.7
step-family **354**.40
stereotyping **369**.3–5, 10, **373**.32–3, **386**.1, **393**.8
  of abuse survivors **388**.30
  of Armed Forces **356**.20
  of bullies **380**.18
  and bullying **380**.6
  and children **364**.28–9, 35–7
  and discrimination **376**.11–12
  by gender **364**.27–39, **386**.3, 27–8, 41
  and homelessness **398**.4, 7
  of older people **378**.22
  racial **308**.1–2, 7, 16, 31–2
  and skin colour **386**.7–8
steroids **301**.14, **343**.28, **373**.4, 22
  classification and penalties for possession **301**.19, 22
  cosmetic uses **301**.14
  criminalisation of use **301**.15
  global misuse **301**.14
  harmful effects **301**.12, 14–15

  and image-enhancing drugs (SIEDs) **301**.15–16
  injecting **301**.14–15
  needle and syringe programmes **301**.15–16
  user profiles **301**.14–16
stigma **388**.30, **392**.25, **397**.36
  asylum seekers **380**.4
  and eating disorders **390**.17–18
  and homelessness **398**.30
stillbirth **387**.11, **394**.19, 25–7, 41
stimulants **373**.4, 41
STIs (sexually transmitted infections) **309**.2, 3, 5, 9–10, 14–15, 21, 23, **314**.4, **379**.3, 4–5, 14–25, 41
  chlamydia **309**.5, 11
  and decriminalisation of sex trade **318**.2
  difficulty of treatment **309**.3
  and fear **309**.23
  gonorrhoea **309**.10–11
  hepatitis B **309**.10–13
  hepatitis C **309**.13
  herpes **309**.9, 11, 13
  lice **309**.12
  Molluscum contagiosium **309**.12
  in older people **379**.19
  preventing **379**.20–1
  resistance to treatment **379**.21
  scabies **309**.12
  syphilis **309**.9–10, 12
  testing for **379**.23–4
  treating **379**.25
  trichomoniasis **309**.12
  and violence **318**.4
  see also HPV; see also HIV
Stockton-on-Tees **368**.9
Stonewall Workplace Equality Index **356**.17
stop and search **366**.36–8, 41, **372**.8
Stop Circus Suffering campaign **303**.10
Stop Mass Homelessness campaign **398**.6
Stoptober **406**.25
Stormzy **376**.1–2
straight **369**.14
strangers
  as cyberbullies **361**.8
  and racism **308**.4
Strategic Defence and Security Review (SDSR)
  2010 **356**.2
  2015 **356**.1
  targets **356**.1–2
straws **368**.11
streaming **409**.36
street gangs **366**.41
stress **351**.2, 6, 9, 14, 19–20, 41, **380**.32, **395**.6–7, 33, **404**.3, 8–9, 16, 32–4, 41, **409**.34, **415**.9, 19–20, 35
  and bullying **380**.14, 17
  and dreams **389**.9–10
  and exams **353**.15–16, 20–1, **403**.32–5
  exam stress **395**.36–7
  and money issues **391**.23
  post-abortion **302**.17–18
  and religion **358**.21
  and self-harm **400**.17, 21, 41
  and sleep **384**.24, **389**.3–4, 20–1, 27, 33, 36–9
  see also anxiety; post-traumatic stress disorder (PTSD); work-related stress
stretch marks **394**.2

strike action **405**.32, 34

strip searches **412**.37–8

stroke **311**.14–15, **348**.5–6, **392**.34–5, 41, **406**.1, 9, 14

student debt **403**.41

student loans **391**.28–9, 41, **403**.22, 30, 41, **405**.22

students
    care home volunteering **311**.30–1
    and poverty **306**.10–11
    and prostitution **318**.19
    see also education; schools; young people

student unions **403**.41
    and censorship **347**.4

study groups **403**.37

study-related visas **359**.1

stuffy nose **394**.7

styrene acrylonitrile (SAN) **385**.29

sub-Saharan Africa
    and AIDS **314**.14
    and HIV **314**.14–16, 18

substance misuse **348**.2, **392**.23–4, **410**.4, 7, 34–9, **415**.6
    see also addiction

suction abortion **302**.2–3, 6

Sudan, refugee statistics **359**.34

sudden infant death syndrome (SIDS) **394**.10

suffering
    of animals **374**.1, 9, 19
    and euthanasia **362**.27

suffrage **360**.15, 30, 36

suffragettes **364**.10–11, 41

sugar **395**.41, **408**.1, 3, 8–9, **410**.41
    addiction **301**.39, **410**.20–2
    levy **392**.21
    tax **408**.36

suicidal behaviour **380**.28

suicidal feelings **415**.4, 9

suicidal thoughts **369**.19, 34, 36, **375**.16

suicide **308**.26, **348**.2, **364**.18, **369**.34, **404**.2, **411**.14, **415**.17, 29–31
    and the Armed Forces **356**.23–4
    and cannabis use **399**.23
    in children and young people **400**.24–8
    and cyberbullying perpetrators **361**.31
    and cyberbullying victims **361**.19, 23
    and depression **400**.12
    facts and statistics **400**.24
    and gambling **349**.4, 6, 30
    ideation **400**.6
    in men and boys **400**.24
    and mental health **400**.27–9
    myths about **400**.23
    preventing **400**.20
    risk factors **400**.19–20, 24
    safety plan **400**.21–2
    and self-harm **400**.10, 14
    and social media **400**.26, 29
    suicidal thoughts **400**.2, 36
    support after **400**.37
    support for **400**.20–2, 36, 39
    threats of **370**.21–2, **400**.20
    warning signs **400**.20, 36
    in women and girls **400**.24

Suicide Act 1961 **362**.1–2, 8, 10, 12, 14, 18, 28

suicide bombers **355**.2, 4, 7, 20–2

suicide tourism **362**.5

Sukkot **358**.24–5

'summer born' children **353**.10

'sunny disposition' **351**.33

superbugs **348**.31, 41

supercentenarians **378**.4

superfoods **350**.23

superheros **386**.2–3

supermarkets **414**.28–31
    and plastic waste **385**.26–7

Supplementary Vote (SV) **360**.25

supplying drugs **373**.22–3

supported housing
    see also social housing

supported internships **403**.18, 19
    see also internships

support groups **351**.9

Sure Start children's centres **392**.21

surface-to-air missiles **355**.4

surgical abortion **367**.2, 15–16

surrogacy **387**.21, 34–7, 41

surveillance **317**.1, 17–18, 21–4, 26–8, 34–5, 37, **372**.8, 31–2, **383**.41
    and browsing history **317**.19–20
    CCTV **317**.23, 25
    closed-circuit television (CCTV) **383**.14–15, 20, 41
    drones **317**.30
    exports to repressive regimes **317**.27–8
    extended legislation **317**.4–8, 20, 27
    facial recognition **383**.14–15, 17–22
    fibre optic **317**.23
    and genetic research **317**.29
    geodata **317**.17, 23
    health risks **317**.31
    history of **317**.15–16
    homeworking **383**.15–16
    human rights **317**.24
    ICRs **317**.6–8
    insecure data **317**.6
    malware **317**.21–2
    motion data **317**.11
    nudging **317**.18
    personal and global issues **317**.9
    personal messages on work computers **317**.14–15
    powers **383**.17
    and proportionality **317**.26
    and public support **317**.27
    safety risks **317**.13, 31, 37
    and security **317**.1–2
    technology company assisted **317**.6
    voice data **317**.13, 34, 37
    wearable technology **317**.15–16
    at work **383**.21
    see also smart speakers

surveillance technologies **401**.7

sustainability **306**.30, **350**.41, **365**.41, **381**.26–8, **385**.41, **396**.34–5, **414**.19, 20, 24, 41
    and cannabis production **399**.29
    and climate emergency **357**.2
    definition **368**.1, 41
    and diet **368**.5, 33–5, 41
    examples **368**.2
    in fashion **368**.2–3, 11, 26–31
    in food industry **368**.3
    and meat-free diets **350**.9–13, 31, 36–7

principles of **368**.1–2
in technology **368**.2
in transportation **368**.3
waste management **368**.4
in the workplace **368**.3–4
see also eco-homes; energy efficiency
sustainable cities **368**.4
sustainable development **368**.1–2, **372**.9
Sustainable Development Goals (SDGs) **306**.35, 38–9, **348**.1,
3, **368**.6–8, 41, **377**.41
and child poverty **306**.38
and ecosystems **306**.38
and HIV **314**.8–10
and leadership **306**.39
Sustainable Development Solutions Network (SDSN) **368**.8
sustainable living **368**.10–11, 13–15
sustainable population **363**.41
sustainable tourism **365**.1, 36–9, 41
Sutton Trust, on school funding **353**.32
Sweden
database **317**.29
drug policies **301**.28
immigration statistics **359**.4
and prostitution **318**.14
and SDGs **314**.10
sweepstakes **349**.14
see also pool betting
Swiss nationals **359**.1
Switzerland
and assisted suicide **362**.8, 28, 34, 36, 39
immigration statistics **359**.4
waste statistics **385**.3
swollen breasts **394**.4
symptoms **351**.1–2, 20–1, 37
synthetic
biology **352**.7–8, 41
food **352**.19
synthetic biology **402**.7
synthetic cannabis **301**.6–7, 31, **373**.20–1, 22, 28
syphilis **309**.9–10, 12, **379**.3, 14–15, 20, 24, 25
Syria
refugees **300**.20, **359**.31
and surveillance **317**.27–8
war and conflict **401**.5, 13–15, 30–1

systemic racism **376**.15–16, 41

T

tagging **366**.39
tai chi **343**.7
Taiwan, and animal research **303**.39
Tajikistan **377**.21–2
Taliban **355**.14–15, 41, **401**.5, 17, 19, 24, 31–2, **412**.39
talking therapies **351**.24, **400**.41, **404**.16, 27, 36–9, 41,
410.41, **415**.2, 21, 23
see also cognitive behavioural therapy; cognitive
behavioural therapy (CBT); counselling
Talmud **358**.31
Tamil Tigers **355**.2
Tanakh **358**.13, 31
Tanzania **377**.22–3
Taoism **358**.4, 10, 31
tap water **350**.36, **368**.35
tar **406**.32, 41
tariffs and abolition **305**.13
taxation **377**.32–3, **391**.21–2
history of **306**.5
and international trade **305**.6, 29
and marriage allowance **354**.3
tax avoidance **381**.36–9
tax evasion **381**.41
tax havens **381**.37–9
TB (tuberculosis), and death **314**.3
teaching, cuts to **353**.32
teaching hospitals **392**.1
teasing
and body image **307**.1–2
and bullying **380**.2
Technical Awards **403**.4
technical qualifications **403**.20–1
technicians **405**.2
technology
and anxiety **351**.14
sustainability in **368**.2
technology addiction **410**.9–11
technology colleges **353**.4
teetotalism **397**.36–7, 41

Vol. numbers appear first (in bold) followed by page numbers; a change in volume is preceded by a semi-colon.

Vol. 305	Globalisation – Good or Bad?	Vol. 368	Sustainable Living	Vol. 392	National Health
Vol. 314	HIV & AIDS	Vol. 369	LGBT+ Issues	Vol. 393	Disability
Vol. 316	Marriage	Vol. 370	Domestic Violence and Abuse	Vol. 394	Pregnancy
Vol. 347	The Censorship Debate	Vol. 371	The Internet and Us	Vol. 395	Teen Self-Care
Vol. 348	World Health	Vol. 372	Our Human Rights	Vol. 396	UK Housing
Vol. 349	Gambling Culture	Vol. 373	Drug Use and Abuse	Vol. 397	Alcohol Issues
Vol. 350	Lifestyle Diets	Vol. 374	Animal Rights	Vol. 398	Homelessness
Vol. 351	The Anxiety Epidemic	Vol. 375	Body Image	Vol. 399	Discussing Cannabis
Vol. 352	Biotech & Bioethics	Vol. 376	Racism	Vol. 400	Suicide & Self-Harm
Vol. 353	Education	Vol. 377	Poverty	Vol. 401	War & Conflict
Vol. 354	Relationships	Vol. 378	Ageing	Vol. 402	Endangered Species
Vol. 355	Terrorism	Vol. 379	Understanding Sexual Health	Vol. 403	Student Options
Vol. 356	British Armed Forces	Vol. 380	About Bullying	Vol. 404	Depression
Vol. 357	The Climate Emergency	Vol. 381	Business	Vol. 405	Employability
Vol. 358	Religion Today	Vol. 382	Active Citizenship	Vol. 406	Smoking
Vol. 359	Migration & Immigration	Vol. 383	The Privacy Debate	Vol. 407	Bereavement
Vol. 360	Government	Vol. 384	Health & Fitness	Vol. 408	Healthy Eating
Vol. 361	Cyberbullying	Vol. 385	Waste & Recycling Issues	Vol. 409	Online Safety
Vol. 362	Euthanasia	Vol. 386	Sexualising Society	Vol. 410	Addiction
Vol. 363	Population Change	Vol. 387	Fertility Issues	Vol. 411	Sport
Vol. 364	The Gender Equality Debate	Vol. 388	Discussing Child Abuse	Vol. 412	Rights of the Child
Vol. 365	Tourism Today	Vol. 389	Sleep	Vol. 413	Energy
Vol. 366	Crime in the UK	Vol. 390	Eating Disorders	Vol. 414	Consumerism
Vol. 367	Discussing Abortion	Vol. 391	Money	Vol. 415	Mental Health

Teletext **365**.11
television *see* TV
temperature
changes **394**.4–5
heatstroke **357**.29
rising **357**.1–2, 8, 28–9
'wet bulb' **357**.28
temporary accommodation **398**.2–3, 11, 23, 25–6, 33
temporary basic income (TBI) **377**.35–6
tenancy agreement **396**.2, 17, 41
tenants
and poverty **306**.7
see also rented accommodation
Ten Commandments **358**.13
tennis **411**.32–3
tension **351**.36
Terasem **358**.4
terminal illness **362**.41
and assisted suicide **362**.18, 20, 30, 32–6
terminally ill people *see* assisted suicide; end-of-life care;
euthanasia; hospices
termination *see* abortion
Terrence Higgins Trust **314**.1, 24
on HIV **314**.1–2, 24, 26, 34
on sexually transmitted infections (STIs) **379**.15
on SRE **314**.24
Territorial Army **356**.41
territorial gain **401**.1–2
terror attacks
7/7 bombings **355**.41
Ankara **355**.4
in the EU **355**.13
Manchester Arena **355**.7
New Zealand **355**.2
Oslo **355**.2
Paris **355**.3, 4, 13
Pittsburgh **355**.17
South Carolina **355**.2
Tunisia **355**.4
Twin Towers **355**.3
terrorism
arrest statistics **355**.8–11, 34
in Britain **355**.7–8
countering **355**.3, 12, 30, 39
definition **355**.1, 3, 41
female **355**.18, 25–7
financing of **355**.12
history of **355**.7
international **355**.3
legislation **355**.10, 12, 37–8
methods of attack **355**.3–4
purpose of **355**.2
Terrorism Act 2000 **355**.10, 12, 37, **366**.36, **372**.8
terrorists and terrorist groups **355**.3, 14–16
African National Congress (ANC) **355**.2
al-Qaeda **355**.3, 4, 5, 41
Al-Shabaab **355**.15–16
anarchists **355**.6
Boko Haram **355**.15–16
ethno-nationalists **355**.6
Irish Republican Army (IRA) **355**.2, 4, 7
Islamic State (IS) **355**.3, 4, 5, 14–15
jihadists **355**.5–6
left-wing extremists **355**.6
motivation **355**.6
Provisional IRA **355**.3
radical Muslims **355**.2
right-wing extremists **355**.6, 17
separatists **355**.6
single-issue extremists **355**.6
Taliban **355**.14–15
Tamil Tigers **355**.2
TE-SAT categorisation **355**.6
white supremacists **355**.2
test and trace programme **383**.22–3
testicles **387**.2
testicular cancer **395**.17
testosterone **309**.8, **378**.8, **395**.27, **397**.2, **411**.22–3
test tube babies *see* IVF
tetrahydrocannabinol (THC) **373**.20
textile industry, child labour **412**.19
THC (tetrahydrocannabinol) **399**.2, 5, 13, 14–15, 17, 19, 20,
27, 30, 33, 41
theft **366**.1–2, 3
theocratic states **358**.3–4
therapeutic touch **343**.7, 41
therapy
art **343**.6
group **343**.7
music **343**.7
types of **343**.2–17
see also therapies by name
third trimester **394**.2
Third World *see* developing countries
Thirty Years' War (1618-1648) **401**.2
Thomas Cook **365**.9–10
threats **388**.8
throwaway society **385**.41, **414**.41
Thunberg, Greta **357**.1–2, 31–2, **372**.31, 37, **382**.17
tidal power **413**.2
tigers, captive **374**.36–7
Tigray People's Liberation Front (TPLF) **401**.19
TikTok **371**.10, **375**.23, **409**.2–4, 37
Timberlake, Justin **386**.9
Time for Change Edinburgh **398**.24
time management **395**.33–4
tiny home living **368**.14, **396**.20–1, 41
Tisha B'Av **358**.24
tissue engineering **352**.18
T Levels **403**.14–15
TNCs *see* transnational corporations
tobacco **373**.16, **399**.9, 15, **406**.8, 41
advertising **392**.23
costs of **406**.3
industry **406**.1, 3
taxation **406**.35–6
see also cigarettes; smoking
tofu **408**.12
To Kill a Mockingbird **308**.9
tokophobia **394**.34
Tokyo 2020 Olympic Games **411**.3–4, 10, 29
tooth jewellery **395**.25
Torah **358**.25
torture **372**.4, 6, 33–4, 41
Amnesty International campaign against **300**.17–18, 21
convention against **300**.2, 17, 21
countries using **300**.18, 21
total fertility rate (TFR) **363**.3, 10–11, **387**.11–13

see also fertility rates
tourism
  and animal rights **303**.27
  and animal welfare **303**.29
  and Brexit **365**.7
  and carbon footprint **365**.27
  categories of **365**.1
  day trips **365**.11
  domestic **365**.1, 4
  ecotourism **365**.1, 28–9
  and the environment **365**.27–37
  global **365**.6
  and global economy **365**.6
  history of **365**.7, 10
  impact of **365**.8
  impact on endangered species **402**.27–8
  inbound **365**.1, 3, 6–7
  international **365**.1
  outbound **365**.1, 12–13
  overtourism **365**.8, 17–18
  popular destinations **365**.5, 12–13
  responsible **365**.18–39
  sex tourism **318**.10
  sustainable **365**.1, 36–9, 41
  trends **365**.2–5, 11–12
  see also holidays; travel
tourists
  behaviour of **365**.14–16, 35
  experiences of **365**.23
toxic masculinity **364**.34, 38–9, 41, **386**.3
toxins **348**.19
toxoplasmosis **348**.19, **394**.9
toys, and gender equality **364**.35–7
TPP (Trans-Pacific Partnership) **305**.13
tracheostomy **393**.29
trade and inequality **306**.27, 34
  see also international trade
trademarks **381**.2
Trade Union Act 2016 **405**.34
trade unions
  and international trade **305**.13
  and prostitution **318**.24–5
Trading Standards **414**.7
traditional medicine **343**.2

trafficking **300**.3–5, 7–8, **388**.6, 18
  human **359**.38, **372**.14–22
  see also child trafficking; forced labour; sex trafficking; slavery
trafficking of wildlife see wildlife trade
traineeships **403**.1, 18–19
training, military **356**.11, 14
trains see railways
tranquillisers **301**.12, **351**.24, **373**.5
Transatlantic Trade and Investment Partnership (TTIP) **305**.10–13
transcranial magnetic stimulation (TMS) **404**.16
trans-fats **408**.1–2
transformational photographs **375**.17
transgender athletes **411**.9–10, 22–5
transgender people **369**.1–2, 6–7, 9, 12, 34
  and bullying **380**.6
  and HIV **314**.16
  and the human papillomavirus (HPV) vaccination **379**.6
  and prostitution **318**.4–5
  voting rights **360**.36
  see also gender dysphoria; LGBTQIA+ community; non-binary people
transitioning **369**.2, 7–8, 37
Trans-Pacific Partnership (TPP) **305**.13
transphobia **347**.4, **369**.30–1, 41, **380**.6
transport **311**.26
  costs **305**.27
  electrification of **357**.36
  and health **392**.22
  net zero targets **357**.37
  sustainability in **368**.3
  see also air travel; cars and driving; public transport; railways
transport poverty **306**.13
transsexual people **369**.2, 38
  and private life **317**.3
  see also gender dysphoria
trauma **373**.3, 32, **377**.2
  and anxiety **351**.2
  and bullying **380**.17
  see also post traumatic stress disorder (PTSD)
travel
  business **365**.1, 3–4

Vol. numbers appear first (in bold) followed by page numbers; a change in volume is preceded by a semi-colon.

Vol. 305	Globalisation – Good or Bad?
Vol. 314	HIV & AIDS
Vol. 316	Marriage
Vol. 347	The Censorship Debate
Vol. 348	World Health
Vol. 349	Gambling Culture
Vol. 350	Lifestyle Diets
Vol. 351	The Anxiety Epidemic
Vol. 352	Biotech & Bioethics
Vol. 353	Education
Vol. 354	Relationships
Vol. 355	Terrorism
Vol. 356	British Armed Forces
Vol. 357	The Climate Emergency
Vol. 358	Religion Today
Vol. 359	Migration & Immigration
Vol. 360	Government
Vol. 361	Cyberbullying
Vol. 362	Euthanasia
Vol. 363	Population Change
Vol. 364	The Gender Equality Debate
Vol. 365	Tourism Today
Vol. 366	Crime in the UK
Vol. 367	Discussing Abortion

Vol. 368	Sustainable Living
Vol. 369	LGBT+ Issues
Vol. 370	Domestic Violence and Abuse
Vol. 371	The Internet and Us
Vol. 372	Our Human Rights
Vol. 373	Drug Use and Abuse
Vol. 374	Animal Rights
Vol. 375	Body Image
Vol. 376	Racism
Vol. 377	Poverty
Vol. 378	Ageing
Vol. 379	Understanding Sexual Health
Vol. 380	About Bullying
Vol. 381	Business
Vol. 382	Active Citizenship
Vol. 383	The Privacy Debate
Vol. 384	Health & Fitness
Vol. 385	Waste & Recycling Issues
Vol. 386	Sexualising Society
Vol. 387	Fertility Issues
Vol. 388	Discussing Child Abuse
Vol. 389	Sleep
Vol. 390	Eating Disorders
Vol. 391	Money

Vol. 392	National Health
Vol. 393	Disability
Vol. 394	Pregnancy
Vol. 395	Teen Self-Care
Vol. 396	UK Housing
Vol. 397	Alcohol Issues
Vol. 398	Homelessness
Vol. 399	Discussing Cannabis
Vol. 400	Suicide & Self-Harm
Vol. 401	War & Conflict
Vol. 402	Endangered Species
Vol. 403	Student Options
Vol. 404	Depression
Vol. 405	Employability
Vol. 406	Smoking
Vol. 407	Bereavement
Vol. 408	Healthy Eating
Vol. 409	Online Safety
Vol. 410	Addiction
Vol. 411	Sport
Vol. 412	Rights of the Child
Vol. 413	Energy
Vol. 414	Consumerism
Vol. 415	Mental Health

leisure **365**.1, 3–4
responsible **365**.24
trends **365**.2–5, 11–12
visiting friends and relatives (VFR) **365**.1, 3–4
see also air travel; tourism; transport
Traveller communities **308**.5–7, **376**.23–4, 41, **380**.4–5
treason **355**.41, **382**.3
trepanation **343**.25–6
trial, right to **372**.4
Triassic mass extinction **402**.1–2
trichomoniasis **309**.12, **379**.24, 25
trickery **361**.6
tricyclic antidepressants (TCAs) **404**.3
triggers **351**.18–20, 30, 37
for self-harm **400**.1
Trinidad & Tobago, CO_2 emissions **357**.4
Trinity Sunday **358**.22
trolling **361**.5, 6, 12–13, 20–1, 36–7, 41, **380**.41, **409**.41
see also cyberbullying; cyber-bullying
trophy hunting **374**.28–9, 41
Trump, Donald **367**.33–4, **401**.4, 5
on climate change **357**.6, 32
and immigration **359**.33
support of evangelical Christians **358**.5
Trussell Trust **306**.20
on food banks **377**.4–6, 18–19
trust **354**.28, **379**.28
trust schools **353**.2
tuberculosis **348**.13, 41, **392**.1
Tu B'Shevat **358**.24
tuition fees **403**.41
Turin, as 'vegan city' **350**.7
Turkey
CO_2 emissions **357**.3
immigration statistics **359**.3
refugee statistics **359**.34
turnover **381**.41
turtles **357**.19
TV
and divorce **316**.35
normalising alcohol **397**.35
and racial stereotyping **308**.7
streaming **347**.28–9, **371**.11
and surveillance **317**.13, 23, 25, 34–5
watching statistics **409**.36–7
see also film censorship; video classification
Twin Towers *see* 9/11
Twitch **371**.10, **409**.33–4
Twitter **371**.26, **409**.2–3
as anti-racist **308**.37
cyberbullying on **361**.8
and hate crime **308**.8
and racial slurs **308**.14
and rape **318**.36
reporting/dealing with abuse on **361**.32
see also see also cyberbullying; social networking
two-House system **360**.5
two-signature rule, abortions **302**.5, 25, 33
typhoons **357**.13

U

U3A (University of the Third Age) **311**.29
Uber, on popular destinations **365**.6
UCAS (Universities and Colleges Admissions Service) **403**.41
A-level points **403**.10
personal statement **403**.26–8
Scottish Highers points **403**.12
vocational qualifications points **403**.14
Uganda **360**.33, **377**.21
censorship in **347**.11
and HIV **314**.33
refugee statistics **359**.34
UK population
ageing **363**.4–5, 6, 12
birth rates **363**.2–3, 7–11, 36
death rates **363**.3, 13–17
emigration **363**.2, 3–4
future growth **363**.6
growth **363**.1–2
immigration **363**.2, 3–4
life expectancy **363**.5, 13–18
natural change rates **363**.2–3
net migration **363**.3–4, 6
overview **363**.1
Ukraine
and dark tourism **365**.22
family separation **412**.14–15
immigration statistics **359**.3
war and conflict **401**.8, 15–16, 18
ultra-low emission zone (ULEZ) **392**.22
ultra-processed foods **350**.22, **408**.16–17, 19–20, 41
UN *see* United Nations
Uncaged **374**.16
uncodified constitution **360**.4
unconditional acceptance **395**.2
unconscious bias **364**.3, **376**.17
underage drinking **397**.26–34
undergraduates *see* students
undertaker **407**.41
undescended testis **387**.20
unemployment **377**.2, 3, 8, **405**.18–25
and homelessness **398**.14
and overpopulation **363**.23
poverty **306**.7
state benefits **306**.9
see also benefits system
UNESCO world heritage sites **365**.8
Unicef
on air pollution **348**.10
on child poverty **377**.29
on immunisation **348**.30
on inequality in education **353**.30
on refugee resettlement **359**.34
uniform (school)
cost of **353**.35
and freedom of expression **353**.34
United Arab Emirates (UAE)
censorship in **347**.26
CO_2 emissions **357**.4
immigration statistics **359**.3
waste statistics **385**.3
United Kingdom (UK)
attitudes to immigration **359**.15–17, 22–5
immigration from European Union (EU) **359**.6–7

immigration statistics **359**.3–4, 5
migration from **359**.5, 8–10
refugee statistics **359**.30–1, 35–6
United Nations (UN) **306**.38, **372**.2, 9, **401**.4, 6, 26
   and abortion **302**.24–5
   CEDAW **300**.2, 23
   Convention on the Rights of the Child **300**.2, 27–8, 38, **306**.22
   on declining population **363**.26
   Emissions Gap Report **357**.6
   Global Goals **306**.30
   and globalisation **305**.30
   High Commissioner for Refugees (UNHCR) **359**.30, 41
   humanitarian relief **306**.38
   on immigration population statistics worldwide **359**.3–5
   and international trade **305**.14
   investigating poverty **377**.18–19
   on population growth **363**.19–21, 30, 34, 36
   UDHR **300**.1, 26–7, **317**.2
   UNAIDS **314**.3, 8–10, 14
   see also peacekeeping
United Nations Convention on the Rights of the Child (UNCRC) **372**.3, 11–13, 41, **412**.1–3, 7, 12, 41
United Nations Development Programme (UNDP) **382**.12
United Nations Millennium Development Goals, and gender equality **364**.5–6
United States of America (USA) **377**.24–7
   and abortion **302**.14–15, 32
   and animal research **303**.39
   and aspirin **311**.14–15
   and assisted dying **362**.9
   attitudes to Armed Forces **356**.3–4
   Bill of Rights **372**.5
   blocking refugees **359**.33
   CO_2 emissions **357**.3
   and democracy **360**.33
   and divorce **316**.24
   employment rights **405**.33
   and globalisation **305**.24–5
   government **360**.37–9
   healthcare **392**.12–13
   and HPV **309**.22
   immigration statistics **359**.3–4
   and international trade **305**.10–14, 26

legalisation of medical marijuana **301**.21, 28
National Day of Prayer **358**.28
and pregnancy **309**.22
prison inmate population for drug offences **301**.30
and privacy **317**.21
privacy laws **383**.2–3, 7
and racial discrimination **308**.30
religion in **358**.20–1
right to bear arms **372**.5
and SRE **309**.22
and surveillance **317**.21–2
surveillance laws **383**.17
and UK 'special relationship' **317**.27
and violence **308**.37–8
visits to UK **365**.3, 6–7
waste statistics **385**.4
see also North America
units of alcohol **397**.2, 41
Universal Credit (UC) **377**.7, 19, 41, **393**.25, **398**.2, 9, 21, **403**.21
   see also benefits system
Universal Declaration of Human Rights (UDHR) **300**.1, 26–7, **317**.2, **372**.1, 9, 41, **398**.5
   history of **372**.2
universality **372**.1
Universal Periodic Review **372**.3
universities
   academic freedom **347**.5
   admissions
     See also tuition fees
   application **403**.26–8
   choosing **403**.24–5, 29
   costs of **403**.22, 29
   and employability **405**.1
   free speech pledge **347**.5
   Free Speech University Rankings 2018 **347**.4
   and A-level results **353**.18
   lifestyle **403**.30
   online harassment **361**.25–6
   and racism **376**.24–5
   university technical colleges (UTCs) **353**.5
   vending machines **314**.39
   see also further education; graduates; higher education; students

---

Vol. numbers appear first (in bold) followed by page numbers; a change in volume is preceded by a semi-colon.

Vol. 305	Globalisation – Good or Bad?	Vol. 368	Sustainable Living	Vol. 392	National Health
Vol. 314	HIV & AIDS	Vol. 369	LGBT+ Issues	Vol. 393	Disability
Vol. 316	Marriage	Vol. 370	Domestic Violence and Abuse	Vol. 394	Pregnancy
Vol. 347	The Censorship Debate	Vol. 371	The Internet and Us	Vol. 395	Teen Self-Care
Vol. 348	World Health	Vol. 372	Our Human Rights	Vol. 396	UK Housing
Vol. 349	Gambling Culture	Vol. 373	Drug Use and Abuse	Vol. 397	Alcohol Issues
Vol. 350	Lifestyle Diets	Vol. 374	Animal Rights	Vol. 398	Homelessness
Vol. 351	The Anxiety Epidemic	Vol. 375	Body Image	Vol. 399	Discussing Cannabis
Vol. 352	Biotech & Bioethics	Vol. 376	Racism	Vol. 400	Suicide & Self-Harm
Vol. 353	Education	Vol. 377	Poverty	Vol. 401	War & Conflict
Vol. 354	Relationships	Vol. 378	Ageing	Vol. 402	Endangered Species
Vol. 355	Terrorism	Vol. 379	Understanding Sexual Health	Vol. 403	Student Options
Vol. 356	British Armed Forces	Vol. 380	About Bullying	Vol. 404	Depression
Vol. 357	The Climate Emergency	Vol. 381	Business	Vol. 405	Employability
Vol. 358	Religion Today	Vol. 382	Active Citizenship	Vol. 406	Smoking
Vol. 359	Migration & Immigration	Vol. 383	The Privacy Debate	Vol. 407	Bereavement
Vol. 360	Government	Vol. 384	Health & Fitness	Vol. 408	Healthy Eating
Vol. 361	Cyberbullying	Vol. 385	Waste & Recycling Issues	Vol. 409	Online Safety
Vol. 362	Euthanasia	Vol. 386	Sexualising Society	Vol. 410	Addiction
Vol. 363	Population Change	Vol. 387	Fertility Issues	Vol. 411	Sport
Vol. 364	The Gender Equality Debate	Vol. 388	Discussing Child Abuse	Vol. 412	Rights of the Child
Vol. 365	Tourism Today	Vol. 389	Sleep	Vol. 413	Energy
Vol. 366	Crime in the UK	Vol. 390	Eating Disorders	Vol. 414	Consumerism
Vol. 367	Discussing Abortion	Vol. 391	Money	Vol. 415	Mental Health

university degrees **403**.1, 18, 21, 22–4
University of the Third Age (U3A) **311**.29
unlicensed family entertainment centres (UFECs) **349**.1
unprotected sex **379**.4
unsafe abortion **367**.15–17, 26–7
unsaturated fats **408**.1
upcycling **385**.30
urban areas **311**.25, 27
   and community **311**.27
   costs **311**.27
   and driving **311**.27
   housing **311**.25–7
   and public transport **311**.25, 27
   and social isolation **311**.32
   and walking **311**.25
urbanisation **363**.26
urination **394**.6, 31
urine tests **394**.17
Uruguay and abortion **302**.15
   drug policies **301**.27
user-created content **371**.4
USPs (unique selling points) **381**.1
uterine perforation **367**.16
utility costs **391**.17
Uzbekistan **300**.18, **377**.23

V

vaccinations **348**.2, 29–30, 36–7, **352**.1–2, 30, **392**.2, 22, 41, **395**.10–15
   flu vaccine **395**.13
   human papillomavirus (HPV) vaccine **395**.10, 15–16
   measles, mumps and rubella (MMR) vaccine **395**.10, 11, 13
   MenACWY vaccine **395**.10
   side effects **395**.12
   uptake data **395**.8
vacuum aspiration abortion **302**.2–3, 6
vaginal rings **309**.7, **387**.17–18
Valentine's Day **414**.22
vaping **373**.16–19, **406**.8, 9, 16–24, 41
   see also e-cigarettes
vaping cannabis **399**.2
varenicline **406**.18, 33
vasectomies **309**.7
Vatican **358**.4, 5, **360**.36
Vedas **358**.31
veganism **350**.1, 3, 6–7, 21, 32, 38, 41, **368**.5, 15, **400**.18, **408**.12
   and animal welfare **350**.8–9
   as a belief **358**.16–17
   benefits of **350**.2
   costs of **350**.4–5, 15–16
   and disordered eating **350**.18–20
   effects of **350**.14–16
   and the environment **350**.9–13
   growing popularity of **350**.35
   and pollution **350**.9
   and restaurants **350**.7
   see also vegetarianism
Vegan Society **350**.6
Veganuary **350**.6, 15, 41
'Vegan Wool' **350**.7
vegetables **408**.1–2, 9
   see also fruit and vegetables
vegetarianism **350**.3, 21, 32, 35, 38, 41, **400**.18, **408**.12
   and animal welfare **350**.8–359
   benefits of **350**.2
   costs of **350**.4–5
   and disordered eating **350**.18–20
   effects of **350**.16–17
   and the environment **350**.10–11
   and obesity **350**.16–17
   and restaurants **350**.7
   types of **350**.1
vegetative state **362**.5
   see also persistent vegetative state (PVS)
ventilation **406**.15
verbal abuse **361**.41, **393**.16–17
verbal bullying **380**.1
veteran homelessness **398**.34–5
veterans
   Commonwealth **356**.28
   definition **356**.41
   female **356**.34–6
   perception of **356**.32
   support for **356**.28, 32
   transition to civilian life **356**.30–9
   see also ex-service personnel
Veterans Aid **356**.32–3
Veterans Day **356**.3
victim blaming **371**.14, **386**.36
victimisation **393**.16–17, 21
victimization **361**.10, **376**.4
victims
   of knife crime **366**.18
   reporting crime **366**.7
Victorians, and pets **374**.12
video calling **371**.1–2
video classification **347**.24, 40
video gaming **410**.14–17
   and gambling **349**.24
   see also online gambling
Vienna World Conference on Human Rights 1993 **372**.1
Vietnam, and MDGs **306**.29–30
Vietnam War **401**.14
villagization **377**.30–1
violations of human rights **412**.13–14, 28–39
violence **308**.34, **318**.2, 4–6, 20–1, **370**.9–10, 12, **386**.1, 3, 6, 19–20, **392**.28, **401**.11–12, **415**.33
   and apps **308**.37–8
   in bullying **361**.11
   and bullying **380**.17, 38
   and censorship **347**.17
   and decriminalisation of sex trade **318**.6–7, 9
   and eviction **318**.4
   gender-based **364**.7
   and lack of choice **318**.37
   and overpopulation **363**.23
   and protest **308**.26
   reducing **348**.3
   and terrorism **355**.1–2, 12, 41
   and vulnerability **318**.5–6
   see also abuse; domestic violence; hate speech; rape
violence against women and girls (VAWG) **370**.12–13
violent offences **366**.1, 3, 6–9
virginity **386**.2, 9
Virgin Mary **358**.23

virtual consultations **392**.7

virtual currencies *see* digital currencies

virtual reality (VR) **352**.34, **409**.20, 22–3

    see also metaverse

virtual volunteering **382**.34

virtue signalling **361**.19

visas **359**.41

    extension of stay **359**.2

    family-related **359**.1

    study-related **359**.1

    upward trend in **359**.1

    work-related **359**.1

visiting friends and relatives (VFR) **365**.1, 3–4

visualisation **343.7**

vitamin A **394**.11

vitamin B **351**.38

vitamin B12 **350**.38–9, **408**.13, 15

vitamin C **351**.39, **375**.15, **408**.14, 17

vitamin D **350**.38, **394**.8–9, 13, **408**.9, 17

vitamin E **373**.16–17, **406**.16

vitamins **350**.38–9, **352**.2, **387**.23, 29

vivisection **374**.14–25, 41

    see also animal research and experiments

vocational

    learning **353**.41

    qualifications **353**.4

    subjects **353**.19

vocational qualifications **403**.4, 6, 8–9, 14

voice assistants *see* smart speakers

voluntary aided schools **353**.2

voluntary discharge **356**.10

voluntary euthanasia **362**.1, 16, 19, 41

    see also assisted suicide

Voluntary National Review (VNR) **368**.6–7

voluntary returns **359**.2

'volunteer effect' **382**.22

volunteering **311**.17, 29, **405**.3

    benefits of **382**.26–7, 38–9

    and communication **311**.30–1

    demographics **382**.13–14, 25

    as experience **382**.39

    how to start **382**.35

    and intergenerational communities **311**.30, 31

    virtual **382**.34

    and wellbeing **306**.18

    worldwide **382**.26

    young people **382**.14, 18–22

voluntourism **365**.1, 39, 41

vomiting **394**.6

Voss, Sarah **386**.26

voting **300**.30–1, **354**.1, **372**.7–8

    abstaining **360**.19

    age **360**.21–3

    compulsory **360**.16–17

    gender imbalance in **360**.36

    history of **360**.14–15

    importance of **382**.37

    mandatory voter identification **360**.18

    manipulation of **360**.29

    right to **382**.2

    right to vote **360**.20

    systems **360**.24–5

    and women **360**.15, 30, 36

    and young people **382**.22–4

VPNs (virtual private networks) **383**.6

Vulnerable Person Resettlement Scheme (VPRS) **359**.2

vulnerable pupils **353**.24–7

W

wages **305**.16

    and health **317**.15–16

    and living wages **305**.17

    London Living Wage **306**.7

    see also earnings; income; salaries

Wales

    and abortion **302**.1, 10

    and animal welfare **303**.26

    devolved government **360**.2, 3, 9

    and divorce **316**.28

    identity **382**.7

    and marriage **316**.6, 10

    natural change in population **363**.3

    population growth **363**.2

walking **311**.25

    see also exercise and activity

Walk to School Week **384**.35

Vol. numbers appear first (in bold) followed by page numbers; a change in volume is preceded by a semi-colon.

Vol. 305	Globalisation – Good or Bad?	Vol. 368	Sustainable Living	Vol. 392	National Health
Vol. 314	HIV & AIDS	Vol. 369	LGBT+ Issues	Vol. 393	Disability
Vol. 316	Marriage	Vol. 370	Domestic Violence and Abuse	Vol. 394	Pregnancy
Vol. 347	The Censorship Debate	Vol. 371	The Internet and Us	Vol. 395	Teen Self-Care
Vol. 348	World Health	Vol. 372	Our Human Rights	Vol. 396	UK Housing
Vol. 349	Gambling Culture	Vol. 373	Drug Use and Abuse	Vol. 397	Alcohol Issues
Vol. 350	Lifestyle Diets	Vol. 374	Animal Rights	Vol. 398	Homelessness
Vol. 351	The Anxiety Epidemic	Vol. 375	Body Image	Vol. 399	Discussing Cannabis
Vol. 352	Biotech & Bioethics	Vol. 376	Racism	Vol. 400	Suicide & Self-Harm
Vol. 353	Education	Vol. 377	Poverty	Vol. 401	War & Conflict
Vol. 354	Relationships	Vol. 378	Ageing	Vol. 402	Endangered Species
Vol. 355	Terrorism	Vol. 379	Understanding Sexual Health	Vol. 403	Student Options
Vol. 356	British Armed Forces	Vol. 380	About Bullying	Vol. 404	Depression
Vol. 357	The Climate Emergency	Vol. 381	Business	Vol. 405	Employability
Vol. 358	Religion Today	Vol. 382	Active Citizenship	Vol. 406	Smoking
Vol. 359	Migration & Immigration	Vol. 383	The Privacy Debate	Vol. 407	Bereavement
Vol. 360	Government	Vol. 384	Health & Fitness	Vol. 408	Healthy Eating
Vol. 361	Cyberbullying	Vol. 385	Waste & Recycling Issues	Vol. 409	Online Safety
Vol. 362	Euthanasia	Vol. 386	Sexualising Society	Vol. 410	Addiction
Vol. 363	Population Change	Vol. 387	Fertility Issues	Vol. 411	Sport
Vol. 364	The Gender Equality Debate	Vol. 388	Discussing Child Abuse	Vol. 412	Rights of the Child
Vol. 365	Tourism Today	Vol. 389	Sleep	Vol. 413	Energy
Vol. 366	Crime in the UK	Vol. 390	Eating Disorders	Vol. 414	Consumerism
Vol. 367	Discussing Abortion	Vol. 391	Money	Vol. 415	Mental Health

war and conflict
  causes of **401**.1–3
  consequences of **401**.25–39
  definitions of war **401**.1
  girls in **412**.14
  and immunisation **348**.29
  impact of religion **358**.5
  impact on mental health **356**.11, 21–6
  injuries **356**.27
  preventing **401**.9
  reducing **348**.3
  war guilt **356**.3–4
  war zones **412**.3
  see also armed forces; Armed Forces; soldiers; weapons
war crimes **401**.33–6, 38–9, 41
war on drugs **301**.23–4, 28–9, **373**.29–30
war on terror **355**.39, **401**.3, 4, 6, 29–31
  see also counter-terrorism
Warsaw, and diversity **308**.10–11
warts
  genital **309**.11
  vaccination **309**.25
war veterans see ex-service personnel; veterans
Warwick University, 'rape chat' group case **361**.26
war zones
  and animal welfare **303**.15
  and civilian suffering **300**.20, 21
waste **368**.11, **413**.37
  'Blue Planet' effect **368**.19, 23
  by country **385**.2–4
  decomposition of **385**.12–13
  electronic waste **368**.38–9
  as energy source **413**.2, 19, 38–9
  food waste **368**.32, 36
  household **385**.1
  incinerators **385**.16–17
  in landfills **385**.12–15
  management **368**.4
  net zero targets **357**.37
  salvaging from dumps **306**.32
  trading **385**.1, 16–17, 22–3
  zero waste **368**.3, 18–19
  see also household waste; see also household waste
water
  access to **348**.3
  dehydration **408**.5
  hydration **408**.5–7
  tap **350**.36
water birth **394**.28
watershed **347**.28, 40
watershed restrictions **386**.41
water supplies, and drinking water access **306**.26
wealth **306**.3, 33–4
  and ageing **378**.21
  and banks **306**.34
  and food poverty **306**.21
  and income **306**.2
  inequality **377**.32–3
  see also rich-poor gap
weapons **366**.1, 3, 6, **401**.16
  chemical **401**.41
  contracts **401**.10–11
  nuclear **401**.8, 18, 20, 41
  see also knife crime

weather
  extreme **357**.1, 13
  hurricanes **357**.13–15
  and mental health **415**.33–4
  see also temperature
web piracy **371**.27
websites see internet
Webster, George **393**.32
weddings **354**.3
  see also marriage
weed **399**.1
  see also cannabis
weight
  anxiety about **384**.38
  healthy range **384**.4
  in pregnancy **394**.17
  see also body mass index (BMI); obesity; overweight
weight-bearing exercise **384**.22
Weight Watchers **375**.17
welfare benefits see benefits system
Welfare of Animals (Northern Ireland) Act 2011 **374**.5
Welfare Reform Act 2012 **377**.41
welfare support see state benefits
well-being, impact of bullying **380**.11, 14
wellbeing **306**.1, 14, 18, **356**.41
  5 steps to **415**.38
  definition **415**.35
  and inequality **306**.14–15
  and self-care **395**.6–7
  and social media **409**.5–8, 35–7
  see also health and wellbeing; mental health
Wellbeing of Future Generations Act 2015 **392**.23
Wellcome Sanger Institute **374**.19
wellness tourism **365**.1
Wellspring trust **353**.26–7
Werner's syndrome **311**.18
'wet bulb temperature' **357**.28
wet dreams **395**.27
whales, and slaughter **303**.14
WhatsApp **361**.33, **371**.10, 38, **409**.2
What's Underneath Project, The **307**.18
whistleblowers **347**.1
whiteheads **395**.22
White Papers **360**.6
white privilege **376**.18
white rhinoceros **402**.20
white supremacists **355**.2, 17
Whit Monday **358**.22
wholegrain bread **408**.12–13
whole grains **350**.36
Wicca **358**.31
widowed people **316**.4
widows/widowers **378**.41
WikiLeaks, on surveillance **317**.21
wild animals
  circuses **374**.26
  conservation **374**.28–9
  safari parks **374**.35
  trophy hunting **374**.28–9
  zoos **374**.33–5
Wild Animals in Circuses (Prohibition) Bill **303**.10, 26–7
Wild Animals in Circuses Bill **374**.41
wildfires **402**.2
wildflower lawns **357**.33

wildlife, protecting **357**.33–5
wildlife sanctuary **374**.35
wildlife trade **402**.14–17, 32–3, 41
William of Orange **360**.14
wills
    and estate planning **407**.10–11, 41
    and marriage **354**.3
wind power **413**.2, 5–6, 9, 31, 33, 37, 41
Windrush **359**.14, 22, 41, **376**.18–19, **382**.1, 4
wine, synthetic **352**.20
Winograd, N. **374**.39
winter blues *see* seasonal affective disorder (SAD)
winter fuel payment **378**.41
withdrawal **373**.1, 3, 41, **397**.11, **406**.9, 26–7, 32, 41
withdrawing food and fluids **362**.2
    see also clinically assisted nutrition and hydration (CANH)
withdrawing life-sustaining treatment **362**.1
wokefishing **409**.29
women **306**.5
    in Africa **364**.1
    and AIDS **314**.14
    in the Armed Forces **356**.1, 7, 12–16
    bill of rights for **372**.1, 3
    birth rates **358**.3
    and body image **307**.4, 13, 20, 22–3, 27–8
    body image issues **375**.4–5, 10, 28–9
    in business **381**.33–5
    care for older parents **311**.13
    CEDAW **300**.2, 23
    and commercial sexual exploitation **318**.29
    and death **311**.34
    with disabilities **393**.2
    discrimination against **300**.22–3
    discrimination of **372**.33
    and domestic violence **318**.28
    equality for **372**.9–10
    equality in sport **364**.20–1
    equal pay **411**.26–7
    equal rights at work **364**.2, 30–1
    exercise **384**.15–17, 26–9, 33
    female genital mutilation (FGM) **358**.35–6, 41, **372**.23–6
    female sex chromosome **369**.1
    in film and theatre **364**.2
    football **411**.1–2, 21, 26–8, 31
    for forced labour **300**.7
    freedom to travel **372**.30
    and gaming **364**.25–6
    gender pay gap **364**.9–10, 15–16
    gender stereotyping **364**.28–9
    and global poverty **306**.32, 38
    and HIV **314**.14
    and homelessness **398**.1, 4, 5, 22–4
    human rights violations **412**.13–14
    impacts of war **401**.32–3
    International Women's Day **364**.1, 8, 22
    landmark dates for **364**.11
    life expectancy **311**.4, **378**.1–3, 8, 36
    and mental health **351**.17–18, 22–3
    netball **411**.19–20
    obesity **384**.6–8
    in Parliament **360**.34–5
    and pensions **311**.8
    as 'persons in their own right' **364**.12
    'pink tax' **364**.24, 41
    prejudice against **364**.3
    and property **364**.12
    and prostitution **300**.3, 8, **318**.2, 5–9, 15, 26
    and rape **318**.36
    rights of **364**.10–12
    rugby union **411**.24–5
    and sex trafficking **318**.5
    and sexual abuse **300**.24
    and sexual assault **309**.27–8
    sexualisation of **411**.29–31
    in sport **411**.21–2, 26–7, 29–31
    state pension **378**.15–17
    suffrage **360**.15, 30, 36, **364**.10–11, 41
    veterans **356**.34–6
    Yazidi women **300**.23–4
    see also equality; feminism; girls; girls and young women; mothers; Muslim women; pregnancy
Women's Aid **370**.3, 14
Women's Equality Party **360**.31
work
    and child poverty **306**.11
    and income **306**.21
    low-skilled jobs **359**.19
    migrant workers **359**.18–19

Vol. numbers appear first (in bold) followed by page numbers; a change in volume is preceded by a semi-colon.

Vol. 305	Globalisation – Good or Bad?
Vol. 314	HIV & AIDS
Vol. 316	Marriage
Vol. 347	The Censorship Debate
Vol. 348	World Health
Vol. 349	Gambling Culture
Vol. 350	Lifestyle Diets
Vol. 351	The Anxiety Epidemic
Vol. 352	Biotech & Bioethics
Vol. 353	Education
Vol. 354	Relationships
Vol. 355	Terrorism
Vol. 356	British Armed Forces
Vol. 357	The Climate Emergency
Vol. 358	Religion Today
Vol. 359	Migration & Immigration
Vol. 360	Government
Vol. 361	Cyberbullying
Vol. 362	Euthanasia
Vol. 363	Population Change
Vol. 364	The Gender Equality Debate
Vol. 365	Tourism Today
Vol. 366	Crime in the UK
Vol. 367	Discussing Abortion
Vol. 368	Sustainable Living
Vol. 369	LGBT+ Issues
Vol. 370	Domestic Violence and Abuse
Vol. 371	The Internet and Us
Vol. 372	Our Human Rights
Vol. 373	Drug Use and Abuse
Vol. 374	Animal Rights
Vol. 375	Body Image
Vol. 376	Racism
Vol. 377	Poverty
Vol. 378	Ageing
Vol. 379	Understanding Sexual Health
Vol. 380	About Bullying
Vol. 381	Business
Vol. 382	Active Citizenship
Vol. 383	The Privacy Debate
Vol. 384	Health & Fitness
Vol. 385	Waste & Recycling Issues
Vol. 386	Sexualising Society
Vol. 387	Fertility Issues
Vol. 388	Discussing Child Abuse
Vol. 389	Sleep
Vol. 390	Eating Disorders
Vol. 391	Money
Vol. 392	National Health
Vol. 393	Disability
Vol. 394	Pregnancy
Vol. 395	Teen Self-Care
Vol. 396	UK Housing
Vol. 397	Alcohol Issues
Vol. 398	Homelessness
Vol. 399	Discussing Cannabis
Vol. 400	Suicide & Self-Harm
Vol. 401	War & Conflict
Vol. 402	Endangered Species
Vol. 403	Student Options
Vol. 404	Depression
Vol. 405	Employability
Vol. 406	Smoking
Vol. 407	Bereavement
Vol. 408	Healthy Eating
Vol. 409	Online Safety
Vol. 410	Addiction
Vol. 411	Sport
Vol. 412	Rights of the Child
Vol. 413	Energy
Vol. 414	Consumerism
Vol. 415	Mental Health

and poverty **306**.5, 7, 10
PTSD **318**.27–8
and self–esteem **307**.30
see also careers; child labour; employment; globalisation;
   migration
Work Capability Assessment **393**.25
work experience **403**.18, **405**.11–12
workhouses, history of **306**.5
Working Time Regulations Act 1998 **405**.34
work-life balance **351**.15, 41, **389**.36–7, **395**.33, **405**.30, 41
workplace bullying **380**.18–19, 20, 29–39, **405**.36–7
Workplace Bullying Institute **380**.18
workplace cyberbullying **361**.14–15, 29–30
workplace sustainability **368**.3–4
work-related visas **359**.1
World AIDS Day **314**.24
World Animal Protection **374**.6–7, 33
World Association of Zoos and Aquariums (WAZA) **374**.33
World Bank
   on global poverty **306**.27–8
   on updating terms **306**.27–8
   waste report **385**.2
World Cup, and gambling **349**.14
World Economic Forum's Inclusive Development Index
   (2018) **377**.19
World Health Organization (WHO)
   on adolescent nutrition **408**.29
   on AIDS **314**.30
   on air pollution **348**.5
   on animal experimentation **374**.16
   on childhood obesity **384**.3, 9–10
   on depression **404**.20
   on e-cigarettes **406**.21
   on exercise **384**.15, 22
   Framework Convention on Tobacco Control (FCTC) **348**.2
   on gambling **349**.5
   on gender **369**.3
   Global Strategy on Diet, Physical Activity and Health **408**.4
   on HIV **314**.7, 14, 30–1
   Mental Health Action Plan **404**.3
   on nicotine **406**.9
   obesity statistics **384**.1–2
   on sexual health **309**.1–2
   on STIs **309**.9–10
   on unsafe abortions **367**.15–17
world health statistics **348**.5
   health and wellbeing **348**.1
World Press Freedom Index 2018 **347**.12, 14, 16
World Refugee Day **359**.38–9
world religions **358**.8–11
World Tourism Organization (UNWTO), on holiday travel
   365.6
world trade *see* international trade
World Trade Center attacks **401**.3, 5, 29–31
World Trade Organisation (WTO) **305**.18–19
   and dispute resolution **305**.19
World War I (1914-1918) **360**.15, **401**.3, 8–9
World War II (1939-1945) **401**.3, 8–9, 14
World Wide Fund for Nature (WWF) **357**.18
World Youth Skills Day **405**.3
worry **351**.21

X
xenophobia **358**.1, **376**.24, 41

Y
yawning **389**.5
Yazidi women, abuse of **300**.23–4
Y chromosome **352**.29–30
Yemen **377**.22
   war and conflict **401**.6, 21, 31
Yik Yak **361**.18
yoga **343**.7, 41, **350**.15, **358**.1
YOLO, social media app **361**.18
Yom HaAtzmaut **358**.24
Yom HaShoah **358**.24
Yom Kippur **358**.24
YouGov
   on achievement of gender equality **364**.8–9
   on attitudes to Armed Forces **356**.3
   on body image issues **375**.4–5, 16, 25
   on cyberbullying **361**.22
   Death Study **407**.6–7, 34–5
   on female veterans **356**.34–5
   on immigration **359**.15–17
   on 'microcrime' **366**.15–16
   on racism in Britain **376**.4–7
   on religious influence **358**.1
young adults, living with parents **363**.2
young carers **380**.6
Young Gamers & Gamblers Education Trust (YGAM) **409**.33
Young Innovator Award **381**.22
YoungMinds, on cyberbullying **361**.1–2
youth crime **366**.4, 10–14
youth homelessness **398**.14–15
   see also homelessness
youth justice system **415**.17
youth-led movements **372**.31
youth violence **392**.28
YouTube **371**.10, **409**.2, 16–17, 36
   censorship **347**.6
   cyberbullying on **361**.8
   and gambling **349**.25
   reporting/dealing with abuse on **361**.32
Yugoslav Wars (1991-1995) **401**.2

Z
Zelensky, Volodymyr **401**.18
zero-hours contracts **377**.11, **405**.30–1
zero waste **365**.41, **368**.3, 18–19, **385**.1, 34, 41
Zika virus **302**.24–5, **348**.20–1, 28, 37
Zimbabwe **360**.33
zinc **350**.38
Zoom **383**.32–3
zoos
   animal welfare **374**.33–5
   personhood **303**.24–5
   petting **303**.22
   and slaughter **303**.6, 24, 25, 37
   see also conservation
Zoroastrianism **358**.4, 9, 31
Zuckerberg, M. **409**.21